Changing Rural Society in India

Changing Rural Society in India

K Gopalkrishna Rao

AUTHORSPRESS
Publishers of Scholarly Books

Worldwide Circulation through Authorspress Global Network
First Published 2010
by
Authorspress
E-35/103, Jawahar Park
Laxmi Nagar, Delhi-110 092
e-mail: authorspress@yahoo.com

Changing Rural Society in India
ISBN 978-81-7273-542-5

Printed in India at Tarun Offset, Delhi.

PREFACE

Villages constitute the foundational brick of Indian social system. About seventy per cent of the total people live in more than 550,000 villages. They are the principal pivot around which whole Indian social life revolves.

The rural life in India has been steadily changing over the years. With growth in industrialisation a lot of the rural population has shifted to urban areas in search of jobs. Due to migration joint families are giving way to the nuclear set up. Education and the modern influence are loosening the hold of blind faith and superstition.

Ever since our country became a democracy, various development programmes have been implemented at the village level. There are self-help groups for women, better roads are being constructed and electricity being reached to every home. On the social and political front the changes are even more marked. Marginalised sections like the lower caste population and the women also have a voice in local politics and decision making. The age-old caste system is also loosening somewhat. Inter caste marriages are a little better tolerated. The most significant change is in the feeling of togetherness. With more and more population moving at least one member to urban areas the city influence can be seen here.

The feudal system's collapse has lead to better income and life for the small farmers. The land reforms enacted and implemented during the mid-fifties along with technological upgradation played a crucial role in augmenting agricultural production. From a nation dependent on food imports to feed its population, India today is not only self-sufficient in grain production. Tractors have taken the place of traditional ploughing mechanisms. Better irrigation facilities and seeds are leading to better crops. Industrialisation and government schemes have generated better employment opportunities in non-farm sector also.

Communication technology is one of the major driving force of rural development. Traditional media like radio and TV have dominated the development scene. Technological changes further compounded the direction of rural development with information and communication technologies (ICTs). Now ICTs are being used everywhere for information dissemination, management and governance of development.

Despite the huge progress made in the past decades, rural areas are still home to billions of poor people. Most of the rural poor depend on rain-fed agriculture and fragile forests for their livelihoods. Millions of people still face discrimination, abuse, and social and economic marginalisation. The government of India places high priority on reducing rural poverty, rural development, upliftment of backward classes and women empowerment. However, bold action from policymakers will be required to shift away from the existing situation to build a solid foundation for a highly productive, well-educated, empowered and sustainable rural India.

This book provides a comprehensive picture of the changing face of rural India. It has been kept in mind that Indian planners and administrators will be greatly helped rewarded. This volume will also be useful for students, teachers and practitioners who want to learn about the contemporary status and issues of Indian rural life.

K Gopalkrishna Rao

CONTENTS

1

RURAL SOCIETY AND DEVELOPMENTAL CHANGE

Villages constitute the foundational brick of Indian social system. Rural life is the principal pivot around which whole Indian social life revolves. Though there is rapid urbanisation, Indian society is primarily a rural society. Majority of India's people live in rural areas. They make their living from agriculture or related occupations. This means that agricultural land is the most important productive resource for a great many Indians.

Agriculture and culture are closely connected. The nature and practice of agriculture varies greatly across the different regions of the country. These variations are reflected in the different regional cultures. One can say that both the culture and social structure in rural India are closely bound up with agricultural and the agrarian way of life.

For the majority of the rural population agriculture is the single most important source of livelihood. But the rural is not just agriculture. Many activities that support agriculture and village life are also sources of livelihood for people in rural India. However, increasing interconnection of the rural and urban economies have led to many diverse occupations. Many people living in rural areas are employed in, or have livelihoods based in, rural non-farm activities. For instance, there are rural residents employed in government services such as the Postal and Education Departments, factory workers, or in the army, who earn their living through nonagricultural activities.

1.1. Nature of Rural Settlements

Scattered throughout India are approximately 500,000 villages. The Census of India regards most settlements of fewer than 5,000 as a village. These settlements range from tiny hamlets of thatched huts to larger settlements of tile-roofed stone and brick houses. Most are nucleated settlements, while others are more dispersed. It is in villages that India's most basic business—agriculture—takes place. Here, in the face of vicissitudes of all kinds, farmers follow time-tested as well as innovative methods of growing wheat, rice, lentils, vegetables, fruits, and many other crops in order to accomplish the challenging task of feeding themselves and the nation.

Indian village life is far from simple. Each village is connected through a variety of crucial horizontal linkages with other villages and with urban areas both near and far. Most villages are characterised by a multiplicity of economic, caste, kinship, occupational, and even religious groups linked vertically within each settlement. Factionalism is a typical feature of village politics.

Throughout most of India, village dwellings are built very close to one another in a nucleated settlement, with small lanes for passage of people and sometimes carts. Village fields surround the settlement and are generally within easy walking distance. In hilly tracts of central, eastern, and far northern India, dwellings are more spread out, reflecting the nature of the topography. In the wet states of West Bengal and Kerala, houses are more dispersed; in some parts of Kerala, they are constructed in continuous lines, with divisions between villages not obvious to visitors.

In northern and central India, neighborhood boundaries can be vague. The houses of Dalits are generally located in separate neighborhoods or on the outskirts of the nucleated settlement, but there are seldom distinct Dalit hamlets. By contrast, in the south, where socioeconomic contrasts and caste pollution observances tend to be stronger than in the north, Brahman homes may be set apart from those of non-Brahmans, and Dalit hamlets are set at a little distance from the homes of other castes.

The number of castes resident in a single village can vary widely, from one to more than forty. Typically, a village is dominated by one or a very few castes that essentially control the village land and on whose patronage members of weaker groups must rely. In some regions, landowners refrain from using plows themselves but hire tenant farmers and labourers to do this work. In other regions, landowners till the soil with the aid of labourers, usually resident in the same village. Fellow villagers typically include representatives of various service and artisan castes to supply the needs of the villagers—priests, carpenters, blacksmiths, barbers, weavers, sweepers, waterbearers and so on. Artisanry in pottery, wood, cloth, metal, and leather, although diminishing, continues in many contemporary Indian villages as it did in centuries past. Village religious observances and weddings are occasions for members of various castes to provide customary ritual goods and services in order for the events to proceed according to proper tradition.

Aside from caste-associated occupations, villages often include people who practice nontraditional occupations. For example, Brahmans or Thakurs may be shopkeepers, teachers, truckers, or clerks, in addition to their caste-associated occupations of priest and farmer. In villages near urban areas, an increasing number of people commute to the cities to take up jobs, and many migrate. Some migrants leave their families in the village and go to the cities to work for months at a time.

1.2. Caste and Class

Though agriculture is the main source of income for rural people, it is not equally distributed among people living in a particular village or region. Nor does everyone have access to land. In fact, the distribution of landholdings in most regions is highly unequal among households. In some parts of India the majority of rural households own at least some land—usually very small plots.

Women are usually excluded from ownership of land, because of the prevailing patrilineal kinship system and mode of inheritance. By law women are supposed to have an equal share of family property. In reality they only have limited rights and some access to land only as part of a household headed by a man.

Agricultural land is the most important productive resource in rural areas. So, access to land shapes the rural class structure. Access to land largely determines what role one plays in the process of agricultural production. Medium and large landowners are usually able to earn sufficient or even large incomes from cultivation. But agricultural labourers are more often than not paid below the statutory minimum wage and earn very little. Their incomes are low. Their employment is insecure. Most agricultural labourers are daily-wage workers. And do not have work for many days of the year. This is known as underemployment. Similarly, tenants have lower incomes than owner-cultivators. Because they have to pay a substantial rent to the landowner.

Therefore, agrarian society, therefore, can be understood in terms of its class structure. But it is also structured through the caste system. In rural areas, there is a complex relationship between caste and class. This relationship is not always straightforward. We might expect that the higher castes have more land and higher incomes. And that there is a correspondence between caste and class as one moves down the hierarchy. In many areas this is broadly true but not exactly.

The dominant landowning groups are usually middle or high ranked castes. Most of the marginal farmers and landless belong to lower caste groups. In official classification they belong to the Scheduled Castes or Tribes (SC/ STs) or Other Backward Classes (OBCs). In many regions of India, the former 'Untouchable' or dalit castes were not allowed to own land and they provided most of the agricultural labour for the dominant landowning groups. This also created a labour force that allowed the landowners to cultivate the land intensively and get higher returns.

Typically the upper and middle castes also had the best access to land and resources, and hence to power and privilege. This had important implications for the rural economy and society. In most regions of the country, a 'proprietary caste' group owns most of the resources and can command labour to work for them. Until recently, practices such as begar or free labour were prevalent in many parts of northern India.

1.3. Impact of Land Reforms

The agrarian structure has changed enormously over time, from the pre-colonial to the colonial and after independence. While the same dominant castes were probably also cultivating castes in the pre-colonial period, they were not the direct owners of land.

Instead, ruling groups such as the local kings or zamindars controlled the land. The peasants or cultivators who worked the land had to hand over a substantial portion of the produce to them. When the British colonised India, in many areas they ruled through these local zamindars. They also granted property rights to the zamindars. Under the British, the zamindars were given more control over land than they had before. Since the colonisers also imposed heavy land revenue on agriculture, the zamindars extracted as much produce or money as they could out of the cultivators. One result of this zamindari system was that agricultural production stagnated or declined during much of the period of British rule. For peasants fled from oppressive landlords and frequent famines and wars decimated the population.

Many districts of colonial India were administered through the zamindari system. In other areas that were under direct British rule had what was called the raiyatwari system of land settlement. In this system, the 'actual cultivators' rather than the zamindars were responsible for paying the tax. Because the colonial government dealt directly with the farmers or landlords, rather than through the overlords, the burden of taxation was less and cultivators had more incentive to invest in agriculture. As a result, these areas became relatively more productive and prosperous.

Soon after the independence of India, Nehru government implemented many policies to agriculture and industry. The first important legislation was the abolition of the zamindari system, which removed the layer of intermediaries that stood between the cultivators and the state. Of all the land reform laws that were passed, this was probably the most effective, for in most areas it succeeded in taking away the superior rights of the zamindars over the land and weakening their economic and political power. This did not happen without a struggle, of course, but ultimately the effect was to strengthen the position of the actual landholders and cultivators at the local level. However, zamindari abolition did not wipe out landlordism or the tenancy or sharecropping systems, which continued in many areas. It only removed the top layer of landlords in the multilayered agrarian structure.

Among the other major land reform laws that were introduced were the tenancy abolition and regulation acts. They attempted either to outlaw tenancy altogether or to regulate rents to give some security to the tenants. In most of the states, these laws were never implemented very effectively. In West Bengal and Kerala, there was a radical restructuring of the agrarian structure that gave land rights to the tenants.

Land Celling Acts were the third major category of land reform laws. These laws imposed an upper limit on the amount of land that can be owned by a particular family. The ceiling varies from region to region, depending on the kind of land, its productivity, and other such factors. Very productive land has a low ceiling while unproductive dry land has a higher ceiling limit. According to these acts, the state is supposed to identify and take possession of surplus land (above the ceiling limit) held by each household, and redistribute it to landless families and households in other specified categories, such as SCs and STs. But in most of the states these acts proved to be toothless. There were many loopholes and other strategies through which most landowners were able to escape from having their surplus land taken over by the state. While some very large estates were broken up, in most cases landowners managed to divide the land among relatives and others, including servants, in so-called 'benami transfers'—which allowed them to keep control over the land (in fact if not in name). In some places, some rich farmers actually divorced their wives (but continued to live with them) in order to avoid the provisions of the Land Ceiling Act, which allowed a separate share for unmarried women but not for wives.

The agrarian structure, although it has changed substantially from colonial times to the present, remains highly unequal. This structure puts constraints on agricultural productivity. Land reforms are necessary not only to boost agricultural growth but also to eradicate poverty in rural areas and bring about social justice.

1.4. Impact of Green Revolution

To overcome the drawbacks of land reforms, India introduced Green Revolution, which meant to modernise agriculture. Green Revolution programmes were introduced only in areas that had assured irrigation, because sufficient water was necessary for the new seeds and methods of cultivation. It was also targeted mainly at the wheat and rice-growing areas. As a result, only certain regions such as the Punjab, western U.P., coastal Andhra Pradesh, and parts of Tamil Nadu, received the first wave of the Green Revolution package. The rapid social and economic transformations that were seen in these areas stimulated a spate of studies by social scientists, and vigorous debates about the impact of the Green Revolution.

Because of the new technology, agricultural productivity increased sharply. India was able to become self-sufficient in foodgrain production for the first time in decades. The Green Revolution has been considered a major achievement of the government and of the scientists who contributed to the effort. However, there were certain negative social effects that were pointed out by sociologists who studied the Green Revolution areas, as well as adverse environmental impacts.

Green Revolution crops were highly profitable, mainly because they yielded more produce. Well-to-do farmers who had access to land, capital, technology, and know-how, and those who could invest in the new seeds and fertilisers, could increase their production and earn more money. However, in many cases it led to the displacement of tenant-cultivators. For landowners began to take back land from their tenants and cultivate it directly because cultivation was becoming more profitable. This made the rich farmers better off, and worsened the condition of the landless and marginal holders. In addition, the introduction of machinery such as tillers, tractors, threshers, and harvesters (in areas such as Punjab and parts of Madhya Pradesh) led to the displacement of the service caste groups who used to carry out these agriculture-related activities. This process of displacement also increased the pace of rural-urban migration.

The ultimate outcome of the Green Revolution was a process of 'differentiation', in which the rich grew richer and many of the poor stagnated or grew poorer. It should be noted that employment and wages for agricultural workers did increase in many areas, because the demand for labour increased. Moreover, rising prices and a shift in the mode of payment of agricultural workers from payment in kind (grain) to cash, actually worsened the economic condition of most rural workers.

The second phase of Green Revolution is currently being introduced in the dry and semi-arid regions of India. In these areas there has been a significant shift from dry to wet (irrigated) cultivation, along with changes in the cropping pattern and type of crops grown. Increasing commercialisation and dependence on the market in these areas (for instance, where cotton cultivation has been promoted) has increased rather than reduced livelihood insecurity, as farmers who once grew food for consumption now depend on the market for the incomes. In market-oriented cultivation, especially where a single crop is grown, a fall in prices or a bad crop can spell financial ruin for farmers. In most of the Green Revolution areas, farmers have switched from a multi-crop system, which allowed them to spread risks, to a mono-crop regime, which means that there is nothing to fall back on in case of crop failure.

The worsening of regional inequalities was another negative outcome of the Green Revolution strategy was. The areas that underwent this technological transformation became more developed while other areas stagnated. The landed castes and landlords maintain power over the lower castes, landless workers and small cultivators. The sharp caste and class inequalities, together with exploitative labour relations, in these regions has given rise to various kinds of violence in recent years.

Imparting knowledge of 'scientific' farming methods will improve the conditions of Indian farmers. We should remember that Indian farmers have been cultivating the land for centuries, much before the advent of the Green Revolution. They have very deep and extensive traditional knowledge about the land they till and the crops they sow. Much of this knowledge, like the many traditional varieties of seeds that were developed over the centuries by farmers, is being lost as hybrid, high-yielding, and genetically modified varieties of seeds are being promoted as more productive and 'scientific'. In view of the negative environmental and social impact of modern methods of cultivation that has been observed, a number of scientists as well as farmers' movements now suggest a return to traditional, more organic seeds and methods of cultivation. Many rural people themselves believe that hybrid varieties are less healthy than the traditional ones.

Several profound transformations in the nature of social relations in rural areas took place in the post-Independence period, especially in those regions that underwent the Green Revolution.

The capitalist mode of production is based on the separation of the workers from the means of production (in this case, land), and the use of 'free' wage labour. In general, it is true that farmers in the more developed regions were becoming more oriented to the market. As cultivation became more commercialised these rural areas were also becoming integrated into the wider economy. This process increased the flow of money into villages and expanding opportunities for business and employment. But we should remember that this process of transformation in the rural economy in fact began during the colonial period. However, the pace and spread of change rapidly increased after Independence, as the government promoted modern methods of cultivation and attempted to modernise the rural economy through other strategies. The state invested in the development of rural infrastructure, such as irrigation facilities, roads, and electricity, and on the provision of agricultural inputs, including credit through banks and cooperatives. The overall outcome of these efforts at 'rural development' was not only to transform the rural economy and agriculture, but also the agrarian structure and rural society itself.

The process of diversification gave rise to new entrepreneurial groups that moved out of rural areas and into the growing towns of these developing regions, giving rise to new regional elites that became economically as well as politically dominant. Along with this change in the class structure, the spread of higher education, especially private professional colleges, in rural and semi-urban areas, allowed the new rural elites to educate their children—many of whom then joined professional or white collar occupations or started businesses, feeding into the expansion of the urban middle classes.

The growth of migrant agricultural labour was another significant change in rural society. As 'traditional' bonds of patronage between labourers or tenants and landlords broke down, and as the seasonal demand for agricultural labour increased in prosperous Green Revolution regions such as the Punjab, a pattern of seasonal migration emerged in which thousands of workers circulate between their home villages and more prosperous areas where there is more demand for labour and higher wages. Labourers migrate also due to the increasing inequalities in rural areas from the mid-1990s. As a livelihood strategy, men migrate out periodically in search of work and better wages, while women and children are often left behind in their villages with elderly grandparents.

The local landless labourers move out of the home villages in search of work during the peak agricultural seasons, while migrant workers are brought in from other areas to work on the local farms. This pattern is found especially in sugarcane growing areas. Migration and lack of job security create very poor working and living conditions for these workers. The largescale circulation of labour has had several significant effects on rural society, in both the receiving and the supplying regions. For instance, in poor areas where male family members spend much of the year working outside of their villages, cultivation has become primarily a female task. Women are also emerging as the main source of agricultural labour, leading to the 'feminisation of agricultural labour force. The insecurity of women is greater because they earn lower wages than men for similar work. While women toil on the land as landless labourers and as cultivators, the prevailing patrilineal kinship system, and other cultural practices that privilege male rights, largely exclude women from land ownership.

1.5. Impact of Science and Technology

The necessity of harnessing science and technology (S&T) for transforming rural India has long been recognised. In fact, Gandhi had clearly shown an appreciation of this necessity. There are a number of aspects of the growth of post-independence S&T.

i) There has been a phenomenal growth in the total expenditure on R&D.

ii) This growth has been through a marked increase in the number of S&T agencies/organisations.

iii) Several of these agencies have shown a spectacular increase in the number of constituent S&T institutions.

iv) The establishment and development of these institutions necessitated an enormous increase in the number of technical personnel.

Post-independence Indian science became western-oriented and Indian technology focused on the needs of urban settlements, industry, the central government and to much smaller extent, the state governments. Thus, the main thrust of post-independence S&T effort was not in favour of the needs of rural areas. This conclusion is supported by (i) the bias in R&D expenditure, (ii) the bias in the distribution of institutions, (iii) the bias in the distribution of technical personnel, and (iv) the bias in the focus of Plans.

1.5.1. ASTRA—An Institutional Experiment

In the 1970s a number of new attempts arose to reorient Indian S&T towards the needs of rural India. Notable among these were the strings in the institutions of advanced education, science and technology.

Perhaps the most well known of these efforts was effort by the Indian Institute of Science (IISc), Bangalore. In 1974, a presentation on 'The choice of alternative technologies' at the Bangalore meeting to discuss the Science and Technology Plan of the National Committee of Science and Technology evoked a great deal of interest amongst the faculty of IISc. Several of these faculty members were in favour of an attempt to translate the ideas of alternative technology into a practical programme. An opportunity to make a presentation to the IISc's Senate Committee on Research and Academic Policy (SCRAP) was therefore requested. Following this presentation, the Institute accorded permission for the formation of a cell for the Application of Science and Technology to Rural Areas. This cell became known by its acronym ASTRA (which is the word for 'weapon' in Sanskrit) because it was meant to be a weapon against poverty in rural areas. Thus began a pioneering institutional experiment to evolve and apply S&T to rural areas.

The ASTRA institutional experiment was based on a model of technology–rural society interactions. Models are a path to understanding in the face of a complex reality. They are simplified representations of reality serving to discover its essential features. Model building, however, has to be an iterative process. Starting with an initial model, its ability to reproduce the essential features of reality has to be tested empirically. Then, the mismatch between model-based predictions and empirical results has to become the driving force for the improvement of the initial model.

The experiment of ASTRA brought to bear on the challenges the prestige and competence of the Indian Institute of Science, which is one of the premier institutions of education, science and technology in the country. The Institute's infrastructure for technology generation was combined in the ASTRA programme with a new rural development and poverty-eradication perspective. Several key technology areas were identified such as energy (particularly biomass), low-cost housing, drinking water and agro-processing. The scientists and engineers involved quickly became pioneers in the field. There was a tremendous feeling of excitement, as ASTRA became a hub of intellectual activity inspired by sensitivity to social concerns and a moral fervour.

ASTRA has survived for over 25 years. It has the infrastructure for technology generation and micro-diffusion. It has built an excellent reputation in Karnataka, India and abroad for past work. It is sufficiently well funded. It has excellent linkage with state-wide and countrywide technology dissemination agencies.

Moreover, the ASTRA programme of IISc served as a model for emulation and inspired a number of efforts in other institutions such as the IITs. Perhaps even more important was ASTRA's success in placing rural technology on the agenda of national institutions. Thus, towards the late 1970s and the 1980s rural technology started finding a place in the Plan documents.

Several key features of the initial ASTRA model have been validated. First and foremost is the importance of identifying felt needs. Whereas in industrial R&D work, these needs are communicated through the market mechanism, in the case of rural work, one is invariably dealing with sections of the population that do not have the purchasing power to articulate their demands through the market. The rural studies of energy, buildings, water, etc. carried out by ASTRA proved a powerful platform for its work of technology development.

Sustainable development an equitable, self-reliant and environmentally sound development. It is widely believed that the concept of sustainable development must be attributed to the

Brundtland Commission which defined it as 'development that meets the needs of the present without compromising the ability of future generations to meet the future needs'. The concept of sustainable development would never have attained the standing that it has.

With this perspective of sustainable development, ASTRA's objectives have to reckon with the dimensions of economic efficiency, equity, environmental soundness, long-term viability and self-reliance. It is necessary therefore to set rural objectives in the broader framework of sustainable development. The emphasis has to be not merely on rural technologies but on *sustainable* technologies.

1.5.2. Energy for Rural Poor

Energy is the basis of life. All other activities flow from it. Therefore, availability of affordable energy in rural areas is the only way to improve the quality of life of its inhabitants. Energy production via agriculture can produce rural wealth by providing energy, creating employment, increasing wages and providing services to improve people's quality of life. In the development of a viable energy technology and in producing devices, the role of global technological community becomes important.

From agriculture three types of fuels can be produced easily. Liquid fuels such as ethanol, pyrolysis oil, or biodiesel; gaseous fuels like methane, and production of electricity. Though the basic technology for their production exists, much more R&D is needed for increasing their efficiency and making them affordable. This is the challenge for the global technological community.

Ethanol fuel can easily be produced from agricultural crops like sweet sorghum, sugarbeet, sugarcane, corn, etc. However, to produce it in an affordable and environmentally sound manner will require tremendous inputs of biotechnology and good engineering. Thus research is being done in the US and all over the world in converting agricultural residues into ethanol via the enzymatic hydrolysis process.

Likewise, biodiesel can be produced from a horde of oil-producing crops like jatropha, soybean, pongamia, castor, etc. Though the production of biodiesel is quite easy, there is a need to increase the yield of oil-bearing plants and to develop internal combustion engines which can run on a whole bouquet of biodiesels. Presently the high-speed diesel engines require tailored biodiesel.

On the other hand, Pyrolysis oil is produced by rapid combustion of biomass and then condensing rapidly the ensuing vapours or smoke to yield oil which is nearly equivalent to diesel. Pyrolysis oil still requires much more R&D in terms of producing it economically, improving its keeping quality and making it suitable for use in existing internal combustion engines.

In any agriculture only 25–40 per cent of the produce is food. The rest 60–75 per cent forms the agricultural residues. It is these residues which can produce electricity via biomassbased power plants or pyrolysis oil or ethanol fuel. Any marginal farm can produce agricultural residues even if the main food crop fails. This income can give him benefits, even in case of a distress sale of his crop. The farmer is a multipurpose industrialist producing a variety of outputs from the same piece of land.

Around 600 million tonnes of agricultural residues is produced annually in India. Most of these residues are burnt in the fields as a solution to the waste-disposal problem. This not only wastes the precious biomass resource, but also produces tremendous air pollution.

In theory, these residues can produce about 80,000 MW of electric power year round through biomass-based power plants. This power is nearly 50 per cent of the total installed capacity of India. Alternatively, they can produce 156 billion litres of ethanol, which can take care of 42 per cent of India's oil demand for the year 2012. Similarly, the residues can also produce about 400 billion kilograms of pyrolysis oil, which is equivalent to 80 per cent of the total Indian oil demand for 2012. Thus the agricultural residues if properly utilised, can take care of a huge chunk of India's energy needs.

Through bio-digester route, a part of these agricultural residues can also be used to produce fertiliser for the crops and methane gas to either run rural transport, irrigation pump sets or for cooking purposes. Another stream can also be used for producing fodder for animals. Thus the residues can produce fuel, fodder and fertiliser. Which stream of residue conversion technology is eventually followed will depend upon the existing market forces.

If the agricultural residues can be broken down by suitable enzymes to produce ethanol, then both food and fuel can be produced from all food crops. Extensive research in this field is being done by universities and industry the world over and this technology will be very useful for rural areas of the world.

When the farmers are neglected, the long-term sustainability of the country is threatened. When farms produce both food and fuel, then their utility becomes manifold. In India, 65 per cent of its population depends upon farming and with energy from agriculture as a major focus India has the potential of becoming a high-tech farming community.

Technology intervention is required in using local resources to provide products and services to rural people. Filtering-down approach of urban goods to rural areas will not work in the long run because of lack of infrastructure, resources and different local situations.In this technological age, technology plays an extremely important role in our lives. Most of the technological efforts in the past for providing basic facilities to rural areas have been based on a 'tinkering' approach, meaning a small adjustment here and there, and using 'low' or appropriate technology. Therefore, sophisticated or 'high' technology is needed to convert efficiently the locally available resources and materials into useful products. This is the hallmark of evolution, where natural systems evolve into very efficient materials and energy converters. In this process, size reduction and increased complexity of the system take place. Some of our designs and technologies are following the size reduction route.

1.5.3. Strategy for Lighting

The history of civilisation is the history of lighting. Lighting allowed mankind to extend daylight hours and hence increase productivity and commerce. It is a sad state of affairs in India that nearly 60 years after independence, around 60 per cent of the rural population is without electricity. They use a simple but very inefficient hurricane kerosene lantern for lighting. Similar is the story of the rural poor in other parts of the world.

Therefore, NARI has developed a very efficient lantern called Noorie. This lantern produces about 1350 lumens (lm) of light, which is equivalent to that from a 100 W electric bulb and runs either on kerosene, diesel or with slight modification on low-concentration ethanol. It is reasonably priced at US$ 10, is very light-weight, efficient and also doubles up as a cooking device. However, in developing the lantern we became aware that the stumbling block in improving its efficiency was the thermoluminescent (T/L) mantle, which produces light.

Ultimately for decentralised light based on chemical fuels we should try to copy the bioluminescence mechanism of a firefly, where visible light is produced very efficiently and at room temperatures. Similarly, it is possible that mankind one day will develop a strategy where sunlight will photocatalyse two liquids, which when mixed together will produce brilliant light. The time is now to work on this strategy and that is the challenge for the global community. With grid electricity still a distant dream for a major portion of the rural areas, efficient liquid fuel lighting needs to be encouraged.

NARI has pioneered the strategy of biomass-based power plants for providing energy self-sufficiency at the taluka level. The taluka strategy was based on producing power from agricultural residues and wood from fast-growing trees. Thus the biomass available in a taluka could easily support two 15 MW biomass-based power plants. This strategy became a national policy and was implemented by the Government of India from 1996 till 2002.

R&D is needed in biomass gasifier-based plants, steam engines, sterling engines or biogas-based gas turbines. There is a whole array of technologies to be developed so that power is generated from renewable fuels, which are biomass-based, environment-friendly and produced locally. This is the challenge for the global community. There has been a quantum jump in the efficiency of thermoelectric elements—a device which converts heat directly into electricity. These elements can be incorporated into any biomass cook stove and about 40–50 W of power can be produced. This power is enough to run a small fan, so that the combustion efficiency of the cook stove is nearly doubled and part of the power can be stored in ultra capacitors for lighting.

1.5.4. Cooking Energy

Only liquid and gaseous fuels produced renewably can provide clean cooking energy. Two fuels fall into this category. Liquid fuels like ethanol or biodiesel, and gaseous fuel like biogas. Ethanol is an excellent fuel for cooking. NARI has developed a stove which runs on 50 per cent ethanol–water mixture. This mixture is very safe and can be easily distilled in a backyard still with much less energy than that required to distil high concentration of ethanol. The stove has a maximum thermal capacity of 2.5–3 kW and has a flame control for simmer and high settings, so that it works just like an LPG stove. Large-scale testing in the field has been positive and almost all the rural women who have tried it, compare it favourably with an LPG stove. However, in order that ethanol can be used as a rural household fuel, the presently tough excise laws have to be modified. The Noorie lantern also works on 50 per cent ethanol–water mixture. Thus we have developed hightech, environmentally sound cooking and lighting systems which can run on homegrown fuel.

Biodiesel is another fuel which can be grown locally. Various governments all over the world are embarking on a major programme of using biodiesel for running automobiles. However, R&D is required in improving its yield per ha and also its use in cooking stoves. Presently, there are no reliable cooking and lighting devices which can run on biodiesel.

Biogas is a clean gaseous fuel that can be produced from the existing biomass sources. Biogas has been used extensively in the rural areas of India. However, it is produced inefficiently in fixed and floating dome systems and requires considerable amount of cowdung and other nitrogenous material. It is not suitable for a household with less than 3–4 cattle. Besides, there are problems of gas production during winter and improper mixing of mixed inputs like biomass, night soil, cowdung, etc. Biogas, which is a mixture of methane and carbon dioxide, cannot be liquefied and requires high pressure of more than 100 atmospheres to compress it so that it can be used over extended periods.

R&D is necessary in two areas. One is in the development of extremely efficient biogas reactors, so that the production per unit of biomass inputs could be maximised. The second is to develop appropriate storage materials which could store biogas at medium pressures.

Optimisation of biogas production from a reactor requires sophisticated electronics-based controls and biochemical engineering technology. A small utility can afford to do it, whereas for a household it might be too costly. Tinkering around with existing biogas reactors will not solve the problem. A sophisticated science and technology input has to be brought to bear on the problem for optimising biogas production in rural areas. The use of high technology in lighting and cooking energy can result in considerable economic development in rural areas. Since fuel production will be rural-based, it can bring in substantial wealth to these areas both in terms of biomass production and also in processing it to produce fuel.

1.5.5. Water Supply

Supply of adequate water to poor regions of the world is a much bigger challenge than even energy availability, and where the global technological community can play an important role. Not only is there a water shortage, but lack of clean potable water results in millions of deaths every year due to diarrhoea. With the green revolution in India, there has been an extensive use of water, resulting in shortage in some parts of the country. This is despite the fact that there is enough rainfall. Thus theoretically we have enough water, but the rainfall is not evenly distributed over India and it comes in short spells, thereby pointing to the need for rainwater harvesting and storage programmes.

However, there is a need for the local governments to develop policies so that rural water utilities can be set up which can harvest the rainwater, store it and then supply this water to a village throughout the year. These water utilities may also be able to buy water from the government through the existing canal system. Presently, all the water utilities in India are owned by the government and this leads to corruption in supply of water and its very inefficient usage. In 2003, the Government of India passed an electricity act allowing for the first time the private players to produce, sell and distribute electricity anywhere in the country. This act has allowed power producers to break free from the clutches of inefficient and corrupt government power utilities.

Supply of clean water and electricity are two most important issues for rural development are. NARI has developed a strategy, whereby it is shown that a microutility producing 500 kW power for rural areas can easily use the heat of the flue gases of the engine to boil or distil water to make it potable. Nevertheless, R&D is needed in improving the distillation process and developing a compact water-treatment plant, so that potable water can be delivered at affordable price.

1.6. Impact Liberalisation Policy on Rural Society

The liberalisation policy of India have had a very significant impact on agriculture and rural society. The policy entails participation in the World Trade Organisation (WTO), which aims to bring about a more free international trading system and requires the opening up of Indian markets to imports. After decades of state support and protected markets, Indian farmers have been exposed to competition from the global market.

Now, contract farming is very common in the production of specialised items such as cut flowers, fruits such as grapes, figs and pomegranates, cotton, and oilseeds. While contract farming appears to provide financial security to farmers, it can also lead to greater insecurity as farmers become dependent on these companies for their livelihoods. Contract farming of export-oriented products such as flowers and gherkins also means that agricultural land is diverted away from food grain production. Contract farming has sociological significance in that it disengages many people from the production process and makes their own indigenous knowledge of agriculture irrelevant. In addition, contract farming caters primarily to the production of elite items, and because it usually requires high doses of fertilisers and pesticides, it is often not ecologically sustainable.

The globalisation of agriculture also allows the entry of multinationals into this sector as sellers of agricultural inputs such as seeds, pesticides, and fertilisers. Over the last decade or so, the government has scaled down its agricultural development programmes, and 'agricultural extension' agents have been replaced in the villages by agents of seed, fertiliser, and pesticide companies. These agents are often the sole source of information for farmers about new seeds or cultivation practices, and of course they have an interest in selling their products. This has led to the increased dependence of farmers on expensive fertilisers and pesticides, which has reduced their profits, put many farmers into debt, and also created an ecological crisis in rural areas.

Farmers in India for centuries have periodically faced distress due to drought, crop failures, or debt. But, the phenomenon of farmers' suicides appears to be new. Sociologists have attempted to explain this phenomenon by looking at the structural and social changes that have been occurring in agriculture and agrarian society. Such suicides have become 'matrix events', that is, a range of factors coalesce together to form an event. Many of the farmers who have committed suicides were marginal farmers who were attempting to increase their productivity, primarily by practising green revolution methods. However, undertaking such production meant facing several risks: the cost of production has increased tremendously due to a decrease in agricultural subsidies, the markets are not stable, and many farmers borrow heavily in order to invest in expensive inputs and improve their production.

The loss of either the crop (due to spread of disease or pests, excessive rainfall, or drought), and in some cases the lack of an adequate support or market price, means that farmers are unable to bear the debt burden or sustain their families. Such distress is compounded by the changing culture in rural areas in which increased incomes are required for marriages, dowries, and to sustain new activities and expenses such as education and medical care.

Agriculture for many is becoming untenable, and state support for agriculture has declined substantially. In addition, agricultural issues are no longer key public issues, and lack of mobilisation means that agriculturists are unable to form powerful pressure groups that can influence policy making in their favour.

1.7. Economic Transformation

Sustained economic growth is the outcome of dramatic change that occurs in the sectoral composition of an economy. This change leads to a drastic decline in the relative importance of agriculture in the gross domestic product (GDP), and increase in the share of manufacturing and services and associated structural transformation of the economies from rural to urban.

The transformation involves a marked decline of relative shares of the agricultural sector, agricultural employment and the rural economy. So, agriculture and the rural economy have an important role to play in the process of their relative decline. The pattern of the transformation and the speed with which it occurs has significant socioeconomic implications for the rural population. In addition, policy measures taken during the transformation period have profound implications for the development issues in both rural and urban sectors in the post-transformation period.

Also, economic transformation involves significant adjustment costs. If the process is not managed efficiently and effectively, major socioeconomic problems may occur, particularly in rural areas. Sound rural development may be interpreted as a process of managing this structural transformation in such a way as to minimise the adjustment costs, potential for urban–rural dualism in standards of living and intra-rural sector inequalities by turning the economic growth process into one of shared growth through systematically providing the rural population with opportunities and capacity to reap long-term benefits from economic growth and participate in social development. The growth and development shared in this manner with the wider population is considered inclusive and sustainable because it embraces all strata of the society and leads to greater social stability. The international experience of rural development thus differs widely across countries depending on how each has understood and managed, or is managing, the process over time, in addition to the initial conditions of each country, and the global environment within which each country operated or is operating. However, the country experience in general offers important insights for policy makers.

Agricultural development played a critical role in rural development in the economies. Agricultural development contribute capital, labour, and government revenue for the development of other sectors. In addition, it enabled rapid development of rural non-farm economy with the assistance of appropriate government policies. The growth of the rural non-farm economy contributed in particular to reduce potential for sharp income disparities between rural and urban households.

In recent years, India has also begun its economic transformation, with liberal economic policies and reforms introduced in the early 1990s. However, it has been so far driven largely by the rapid growth in the manufacturing and service sectors while agricultural growth has not played as dynamic and spectacular role as it has in the PRC. The growth rate in agriculture has declined since 1997 and remains low. Rapid population growth appears to have significantly negated the positive impact of economic growth on reduction of the absolute number of rural poor.

Even though, the region has impressively reduced rural poverty, rural development record remains mixed across countries and majority of the poor in the region continues to live in rural areas. In most countries, poverty levels continue to be much higher in rural than in urban areas.

Rising income inequality is the other problem which related economic growth. High incidence of landlessness, poor access to quality education facilities in rural areas, inequalities in access to institutional sources of financial services, and inequalities in social indicators have a significant bearing on these income inequalities.

Non-income poverty further reinforces concerns about inadequacies in rural development of many countries. First, most people with low social development are concentrated in rural areas. Second, significant intra-sectoral disparities in social development exist in rural areas. Third, social development in rural areas continues to be much lower than that in urban areas.

In most developing countries in the region, educational levels and health indicators of the rural population are much lower than those of the urban population. Lack of qualified staff and a high rate of absenteeism among workers aggravate the problems. Other non-income dimensions of poverty are also acute in rural areas.

Rural areas in many developing economies and some middle-income countries continue to face serious environmental problems, threatening the pace of further growth and adversely affecting the quality of life of the rural population, particularly the poor. Lack of inclusiveness in rural development has increased the potential for sociopolitical instability and more negative consequences on overall economic growth and quality of life of both rural and urban populations. Rural-urban income disparities are a significant development issue.

The environmental pollution and environmental vulnerability have increased partly because of the pattern of rural economic growth. Environmental problems include desertification, soil erosion, grassland degradation, salinity on irrigated land, organic matter and fertility loss, burning of crop residues, aquifer depletion, high levels of heavy metals, nitrates and pesticide residues in soils and water, animal waste and loss of biodiversity. Some environmental trends are still in the wrong direction.

Rural-urban inequality is an acute problem in income and all social indicates while the people who have sanitation facility in rural area is very less, it is very high in urban population. In addition, alarmingly high gender disparities remain in education and health and access to most basic services. Infant mortality rates continue to be much higher in rural areas than in urban areas.

Deforestation, soil erosion, water pollution, and land degradation continue to worsen and are hindering economic development in rural India." Many other developing economies in Asia and the Pacific are facing similar rural development issues—high levels of persistent poverty in rural areas, major environmental problems such as land degradation and water pollution and scarcity, unacceptably low levels of social development, wide gaps between urban and rural incomes, regional imbalances and intra-rural sector disparities in income and social development.

The 11 Five Year Plan emphasizes the need to concentrate on economic growth while improving development quality, and aims to solve the problems facing "agriculture, rural areas and farmers." It emphasizes the need to increase rural household incomes by improving agricultural productivity and developing rural nonfarm enterprises. It also aims to improve rural infrastructure—including roads—energy, safe drinking water, education, and public services and to develop rural financial systems. It further seeks to coordinate development between urban and rural areas and pay increased attention to social equity. It also emphasizes the need to increase the pace of change of the patterns of economic growth, promoting balanced development among regions and between economic and social development, and strengthening rural environmental protection.

The plan outlines broad-ranging policy changes, institutional reforms, and new programmes to help refocus on rural areas. These include infrastructure investments; agricultural and other tax reforms; increased emphasis on social development; and better financial services for rural people, including microcredit. The Government of India has also consistently emphasised the importance of rural development in its development plans for over 5 decades.

The Government has recently introduced a number of new major initiatives. These programmes expect to accelerate rural development and reduce both income and non-income rural poverty. Viet Nam announced a 5-year plan to promote rural industries to increase employment and rural incomes. Many other countries have introduced a variety of measures. It is difficult to find a developing economy, including middle-income countries, that does not emphasise rural development. All seek rural development both for its intrinsic value and its instrumental value. This continued emphasis in the context of the severity of rural poverty makes it important to look into potential drivers of rural development in general and inclusive rural development in particular.

1.8. Human Development

Under the British rule, the situation of India was very pathetic. It was a servile state, with its splendid strength caged up, hardly dared to breath freely. After independence, Jawaharlal Nehru envisaged a nation in which there is no space for poverty, ignorance, disease and inequality of opportunity. Mahatma Gandhi had always insisted that India would become truly independent only when the poorest of its people would be free from human suffering. An overwhelming concern for the poor, a multidimensional view of poverty and human deprivations, the focus on freedoms, the need to expand opportunities and ensure its equal distribution are fundamental to a strong human development perspective.

With an objective to raise the nation from the state of hell, India introduced five year plans. The *First Five Year Plan* (1951-56) stated that "the central objective of planning in India is to raise the standard of living of the people and to open them opportunities for a richer and more varied life." Successive five-year plans continued to emphasise poverty eradication, and the attainment of economic equality and social justice as key objectives. The *Eighth Five Year Plan* (1992-97) identified human development as the ultimate goal. It aimed to create jobs, contain population, eradicate illiteracy, universalise elementary education, and provide safe drinking water and primary health care facilities to all.

Since independence several significant changes have taken place in India. Some of these changes are distinctly visible—especially in the economic sphere with adoption of new technologies, diversified production, and sophisticated management. Changes have also taken place in the social sphere—with affirmative action for disadvantaged communities, with the weakening of untouchability and caste discrimination, and with women enjoying by and large more freedoms than ever before. On the political front, India has remained a vibrant democracy with increased participation by women and men in political decision making.

Although, in terms of achievements, India's performance during the past 50 years has been decidedly mixed. From a human development perspective, the glass can be considered half-full or half-empty; much depends upon the eye of the beholder. The country has recorded impressive gains in many areas, significant reductions in the intensity of poverty, but there is still much ground to cover in terms of ending human deprivations.

However, problems of rapidly declining water tables, deteriorating quality and increasing contamination threaten this availability. Despite the narrowing of gender gaps along several fronts, India is one of the few countries where there are fewer women than men a reflection of systematic deprivation and strong anti-female bias that pervades society.

Today, India remains a country of stark contrasts and striking disparities. Some states and districts of India report levels of social advancement similar to leading industrialised countries. Other parts of India report achievement levels that are worse than the average of the poorest countries in the world.

The condition of women is worse than men on most social indicators. A computation of the Genderrelated Development

Index (GDI) for Indian states reveals not only the low levels of human development and the extent of gender inequalities within India, but more importantly, it provides a measure of how badly Indian states are doing vis-a-vis other nations of the world. Similarly, disparities exist between and within communities in India. For instance, communities classified as belonging to Scheduled Castes and Scheduled Tribes have significantly lower literacy and higher child mortality rates than the rest of the population.

1.8.1. Concerns and Priorities

India has always determined to alleviate poverty. In India, half the population lives in object poverty. Such widespread poverty is a challenge which no society in modern times can afford to ignore for long. It must be eradicated on humanitarian grounds and as a condition for orderly progress. Fails to alleviate the conditions of the poor appreciably can hope for the necessary measure of public cooperation and political support in a mature democracy.

As a part of shifting attention is a narrow conception of poverty as income deprivation, the Planning Commission declared: "The stage has now come when we should sharply focus our efforts on providing an assured minimum income to every citizen of the country within a reasonable period of time. Progressively this minimum should be raised as development goes apace."

Economic growth has the potential to reduce income poverty, but equating growth with income poverty reduction is too simplistic. True, there is an association between economic growth and poverty reduction, but this association is, at best, weak.

However, economic growth alone will not bring down the income poverty. Several factors mediate the conversion of economic growth into income poverty reduction. Kerala, for instance, ensured maximum reductions in income poverty despite slow economic growth through political activism and a rapid expansion of equal opportunities. Improvements in infrastructure and access to assets also play an important role in income poverty reduction.

The decline in agricultural output adversely affected rural incomes, but at the same time, a steep rise in the open market prices of wheat and rice worsened their situation. Anticipating a substantial rise in procurement prices, farmers held back stocks and private traders stepped up direct purchases. Market arrivals were greatly reduced; and public stocks of foodgrains fell below the minimum specified norms. Procurement prices of rice and wheat were raised substantially, as were the central issue prices. The urban poor, beneficiaries of the universal public distribution system were hard hit by these price increases. At the same time, with low and depleting public stocks, the urban public distribution system had to be served through procurement from the below normal harvests. As a result, rural grain prices also went up. These price increases adversely affected the rural poor as well.

So, growth is important but the conversion of higher incomes into income poverty reduction is contingent upon several factors: effective public policy interventions, the redistribution of assets, the equitable expansion of physical and social infrastructure; an even and rapid spread of health, education and employment opportunities, and the assurance of people's participation.

Public expenditures have played an important role in India's income poverty reduction. The period from the mid 1970s to the end of the 1980s when income poverty showed a marked reduction was also a decade when public expenditures rose phenomenally. This also corresponded to a period when Government introduced several new poverty alleviation programmes. There was an increased political commitment to poverty eradication which was backed by an increased allocation of resources and by a set of new pro-poor policies. New employment-creation and asset generation programmes for income poverty reduction were introduced.

Government expenditures appear to have strong "trickle down" characteristics, much more distinctly so than income growth. Practically all states that have succeeded in reducing poverty have made sizable investments in poverty alleviation programmes.

To eradicate poverty, it is important to consider the size of government spending and efficiency of such spending. Leakage, corruption and inefficiency in management are frequently reported. Nevertheless, even with a poor record in programme implementation, states that have invested heavily in poverty alleviation programmes seem to do distinctly better in income poverty reduction. This is not to suggest that efficiency of government spending does not matter. In fact, it points to the enormous potential that exists for accelerating income poverty reductions with improvements in the efficiency of spending. Improving the design, administration and management of poverty alleviation programmes are urgently required poverty. With such improvements, overail government expenditures are likely to have larger multiplier effects and India could witness a more rapid reduction in income poverty.

Poverty is not the only one cause of India. The overwhelming attention paid to measuring and monitoring income poverty has resulted in a gross neglect of other serious forms of human deprivation. Some of these deprivations are loud and visible—child labour, illiteracy, damaged environments. Others are largely silent but visible—caste discrimination, discrimination against women and girls, and child prostitution. Many other forms of deprivations are, to this day, silent and invisible. These include for instance issues of women's health, domestic violence, child malnutrition. These deprivations are not related to income or income poverty levels in any predictable manner.

The lack of incomes also fail to measure the richness—or poverty of human lives. Urban poverty rates, for instance, have been consistently lower than rural poverty rates nationwide and across all states. Also, urban income levels are typically higher than rural incomes. Yet visitors to India's major cities will observe that traffic congestion has increased dramatically and so has air pollution. Respiratory problems have gone up and there is a severe shortage of water and electricity. Infant mortality in urban areas has remained stagnant in recent years for the country as a whole, and has gone up in several states. The declining trends in urban income poverty do not capture such dangerously deteriorating living conditions.

Surely, income has a significant role. But people often value other things in life much more than income. Even to the very poor, self-respect and a good reputation mean a lot. They often articulate their immediate needs as a good education for their children, access to good health care facilities, and a safe environment. They detest exploitation and discrimination. To most people, to be treated with dignity and respect matter much more than incomes.

The global community can help in improving the lives of the rural poor around the world in two ways. One is by providing liberally the technologies, knowledge, intellectual property, funds, etc. on extremely soft terms and secondly, by putting their own house in order.

This is the era of globalisation. Here, the whole world is one global village where the actions of one part directly affect those of the others. Thus global warming, environmental pollution and migration of a large number of people from one country to another for better opportunities are all a result of the globalisation process.

Rise of international terrorism is one of the impacts of globalisation. In fact, poverty breeds terrorism which ultimately affects all of us. It is therefore in the interest of the North to help the South, so that wealth is created in its rural areas and poverty removed. This can happen when the North, which has the resources to produce new ideas, technologies and financial instruments, uses them for providing services to rural areas as outlined above. In this process, the US universities, corporations and businesses will need to work with developing-country NGOs and businesses in a meaningful and cooperative relationship. The governments of both the North and South should have a minimal role in such ventures.

The rural population of the world has a great strength of being satisfied with fewer material comforts. Partially this is because they never had many material goods in the first place and partly because they have not been corrupted by the so-called notions of 'good life'. The provision of high technology for meeting the basic needs of rural poor together with their spiritual strength may provide a new model of sustainable development and in the process may teach the North a lesson or two in sustainability.

References

Braun, Joachim von, et al. "Agricultural and Economic Development Strategies and the Transformation of China and India". In Essays:

Lessons Learned from the Dragon (China) and the Elephant (India) Annual Report 2004–2005. Washington DC: International Food Policy Research Institute (IFPRI). 2005.

Burgess, Robin, and Rohini Pande. "Do Rural Banks Matter? Evidence from the Indian Social Banking Experiment". *The American Economic Review* 95(3): 780–795. 2005.

Chaudhuri, S., and M. Ravallion. "Partially Awakened Giants: Uneven Growth in China and India". In *Dancing with Giants: China, India and the Global Economy*, edited by L.A. Winters and S. Yusuf. Washington DC: World Bank. 2007.

Fan, Shenggen, et al. "Government Spending, Growth and Poverty in Rural India". *American Journal of Agricultural Economics* 82(4): 1038–1051. 2000.

Kripalani, Manjeet. "The Digital Village: Fighting Poverty with Technology in India". *Business Week*. 28 June. 2004.

2

FAST-TRACKING RURAL INDIA

Since early nineties India is witnessing a series of changes. Unprecedented numbers of farmer suicides, big corporate houses entering into retail business, land allocation for Special Economic Zones, boom in information technology and IT enabled services, zero growth rates in employment, are among many such events that needs introspection.

The Indian government has made huge investments in development of infrastructure like roads, telecommunication, etc. It has also passed legislation to benefit rural citizens. For example, under universal service obligation, each village should have a village public telephone installed and maintained by the service providers. Also, the "Right To Information Act" passed recently was to make the government system accountable to the citizens. However, civil society organisations are often unaware of such legislation and they fail to leverage the benefits. Corporate houses, private business houses and largely urban citizens are making effective use of the provisions. Thus, the benefits are inequitably distributed between the rural and urban areas. This rural-urban divide in accessing infrastructure services coupled with inability of civil society organisations to utilise the existing provisions has contributed to the slow growth of livelihood opportunities in rural areas.

In the beginning poverty eradication efforts in India concentrated on supply of agricultural technologies, inputs and services that were often 'production' orientated. However, they were not targeted towards the poor or were largely inappropriate to the needs of the poor and the benefits were mostly captured by the wealthy. Later, the approach changed towards 'capacity-building' in sector organisations to equip people and organisations with the skills and resources to do a better job but, overall little has changed since the new skills are not used.

To reduce poverty effectively, understanding the livelihood systems of the poor is crucial. Livelihoods of the poor can never be understood in any one-track logic—be it economic, social, technical, cultural or political. The livelihood systems are made up of very diverse elements which—taken together—constitute the physical, economic, social and cultural universe wherein the families live. Thus, the livelihood system is more than just a set of physicoeconomic preconditions for continued existence. It also encompasses psychosocial dimensions of experience of living. The livelihoods approach puts households of the poor as its central focus. It takes holistic consideration of things that the poor might be vulnerable to, assets and resources that help them thrive and survive, policies and institutions that impact their livelihoods, how the poor respond to threats and opportunities and what sort of outcomes the poor aspire to.

Most of the rural population in India depends on agriculture and allied activities support livelihoods. In recent years, land based livelihoods of small and marginal farmers are increasingly becoming unsustainable, since their land has not been able to support the family's food requirements and fodder for their cattle. As a result, rural households are forced to look at alternative means for supplementing their livelihoods.

2.1 Changing Rural Agriculture

Majority of the Indian farmers depends agriculture for their livelihood. But they shifted their focus to cash crops when the production of food grains give them only poverty and misery. This shift create food in security because the Indian population failed to supply as per the increasing demand for food crops.

Notwithstanding increased availability of milk, fruits, vegetables, fish and other produce, the agricultural sector is facing the new challenges of diminishing land resources, factor productivity decline, threatened loss of bio-diversity, natural resource degradation, widening economic inequality, etc. that have serious implications on the livelihoods of the poor. Indian agriculture has also come under significant adjustment pressure from market liberalisation and globalisation.

The changing consumer preferences have added to the complexities of adjustment. The food consumption pattern in India is diversifying towards high value commodities. The decline in per capita consumption of cereals, in particular coarse cereals, has worsened the nutritional status of the rural poor. Now, the household level food security for the poor households is changing for the worst.

2.2. Food Security

Food security at the national, state or district level does not automatically ensure food security at the household level. Today, commercial crops are being recommended by Agriculture Departments to improve the economic status of farmers without explicit consideration of their household level food security. What most small and marginal farmers often need is food crops such as short duration cereals, millets and fodder crops to meet their family's food and fodder needs.

Modernising agricultural production through technological alternatives seems to emerge as a natural path to food security. Development and dissemination of green revolution technologies are classic examples of the approach for attaining national food sufficiency when hunger and starvation were widespread. Farmers in resource rich regions of India successfully adopted these technologies that account for about 35 percent of the cultivated area. But, in the rainfed areas (65 percent), technology adoption varied considerably. In semi-arid areas, the record is even miserable despite improved technologies being available.

Some small and marginal farmers sought modern agricultural technologies on their own, without any assistance from the extension network; and there is a majority who, despite all extension efforts, refuse to change from their traditional way of farming. Households that face difficulties in ensuring their own food supply, first try to reach this threshold by intensifying production of subsistence crops (maize and pigeon pea). Households that have crossed food security threshold then invest more in commercial crops like tomatoes and brinjal, etc. Evidently, neither the technologies seem inappropriate nor it appears to be a failure of the extension network. The security of the family's livelihood system as a whole plays the determining role in technology adoption or non-adoption.

Livelihood security has to be understood from the farmers' perspective. Food security is a subjective concept defined as an individual farmer's own perception as to whether s/he has been able to support the family's food and fodder requirements adequately round the year using all resources under his control.

Food security is only one (although extremely important) element of livelihood security. But since farmers never make their decisions in a one-track logic, it seems possible that the one-track security based on food alone would have to be enlarged to the more holistic notion of security of livelihood, or speaking even more simply—life-security. Livelihood security encompasses food security, social security and psychic security. Each one of them has some basic minimum threshold level to achieve and maintain and also must be pursued in a balanced way.

Many of the household decisions (e.g. sending children to school, participation in community organisations, etc.) are directly related to whether the households are below or above the food security threshold. In the absence of food security off-farm income from migration becomes a stabilising component in the over all livelihood security. Many development agencies seek to reduce distress migration by providing opportunities to farmers to increase their income from land based activities through commercialisation of agriculture. Often the approaches taken are sectoral and fragmented.

2.3. Migration

Migration is the other biggest problem in India is facing. Every year millions of poor families migrate in search of work. They are forced to migrate due to a livelihoods collapse in the villages. These distress migrants often lock their homes, take a few meager belongings and move across long distances. The children accompanying their parents are forced to drop out of school.

As they are away from their village, they do not belong to the places where they go and increasingly lose acceptance in their own villages. They are disconnected from their community, culture and traditions, unable to take part in festivals, fairs, religious and social functions, which are an integral part of their lives thus losing their sense of identity. The vulnerability of people who cross state boundaries is even greater as they find themselves increasingly at the mercy of their contractors. The family members or children left behind in villages do not know where the family has gone, or how to contact them. Dealing with emergencies, particularly back home is difficult, especially for those who go long distance.

The migrants skills, assets or education. Earnings from migration are survival level and not enough to build assets. On the contrary, medical or other personal emergencies and the unsteady nature of work often push them further into debt. Those who own a few animals have to arrange that they are cared for or just end up selling them off at low prices—thus depleting their assets.

In worksites they also face the lack of basic facilities like water, marketplace, schools, health centres, etc. Migrants are at the mercy of their employers for all their needs. Contractors retain control of labourers not only financially but also physically, forcing them to work even when they are sick or injured. If there resident communities nearby, migrants are usually shunned by local people, and regarded as bad elements or thieves.

Given the difficulties encountered by illiterate and under-informed migrants in accessing provisions that have been made for them by the State, there appears to be a need for support from elsewhere. A number of civil society organisations have taken up the cause of building the capacity of migrants to demand their rights from contractors and government officials.

Given the problems associated with agriculture and distress migration, occupational diversification is a means to make livelihoods sustainable as agriculture alone cannot sustain the growing population in villages, it is imperative that the RNFS (RNFS) is strengthened. The RNFS plays a crucial role in providing livelihood security to the poor.

2.4. Reforms in Non-Farm Sectors

The rural non-farm sector plays a key role in determining future prospects for employment growth and poverty alleviation in the country. It is because, this economy is the backbone of numerous towns scattered throughout India. Also, it is a primary source for of income and employment for many India's poor. The RNFS is closely linked to agriculture. A large share of rural manufacturing involves agro-processing and the production and supply of farm inputs. Agricultural performance therefore tends to influence growth in the non-farm economy. A growing agriculture demands production inputs in addition to supplying raw materials to transport, processing and marketing firms.

Development of the RNFS in the 1980s resulted in a remarkable reduction in poverty. However, this is an area which has received casual treatment from the policy makers, economists, politicians, social activists, entrepreneurs and more importantly, the communities themselves. Despite this neglect, it is said that 90 percent of the additional employment during the reform period was due to the non-farm sector.

Though the RNFS has tremendous potential of removing unemployment in villages, the government has not been serious to address the basic problems plaguing this sector. Major bottlenecks in the holistic development of the RNFS are poor quality of employment and incomes, shortage of skilled manpower, unavailability of credit facilities, absence of marketing networks, poor transportation facilities, low public investment in villages, lack of basic amenities in rural areas, poor law and order scenario, erratic power supply, etc. Besides, not much has been done to develop technologies relevant for the sector. Entrepreneurs are by and large reluctant to invest in the rural non-farm sector. Not many NGOs and political groups are engaged in empowering the rural communities to be proactive and develop RNFS enterprises on their own.

2.5. Impact of Globalisation

Rural livelihoods are affected by the process of Globalisation. Special Economic Zones (SEZ) are created across India to promote exports. The government claims that SEZs will attract global manufacturing through Foreign Direct Investment (FDI), enable the transfer of modern technology and create incentives for infrastructure.

The industrial giants' unquestionable quest for SEZ all over India reduces the area of cultivating lands. Even though the govt promises the growth of Indian economy as well as the betterment of the condition of peasants, it is not true in practical life. Infact, the entire livelihood of farmers, fisherfolk, salt-pan workers, and agriculturalists are depend on farmland. It is an amazing feature of this exclusive area of India where people have farmlands and they also do inland fishing. India's Special Economic Zones have drawn sharp criticism from a wide range of environmental and human rights groups, as well as farmers, villagers, fishing and agricultural workers who face losing their land, homes and livelihoods. Critics point to a lack of transparency and unwillingness to hold open public consultations on the SEZ issue.

Truly, the entry of corporate retail into India is nothing but a hijack of India's vibrant, well organised retail service economy. Corporate retail will not create two million jobs; but it will destroy 38 million livelihoods of people involved in running small shops and street markets. The growth being projected as a new contribution to the economy hides the destruction of the contribution of the 40 million people involved in small retail to the Indian economy. Corporate retail is being described as organised retail. And small scale decentralised and highly networked indigenous retail is being falsely referred to as unorganised. However Indian trade is highly organised and has existed for centuries on the basis of low cost and high efficiency. India needs the self organised skills of our traders, shopkeeper, hawkers and vendors both to provide employment to millions and affordable friendly community service for basic needs to society.

India is a land of retail democracy. Hundreds of thousands of weekly haats and bazaars are located across the length and breadth of our country by people's own self-organisational capacities. India's streets are bazaars—lively, vibrant, safe and the source of livelihood for millions. So, the entry of the giant corporate retail in India's food market will have direct impact on India's millions of farmers and people employed in tiny retail.

2.5.1. Coping Strategy of the Poor

A very small group of medium farmers is able to cope with adverse climatic conditions merely through the sale of available stocks. On the other end of the spectrum, landless labourers can only resort to seasonal migration due to lack of any productive assets or availability of alternative employment options in the village. Small/marginal farmers use a variety of adaptation options such as sale of cattle, shifts to other subsistence crops, wage labour, as well as seasonal migration. This range of options, however, constitutes only temporary coping measures. During adverse periods, farmers have implemented a range of livelihood and coping strategies to reduce their vulnerability.

Options that enhance longer-term adaptive capacity (such as institutional credit, crop insurance, and use of drought-resistant varieties) are not used by farmers due to procedural complexities and stringent eligibility criteria, compounded by lack of awareness.

2.5.2. Social Protection

India gives top priority on poverty alleviation programmes. The role of economic growth in providing more employment avenues to the population has been clearly recognised. The growth-oriented approach has been reinforced by focusing on specific sectors which provide greater opportunities to the people to participate in the growth process. The various dimensions of poverty relating to health, education and other basic services have been progressively internalised in the planning process. Central and state governments have considerably enhanced allocations for the provision of education, health, sanitation and other facilities which promote capacity-building and well-being of the poor. Investments in agriculture, area development programmes and afforestation provide avenues for employment and income. Special programmes have been taken up for the welfare of scheduled castes (SCs) and scheduled tribes (STs), the disabled and other vulnerable groups.

Antipoverty programmes that seek to transfer assets and skills to people for self-employment, coupled with public works programmes that enable people to cope with transient poverty, are the third strand of the larger anti-poverty strategy. The targeted public distribution system (TPDS) protects the poor from the adverse effects of a rise in prices and ensures food and nutrition security at affordable prices. Poverty rates in India have declined over the last decade, but the incidence of poverty remains high. India's surge in growth and rapid expansion in public spending in the past decade has created new possibilities for its social protection system.

In some cases, the basic subsistence needs and services remain the priority but with the need to re-examine delivery mechanisms for traditional safety nets in the changing economy. Other areas face second generation challenges of expanding social protection instruments to deal with economic modernisation, and the new risks and vulnerability it brings.

To alleviate chronic poverty the Government spending remains focused on social protection programmes. Spending on food programmes remains high, and is mostly focused on rural areas. A safety net for the urban poor is very limited. However, these social protection programmes have not reduced poverty as India had hoped they would. Many of the programmes have been subject to frequent adjustments, through re-branding rather than significant change. In addition, these programmes lack crossprogramme coherence. Poor implementation and limited flexibility in responding to the variations in the priority needs of poor households are serious governance have made limited impact on poverty reduction.

Nevertheless, the importance of social protection is growing as it is reflected in the Government's Common Minimum Programme. Increased resources and political priority given to social protection stem from social concerns that India's high growth has not been sufficiently inclusive.

2.5.3. Role of Information Systems

Development interventions are oriented to changing people's lives. They attempt to target those who are marginalised and vulnerable to disruptions. Until recently top-down methods were dominant in which most essential decisions about what issues will be addressed and how the information will be used were made by "specialists" (as opposed to community members). Projects are designed based on information that they have about the people in question, their needs, conditions, and concerns. When organisations base their actions on insufficient or faulty information, the result is a misplaced intervention that has little correspondence to the needs the poor. Such projects may actually have a negative effect on poor as they undermine traditional practices or cause local communities to invest their scarce resources in unviable activities. Vulnerable populations may actually become more destitute as a result of such poorly informed interventions.

For the development of rural areas in India there are many successful information and communication technology (ICT) initiatives. Now this has received due attention of policy makers, implementers for success of e-government projects through National e-governance plan (NeGP). The objective of NeGP is to provide a portfolio of services to the citizens through common services centers (CSC) integrated with e-government backbone to not only set up a good e-governance system but also to establish a support structure for sustainable livelihood opportunities.

The CSCs are meant for optimising transaction cost and time. It is also envisaged that these CSCs will support on-line transactions for government services. This is primarily aimed to reduce the distance that a villager normally travels to transact. A villager usually would prefer a better transaction cycle to happen in the village itself to support their livelihood prospects.

These CSCs are conceptualised on supply-driven model and are expected to provide predetermined services. Experience of such supply driven projects have more failures than successes. This is primarily due to poor sustainability attributed to gap in supply and demand of the services needed by the rural citizens. Therefore there is a need to develop models to capture local demand on participatory mode with a suitable interface with supplydriven government systems.

2.5.4. Transforming Rural Life

The rural livelihoods approach places people at the centre of development, and focuses on building assets and skills so that women and men can access new opportunities for income generation and employment. Supportive policies, robust institutions, and regulatory and incentive structures that both encourage growth and protect the most vulnerable, are essential to improving livelihoods. At the same time, reliable services—such as micro-finance, veterinary and crop advice—and access to agricultural inputs and markets, are necessary to ensure that improvements are sustained.Focused on the watershed based development programmes of the Government of India, initially the next generation of DFID supports in three states. DFID support transformed these from natural resource programmes focus, emphasising physical conservation works and primarily benefiting larger, mostly male, landowners, to people centred programmes, inclusive of all the residents of the watersheds and paying particular attention to landless, women and other vulnerable groups. This has become known as a 'watershed plus' approach. Specific elements of the 'plus' are components for productivity enhancement and micro-enterprise promotion with earmarked funding, as part of a broader approach that includes enhanced participation, capacity building and innovation.

Agriculture or harvesting of natural products, are the main sources of livelihood and many of the poorest are landless, depending on casual labour and are forced to migrate if work is not available. Nonetheless, opportunities exist for the rural poor to build their assets and to improve their sustainable income. The programmes like DFID help the poor to take advantage of such opportunities by supporting village level organisations such as self-help groups (SHGs), building the necessary skills and facilitating access to supplies, technical advice and markets. Diversification of livelihoods helps communities to counter risks as well as to raise incomes.

2.6. Role of Microfinance

The post-nationalisation period in the banking sector, circa 1969, witnessed a substantial amount of resources being earmarked towards meeting the credit needs of the poor. There were several objectives for the bank nationalisation strategy including expanding the outreach of financial services to neglected sectors. As a result of this strategy, the banking network underwent an expansion phase without comparables in the world. Credit came to be recognised as a remedy for many of the ills of the poverty. There spawned several pro-poor financial services, support by both the State and Central governments, which included credit packages and programmes customised to the perceived needs of the poor.While the objectives were laudable and substantial progress was achieved, credit flow to the poor, and especially to poor women, remained low. This led to initiatives that were institution driven that attempted to converge the existing strengths of rural banking infrastructure and leverage this to better serve the poor. The pioneering efforts at this were made by National Bank for Agriculture and Rural Development (NABARD), which was given the tasks of framing appropriate policy for rural credit, provision of technical assistance backed liquidity support to banks, supervision of rural credit institutions and other development initiatives.

In the early 1980s, the GoI launched the Integrated Rural Development Programme (IRDP), a large poverty alleviation credit programme, which provided government subsidised credit through banks to the poor. It was aimed that the poor would be able to use the inexpensive credit to finance themselves over the poverty line.Also during this time, NABARD conducted a series of research studies independently and in association with MYRADA, a leading non-governmental organisation (NGO) from Southern India, which showed that despite having a wide network of rural bank branches servicing the rural poor, a very large number of the poorest of the poor continued to remain outside the fold of the formal banking system. These studies also showed that the existing banking policies, systems and procedures, and deposit and loan products were perhaps not well suited to meet the most immediate needs of the poor. It also appeared that what the poor really needed was better access to these services and products, rather than cheap subsidised credit. Against this background, a need was felt for alternative policies, systems and procedures, savings and loan products, other complementary services, and new delivery mechanisms, which would fulfill the requirements of the poorest, especially of the women members of such households. The emphasis therefore was on improving the access of the poor to microfinance rather than just micro-credit.

To answer the need for microfinance from the poor, the past 25 years has seen a variety of microfinance programmes promoted by the government and NGOs. Some of these programmes have failed and the learning experience from them have been used to develop more effective ways of providing financial services. These programmes vary from regional rural banks with a social mandate to MFIs. In 1999, the GoI merged various credit programmes together, refined them and launched a new programmeme called

Swaranjayanti Gram Swarazagar Yojana (SGSY). The mandate of SGSY is to continue to provide subsidised credit to the poor through the banking sector to generate self-employment through a self-help group approach and the programme has grown to an enormous size.

MFIs have also become popular throughout India as one form of financial intermediary to the poor. MFIs exist in many forms including co-operatives, Grameen-like initiatives and private sector MFIs. Thrift co-operatives have formed organically and have also been promoted by regional state organisations like the Cooperative Development Foundation (CDF) in Andhra Pradesh. The Grameen-like initiatives following a business model like the Grameen Bank. Private sector MFIs include NGOs that act as financial services providers for the poor and include other support services but are not technically a bank as they do not take deposits.

Recently, microfinance has garnered significant worldwide attention as being a successful tool in poverty reduction. In 2005, the GoI introduced significant measures in the annual budget affecting MFIs. Specifically, it mentioned that MFIs would be eligible for external commercial borrowings which would allow MFIs and private banks to do business thereby increasing the capacity of MFIs. Also, the budget talked about plans to introduce a microfinance act that would provide some regulations on the sector.

2.6.1. SHG Movement

While no definitive date has been determined for the actual conception and propagation of Selg-Help Groups (SHGs), the practice of small groups of rural and urban people banding together to form a savings and credit organisation is well established in India. In the early stages, NGOs played a pivotal role in innovating the SHG model and in implementing the model to develop the process fully. In the 1980s, policy makers took notice and worked with development organisations and bankers to discuss the possibility of promoting these savings and credit groups. Their efforts and the simplicity of SHGs helped to spread the movement across the country. State governments established revolving loan funds which were used to fund SHGs.

By the 1990s, SHGs were viewed by state governments and NGOs to be more than just a financial intermediation but as a common interest group, working on other concerns as well. The agenda of SHGs included social and political issues as well.

The spread of SHGs led also to the formation of SHG Federations which are a more sophisticated form of organisation that involve several SHGs forming into Village Organisations (VO) / Cluster Federations and then ultimately into higher level federations (called as Mandal Samakhya (MS) in AP or SHG Federation generally). SHG Federations are formal institutions while the SHGs are informal. Many of these SHG federations are registered as societies, mutual benefit trusts and mutually aided cooperative societies. SHG Federations resulted in several key benefits including:

- Stronger political and advocacy capabilities
- Sharing of knowledge and experiences
- Economies of scale
- Access to greater capital

Some states have developed SHGs further than others.

The latest published estimates from NABARD state that, to date of March 31, 2005, 1.6 million SHGs have benefited from approximately Rs 69 billion in financing. There is no doubt that there has been greater outreach of financial services to the poor through SHGs. Of course the outreach has been good in South India. However, there outreach has been limited in the rest of the country. In addition to the financial analysis of SHGs, the non-financial areas such as social security and gender dynamics are also effected by the SHG Movement. Indeed, poverty reduction is much less an issue of numbers but rather ideas and concepts. The following is an analysis of the non-financial impact of SHGs.

2.6.1.1. Political Engagement

Political engagement includes active involvement by SHGs in government including local assemblies, Lok Sabha or Panchayati Rai Institutions (PRIs). One of the key benefits of SHGs is women's empowerment and this can be seen with the number of women involved in public affairs. While the number of women actually involved in politics is still very low, research has indicated that of those women that stand for election, over 70 per cent had won their seat. And, the female contribution to civil issues ranges from issue of ration cards, laying of pucca roads, building of school, ensuring appointments in vacant positions in schools and health centres, recovery of river bank lands from encroachers and laying of drinking water pipes. As mentioned, the number of women involved in politics is low. But, the trend is definitely moving up. A mere 5 years ago, the likelihood of women contesting panchayat election was extremely low. Their presence today is affecting the perception of women and their role in the political arena. They are being recognised as an important group with serious concerns.

The role of SHGs is both as an inspiration and as a financer. Impoverished women develop greater language and financial skills through the SHG which provides the building blocks for higher levels of confidence to engage the world. Also, the SHG sometimes finances the campaign of its members that stand for election. SHGs not only empower its members but also wield a powerful political role as a group as well. At local village meetings, the leaders of SHGs are often invited to attend and speak.

2.6.1.2. *Social Harmony*

Social harmony encompasses the equality and integrity of relationships between different social groups. To frame the following analysis, SHGs typically consists of the following social groups:

- Schedule Caste (SC)
- Scheduled Tribe (ST)
- Minorities (MN)
- Backward Caste (BC)
- Other Caste (OC)

The composition of SHGs are sometimes exclusively one particular social group or a mix. The impact of SHGs on social harmony has also been mixed. While it has been observed that in groups with mixed membership had group leaders that came from a variety of the social groups. In the vast majority of instances, groups leaders were almost exclusively from the dominant social groups' category. This demonstrates a lack of equality and unity across caste divisions. Given the relatively young history of SHGs, it is to be expected that their impact on bridging centuries old divisions would be slow.

There have been several occurrences of SHGs resolving disputes between members and the community at large. These instances include initiating legal action, arbitration, divorce and others. While there has long been dispute resolution mechanisms in villages, in the past it was controlled by men. Now, there are instances of women, SHG members, being involved in resolving disputes. Whether or not the women are working for their own interests or in the case for justice varies, regardless SHGs' impact on the political arena is certainly being seen also in social justice, albeit in a slow and evolutionary process.

Recent analysis has shown that the impact that SHGs have on the community at large have been minor. There have been few instances of significant contributions from SHGs to education, family planning, eradication of child labour and hygiene.To interpret these findings further it should be noted that such community problems are often large financial commitments which SHGs simply do not have the capacity to afford. Also, of the few instances where there have been significant contributions from the SHGs to the community, the SHG demonstrated a clear leadership role and rallied the support of the entire village. This demonstrates that given the opportunity, SHGs, assuming they have the capacity, can act as a director of community development. The perception of taking of a women's based organisation taking a leading role for the betterment of the greater good has monumental impacts on the local community. Gender dynamics begin to balance in instances such as these.

The loans that SHG members receive are intended to improve their livelihoods so that they can receive greater and more steadier cash flows. In rural areas, livelihoods range from agriculture farming, animal husbandry, dairy and various other goods and services activities. Experience has shown that SHGs have had improved livelihoods to the extent of providing the leveraging needed to start an enterprise. However, the interventions to introduce new livelihoods or refine existing ones that could yield better economic results were done by external agencies.

2.7. Challenges and Opportunities

Adopting a process approach to design and implementation in all DFID rural livelihoods programmes has been important. This has enabled project management to be flexible and responsive to changing demands. This process continues, and as new opportunities and challenges are thrown up, there is capacity to respond accordingly. Currently some of these emerging areas of engagement include:

2.7.1. Improving Development Effectiveness

Rural development accounts for the largest sectoral outlay in the Government of India budget. This development expenditure is channelled through a large number of centrally sponsored schemes. However in spite of substantial expenditure and a plethora of programmes progress in reducing rural poverty has been modest.

There is a strong rationale for "converging" of some rural development programmes to make them more efficient and cost effective. DFID's rural livelihoods programmes are integrated into government systems, and are well placed to play a catalytic role in converging rural livelihoods with other initiatives that are targeted in the same areas.

In the last year, there has been a step change in the way in which Rural Development Departments are looking at convergence. DFID's rural livelihoods programmes are well placed to assist these innovative approaches to improving the delivery of rural development programmes through integrated structures, budgets and approaches.

The National Rural Employment Guarantee Scheme (NREGS) is a particularly obvious target for convergence with rural livelihood programmes. NREGS a safety net programme providing a guarantee of employment for each household up to 100 days/year, and much of this work is based on implementing soil and water conservation activities. DFID livelihoods programmes work closely with the NREGS to improve the quality of implementation, and monitor its effectiveness. MPRLP is responsible for implementation of NREGS in the eight districts where the programme operates, while in Andhra Pradesh the

Commissionerate for Rural Development is responsible for both APRLP and NREGS implementation.

2.7.2. Food Security

Progress on reducing hunger has lagged behind reduction of income poverty. Child malnourishment is the most commonly used indicator to measure food security. There are currently more hungry people in India than in the whole of Africa. On the basis of the progress made during the last thirteen years, India is highly unlikely to come close to the MDG target by 2015.

Rural livelihoods programmes have improved people's access to nutritious food, either through improvements in crop or livestock production, by helping people get jobs or set up micro-enterprises, or in cases of extreme poverty or response to disasters by supporting food for work initiatives. Such measures have resulted in some modest improvements to food security, assessed in terms of a decrease in the period when food shortages are experienced. Rural livelihoods approaches have a role to play in revitalising progress towards food security.

DFID programmes are looking at ways of protecting, as well as promoting, the livelihoods of vulnerable people. This includes a strong emphasis on social protection schemes which can reduce risk and vulnerability. Areas being considered include areas of weather or crop insurance, or a price stabilisation fund to benefit gatherers of forest products. Improved personal insurance against sickness, accident or death, are other examples that would ensure that resources do not flow out of productive activity in response to shocks or stresses. MPRLP aims to improve people's understanding of their entitlements and ability to demand their rights—to government schemes such as the Rural Employment Guarantee Scheme or the Targeted Public District Scheme. MPRLP has developed some innovative legal literacy tools to help build awareness of rights and entitlements.

2.7.3. Climate Change

Climate change is increasingly important as a policy issue for both the international community and for India. It is likely to impact on rural India in two ways:

- Changes in temperature, rainfall regime, more variable weather and increased frequency and severity of natural disasters will affect the livelihood strategies of rural people;
- The market for carbon offsets may create new opportunities for resource flows to poor rural communities.

Climate change poses a new challenge to rural livelihoods in India. Programmes need to identify the increased risks resulting from climate change and assess their significance for design and implementation.

Rural livelihood programmes emphasise sustainable management of natural resources and diversification of livelihood opportunities and are operating in areas where seasonal and inter-annual variability are key determinants of production and income. The rural livelihoods approach promoted by DFID is consistent with adapting to climate change.

International recognition of climate change as a global problem has resulted in the creation of a market for carbon offsets, through which carbon credits can be created, either by avoided emissions of greenhouse gases (GHGs) or by sequestering carbon in vegetation or soils. To date almost all of the benefits of the carbon market have been captured by medium and large scale industry and very few have flowed to the poor. However as custodians of natural resources that can be used to either reduce or increase carbon dioxide emissions, the rural poor could potentially earn significant revenue from the sale of carbon credits provided the current barriers to the carbon market can be addressed.

Such barriers include a currently limited methodological framework for appraising projects on avoided deforestation, compensated conservation or land use change and the high transaction costs associated with large numbers of small projects. The voluntary carbon market offers a partial solution to these constraints but this is less well developed and usually commands a lower carbon price than the formal Clean Development Mechanism approved under the Kyoto Protocol.

2.7.4. Further Concerns

India is rapidly attaining economic growth and development. But it does not mean to miss out the rural poor. The challenge is to make this growth more inclusive, and, given the growing pressure on natural resources and the mounting threat posed by climate change, to make it more sustainable. New technologies, including those associated with information and communications can help to drive this change and to accelerate the transition out of poverty in rural areas. The private sector is now the major driver of growth in the Indian economy and could potentially play an increasingly important role in opportunities for the rural poor to become key players in India's economic growth. While some work has been initiated on information technology and on engaging the private sector in promoting new technologies and linking the poor to markets, we see both of these issues playing an increasingly important role in rural livelihoods approaches in the future.

References

Andy Hall. *Challenges to Strengthening Agricultural Innovation Systems: Where Do We Go from Here?* United Nations University. UNU-MERIT Working Paper Series. 2007-38. 2007.

Ruedi Baumgartnet and Ruedi Hogger. (eds). *In Search of Sustainable Livelihoods: Managing Resources and Change.* Sage Publications. New Delhi. 2004.

Praduman Kumar, Mruthyunjaya, Madan. M Dey. "Long-term Changes in Indian Food Basket and Nutrition". *Economic and Political Weekly,* September 1, 2007. pp: 3567 -3572.

Robert Tripp. *Self-Sufficient Farming: Labour and Knowledge in Small-Scale Farming.* London. Earthscan, 2006.

World Bank. *World Development Report 2008: Agriculture for Development.* Washington, D.C.: World Bank. 2007.

3

CHANGING EDUCATIONAL STRUCTURE

India achieved enviable position in economic development. But the educational achievement of India is in a state of abyssal. India's recent economic growth rates have generated much optimism about its general social and economic development. But has there been accompanying progress in indicators of educational outcomes? How good are Indian educational achievements in relation to China's, the country with which it is increasingly compared? What are the most significant developments in Indian school education and what has been the impact of various education policy initiatives? This chapter presents a critical overview of the school education sector in India using newly released data and a survey of existing studies.

India has 22 per cent of the world's population but 46 per cent of the world's illiterates, and is home to a high proportion of the world's out of school children and youth. On the positive side, it has made encouraging recent progress in raising schooling participation. While the base of India's education pyramid may be weak, it has emerged as an important player in the worldwide information technology revolution on the back of substantial (absolute) numbers of well educated computing and other graduates.

3.1. Status of Education in Rural Areas

In India, rural education is not in a very good condition. There are very few schools in the rural areas. Children have to walk miles to reach their schools and to write their exams. A study of 188 government-run primary schools found that 59 per cent of the schools had no drinking water and 89 per cent had no toilets. If this is the condition, how can we improve the quality of education. Most of the time the teachers are either absent or they are not teaching. They take private tuitions and earn money. The child that fails to take tuition, fails in the exams as well. So this is the present scenario of rural education in India.

The socioeconomic conditions in rural India have constrained the process of primary education and the social inequalities of caste, class and gender have been identified as the major causes of educational deprivation among children in India. Educational disparities, which contribute a great deal to the persistence of massive inequalities in Indian society, also largely derive from more fundamental inequalities such as those of class, caste and gender. A large proportion of children from the economically poor and socially disadvantaged groups and girls, especially in rural areas, are either denied access or are failing to complete even five years of basic education. The goal of universal elementary education remains a challenge to achieve even after five decades of independence.

The spread of education has been uneven not only in terms of inter state variations, but also between rural and urban areas, with urban areas being at an advantage compared to the rural areas. Social inequalities of caste, class and gender have manifested themselves in primary school participation and completion, as a result of which, certain segments of society, such as the SCs, STs, and girls in rural areas, have continued to lag behind the general population.

3.1.1. Schooling Access

India inherited a legacy of large-scale illiteracy and lack ot proper provision for education at independence. At the first post-Independence Census of 1951, only 9 per cent of women and 27 per cent of men were literate. It was resolved by the framers of the constitution that the new Indian state would endeavour to provide free and compulsory education to all children up to age 14 by 1960. This goal turned out to be elusive and the deadline for its achievement has been put back repeatedly in the past 55 years. While even today this goal remains unfulfilled, there has been very encouraging progress in schooling participation and other educational outcome indicators in recent times.

3.1.2. School Enrolment Rates

A per the findings of the 2006 Annual Status of Education Report (ASER) on rural India brought out by Pratham, a NGO appreciates the Government efforts in Sarva Shiksha Abhiyan, 93.4 per cent of all elementary school age children (6-14 year olds) were enrolled in school, an encouraging statistic, reflecting a good deal of progress compared to enrolments in the early 1990s. Among children 11-14 years old enrol was lower: 10.3 per cent of girls and 7.7 per cent of boys were out of school (either never enrolled in school or dropped out). Among 15-16 years olds, the corresponding out-of-school figures rose steeply to 22.7 per cent and 20.2 per cent respectively for girls and boys.

Schooling participation depends on both the extent of demand for and the availability of supply of schooling. According to Seventh All India Education Survey, in 2002, there were only one-fifth as many secondary schools (those with grade 10 classes) as the number of primary schools. So, it seems likely that secondary school enrolment rates are low partly because of the lack of supply of nearby secondary schools. However, despite supply constraints, demand for secondary education has risen and is likely to rise because it is lucrative level of education to acquire. The education-wage relationship is convex in India, i.e. returns to secondary and higher education are significantly greater than to primary and middle levels of education.

Gender inequality is another biggest problem in education sector. An important part of the reason for gender inequality is to be found within the household, as opposed to institutional explanations. Using household fixed effects equations, she finds strong within-household bias against daughters in terms of enrolment and household educational expenditure.

3.1.3. School Attendance Rates

Current attendance rates are a more reliable indicator of schooling participation than enrolment rates, since large enrolment rates measured at the start of the school year can mask non-attendance and/or drop-out later in the school year. Table 3.1 shows current school attendance rates from the Annual Status of Education Report (rural) 2009. While enrollment has improved, the attendance rate of children has not improved.

Table 3.1. School Attendance Rates in Rural India

ASER 2009	Based on household survey data	Observed on a random day in the school year (Age 6-14) in all school (govt+pvt)	
States	Total school enrollment (Age 6-14) in all school (govt+pvt)	Primary schools Std 1-4/5: % enrolled children attending(average)	Upper primary schools Std 1-7/8 : % enrolled children attending (average)
Goa	99.8	96.4	92.2
Kerala	99.9	91.9	91.7
Tamil Nadu	99.1	91.7	90.1
Maharashtra	99.0	90.6	90.6
Himachal P.	99.3	90.4	90.2
Karnataka	96.8	88.0	79.6
Jammu&Kashmir	98.2	86.7	90.0
Arunachal P.	96.6	86.0	88.0
Mizoram	98.7	85.8	85.9
Sikkim	97.7	84.8	88.5
Punjab	94.6	84.4	86.1
Uttarakhand	98.7	84.2	76.3
Nagaland	97.6	84.1	87.1
Haryana	96.9	83.7	84.9
Gujarat	95.7	83.5	83.1
Chhattisgarh	96.7	76.7	73.3
Tripura	98.1	76.2	71.1
AP	93.9	76.0	77.3
Meghalaya	96.2	75.6	80.5
Orissa	93.7	74.4	72.9
Manipur	98.9	74.0	77.1
Rajasthan	93.4	72.0	74.0
Assam	95.7	70.6	66.1
Madhya Pradesh	97.7	67.9	67.1
Jharkhand	94.6	62.8	63.6
West Bengal	94.3	65.9	66.4
Uttar Pradesh	95.1	59.8	60.9
Bihar	96.0	57.4	57.6
Total	96.0	74.2	76.6

Although enrollment is nearing 96 per cent in Bihar, the attendance in Bihar schools averages still under 60 per cent. Bihar is not alone in this. Excepting Himachal, Kerala, Tamil Nadu, Karnataka, Goa, Nagaland, and Maharashtra, in all other states, attendance is about 15 per cent to 30 per cent lower than the enrollment rate. The average attendance rate is the true enrollment rate of a state. In India, the average attendance rate seems to be around 75 per cent on any given day.

3.1.4. Literacy Rates

Data from the 1991 and 2001 Indian censuses shows that in the population aged 7 years and older, literacy rates rose substantially in the 1990s from 52 per cent to 65 per cent, an increase of 13 points. This is the highest absolute increase in any decade since records began in 1881. Over this 10 year period, the gender gap also began to close noticeably. Some states experienced particularly rapid literacy increases, e.g. in Madhya Pradesh and Rajasthan, literacy rates rose by 20 and 22 percentage points respectively. The increase in female literacy was also large in these states as well as in Uttar Pradesh and Andhra Pradesh. However, Bihar and Gujarat made poor progress.

But, age-specific literacy data were not available from the 2001 Indian census even in early 2007. During the short 6 year period between 1993 to 1999, literacy rates in the young age groups rose rapidly for girls: taking rural and urban areas together, female literacy in the youngest age group 6-10 rose by nearly 14 percentage points. For rural girls aged 6-19, literacy rates rose by about 15 points. Overall, the national literacy rate for males and females aged 6-19 years increased by about 10 percentage points.

Any major improvement in national literacy in the future will depend crucially on its progress among young persons in the four large north Indian states of Bihar, Madhya Pradesh, Rajasthan, and Uttar Pradesh which have lagged behind particularly seriously in the past. Examining recent progress in these states is perhaps the most informative statistic when attempting to foresee the future of literacy in India.

3.1.5. Achievement in Primary Education

Workers productivity and earnings depend not only on years of education acquired but also on what is learnt at school. Unfortunately, no national data on learning achievement levels were available in India until 2006. India's largest educational NGO, *Pratham*, carried out a survey of learning achievement in 2005 and repeated the survey with a bigger sample of about 330,000 household in 2006. It visited 20 homes each in 30 randomly selected villages in each one of 549 Indian districts, and interacted with all children aged 6 to 16 years old in the sample homes. The findings make grim reading. In 2006, nearly 47 per cent of children who were in school and studying in grade 5 could not read the story text at grade 2 level of difficulty. In arithmetic, 55 per cent of grade 5 and 25 per cent of grade 8 children could not solve a simple division problem. In both reading and arithmetic, there was significant inter-state variation in student performance.

Standardised tests of competency in language, mathematics and environmental science were administered and each student's marks were recorded in percentage terms. These tests were administered by the National Council of Educational Research and Training (NCERT) in 2002 and the results published in 2006, soon after the release of the ASER survey. The average percentage mark for India as a whole is 50.3 per cent in science, 46.5 per cent in maths and 58.6 per cent in language.

3.1.6. Achievement in Secondary Education

As the primary level learning is weak, the secondary level of education will also be poor. In cross-country comparison, achievement levels of Indian students appear to be well below the international average, though the latter does include developed countries. While each Indian state examination board sets its own curricula and examinations and there are no national level data based on a common standardised achievement test in India, the Council of Boards of Secondary Education provides pass rates in the High School and Intermediate (senior secondary) examinations in different states.

However, the high school pass rates cannot be taken at face value as they are much inflated due to the phenomenon of wide-spread cheating, if the experience of Uttar Pradesh can be generalised. While the true levels of learning achievements in secondary education are generally hidden, fortuitously they became visible one year in Uttar Pradesh.

When the Kalyan Singh government brought in an anti-cheating rule and installed police at all examination centres in 1992 to prevent the mass-cheating that routinely takes place at board examinations in Uttar Pradesh, the pass rate in the High School exam fell from 57 per cent in 1991 to a pitiful 14.7 per cent in 1992. This is when the bar for passing is set very low, i.e. a student only needs on average 33 per cent marks in their various subjects in order to pass High School. This suggests the true extent of the problem of low achievement levels in secondary education, though it is possible that achievement levels in Uttar Pradesh are lower than those in other states.

3.1.7. School Quality

The impact of cognitive achievement on earnings, productivity and economic growth highlights the importance of school quality. The Public Report on Basic Education (PROBE) was the first serious evidence-based study of the state of primary schooling quality in India. It is based on a survey of schooling facilities in 242 villages across five north Indian states. Bihar, Madhya Pradesh, Rajasthan, Uttar Pradesh and Himachal Pradesh in 1996. PROBE found very poor school infrastructure, e.g. 26 per cent of schools did not have a blackboard in every classroom, 52 per cent had no playground, 59 per cent no drinking water, 89 per cent no toilet, 59 per cent no maps or charts, 75 per cent no toys, 77 per cent no library and 85 per cent no musical instruments.

The District Primary Education Project.(DPEP) started with donor assistance in the mid-1990s in districts with below national mean literacy rates. One of the explicit objectives of the DPEP was to construct schooling facilities and upgrade school infrastructures. While DPEP and its successor programme Sarva Shiksha Abhiyan (Campaign for Education for All) have obviously helped, the current state of school facilities is nevertheless clearly far from satisfactory, with substantial proportions of primary schools still without the most basic essentials such as drinking water, toilets, furniture, teaching aids and books, let alone more advanced resources such as fans, playground, musical instruments, computers etc.

The negligence of teachers in schools is equally worrying. Firstly, teacher absence rates are high. Kremer et. al.'s survey of teacher absence in rural India in 2003 made three unannounced visits to each one of 3700 schools in 20 major states of India. They found that, on average, 25 percent of teachers in government primary schools were absent from school on a given day. Secondly, and more disturbingly, even among teachers who were present, only about half were found engaged in teaching. The PROBE survey had similar findings of low level of teaching activity in schools. PROBE Team states that the extreme cases of teacher negligence were less devastating than the quiet inertia of the majority of teachers. In half of the sample schools, there was no teaching activity at the time of the investigators' visit. Inactive teachers were found engaged in a variety of pastimes such as sipping tea, reading comics, or eating peanuts, when they were not just sitting idle. Generally speaking, teaching activity has been reduced to a minimum in terms of both time and effort.

3.2. Role of Private Schooling

The debate on whether private schools provide better quality primary education as compared to government schools is heating up in India. This is completely understandable in the current scenario. On the one hand, for almost ten years, through Sarva Shiksha Abhiyan, the government has intensified the move towards universalising elementary education and more recently the Right to Education Bill has been passed in the Parliament. This push has led to impressive increases in provision and enrolment. On the other hand, ASER as well as other data show a clear rising trend in private school enrolment in rural India.

At the all India level, private school enrollment increased from 16.3 per cent in 2005 to about 22.6 per cent in 2008 – an increase of about 40 per cent. In the last year, between 2008 and 2009, private school enrollment has marginally dropped to 21.8 per cent in rural India. There is considerable variation across states. On the one end of the spectrum are states like UP, Haryana, Punjab and Kerala where private school enrollment is as high as 40 per cent and on the other end of the spectrum are states like Bihar and West Bengal with enrollment in private school closer to 5 per cent. However, what is clear is that whether enrollment in private schools is high or low, it has been increasing over time.

What has led to this shift towards private schools in rural areas? The standard answer and the common perception is that private schools provide a better quality education. This trend was started by parents living in urban areas – the elite having opted out of the government school system and the middle and lower income classes trying their level best to send their children to private schools – and now their rural counterparts are coming to the same conclusion. After all teacher attendance is much better in private schools and these schools often give instruction in English, mastery of which leads to better job prospects in the future.

For instance, richer households can afford to pay for additional tuition for their children. It is also well established that a larger proportion of children from more affluent homes attend private schools. In this case, part of the observed learning differential between government and private schools would be due to the extra help that private school children were getting at home and not because of the better quality of education being imparted in private schools. Therefore, it becomes important to try and estimate the learning differential once other things that impact learning are taken into account.

A larger number of siblings, presumably, reduces time spent on learning and reduces learning outcomes. Education of both parents is positively correlated with their children's learning level. Further, the impact of parents' education rises monotonically with their education level. Tuition has a large impact on learning – almost as large as the impact of mother's education. Finally, all household characteristics signifying greater affluence are positively correlated with learning outcomes.

Table 3.2 gives the learning differentials between government and private schools for the two learning outcomes. The "Uncontrolled" difference refers to the observed learning difference in a simple cross-tabulation, while the "Controlled" difference refers to the difference once other factors that affect learning are taken into account. In the case of reading in the local language, in many cases most of the learning differential disappears once other factors are controlled for – Uttarakhand, Chhattisgarh, Madhya Pradesh, Maharashtra, Andhra Pradesh, and Tamil Nadu. In the case of Madhya Pradesh, the difference is actually reversed – once other factors are controlled for government schools perform better than private schools. In the case of Andhra Pradesh and Tamil Nadu, where government schools had higher learning levels to start with, the gap widens once other factors are taken into account. On the other hand, in the case of Himachal Pradesh and West Bengal controlling for other factors widens the gap between government and private schools. Both these states have very different private school enrolment rates – since 2006 Himachal has had private school enrolment of about 22 per cent, while the number is closer to 5 per cent in West Bengal.

Table 3.2. Learning Differentials between Government and Private Schools

States	Reading in own language		Reading in English	
	Uncontrolled Difference	Controlled Difference	Uncontrolled Difference	Controlled Difference
J&K	15.84	11.08	11.61	6.49
Him.P.	-1.39	0.75	5.66	4.45
Punjab	27.78	15.06	44.89	31.65
Uttarakhand	7.90	2.15	20.74	13.32
Haryana	17.09	12.24	21.92	16.07
Rajasthan	13.07	9.55	15.11	11.15
U.P.	16.66	9.15	16.96	9.92
Bihar	17.87	9.12	23.50	14.41
Assam	14.59	8.52	20.64	14.27
WB	5.99	8.05	23.45	22.26
Jharkhand	19.76	13.29	20.99	14.35
Orissa	10.10	4.43	14.38	7.44
Chhattisgarh	2.35	0.86	5.86	1.89
MP	2.10	-3.39	9.72	3.26
Gujarat	22.50	10.81	27.27	14.85
Maharashtra	18.11	1.94	27.56	14.88
Andhra P.	-3.06	-7.00	21.03	15.77
Karnataka	5.45	2.44	28.02	22.86
Kerala	3.99	2.16	13.76	10.81
TamilNadu	-3.62	-4.91	20.39	16.99

In the case of English, in most states, the starting differentials are greater and the narrowing of the differential smaller as was the case for All India. However, there are still states like Chhattisgarh and Madhya Pradesh where $2/3^{rd}$ of the learning difference is attributable to factors other than private schooling. This analysis is based on the provisional ASER 2009 data for rural India. The wide variations acrcss states indicate that there is more beyond the type of village, type of school or type of family that determines the educational destiny of the child.

While the debate over private and government schools heats up and opinions and perceptions accumulate, India is also seeing more empirical evidence being gathered. Not only is more and better data needed for "controls" for explanatory variables on the right hand side of the equation but the left hand side – "children's learning" also needs to be measured much more comprehensively.

3.2.1. Quality Concerns

The last two or three years have witnessed a fairly vigorous debate in the education space over the role of the private sector in education, particularly at the elementary level, and its merits and/ or otherwise. The somewhat contentious provisions of the then Draft Right to Education Bill, 2005, recently passed as The Right of Children to Free and Compulsory Education Act, 2009, also contributed to this debate. Among other things, the Act stipulates that even unaided schools under private management would be responsible for providing free education to disadvantaged children between the ages of six and fourteen years from their immediate neighbourhood, at least to the extent of 25 percent of their strength in the entry class.

Although the Act has yet to be notified, not surprisingly, this provision has managements of recognised private schools up in arms. Joining them, albeit for very different reasons, are the proprietors of the unrecognised private schools, who risk monetary fines and jail terms if they continue to operate their schools without seeking recognition as prescribed under the Act. Ironically therefore, an Act that seeks to universalise elementary education for children in India has succeeded in alienating a significant proportion of those who are engaged in contributing to that very objective.

While the numbers offered by different sources vary slightly, it does appear to be more or less agreed that private schools in India account for anything between 15-25 percent of available schools. The District Information System for Education (DISE) data for 2007-08, released in November 2009, places the number of schools under private, unaided management at 173,282 out of a total of 1,250,775 schools in India, or about 14 percent. If one adds the number of aided schools under private management, we arrive at a figure of nearly 20 percent. According to NCERT's 7th All-India Educational Survey based on figures for 2002, enrolment in such private schools was 15 percent and 19 percent at the primary and upper primary stages respectively. While NUEPA and NCERT data capture the picture as related to recognised schools, ASER only notes the fact of private school enrolment without distinguishing between recognised or otherwise, thus providing the slightly higher figure of 21.8 percent children enrolled in private schools in 2009.

While there are minor variations in the private school enrolment indicated by ASER between 2007-2009, it would seem to be fairly clear that roughly one-fifth of elementary schools in India are under private management. If one adds the number of unrecognised private schools, about which little data is available, the percentage of children enrolled in what may be called non-government schools may be conservatively assumed to be between 25-30 percent, if not more. A study in 2006 showed that even in rural areas, almost 28 percent of the population had access to fee-charging private schools. In 2009, ASER data indicates that nearly 44 percent villages have access to private schools, and it would seem safe therefore to assume that this is a sector that is now well established.

At the same time, it may not be correct to presume that private schools are coming up in the absence of government schools; in many cases, they come up in areas with poor government school performance. Various studies have shown that while the private school sector has grown in recent years, leading to a decline in the relative enrolment in government schools, the former do not necessarily compete with the latter in terms of addressing unmet demand. Rather, in establishing themselves in areas where government schools already exist, these private schools meet differentiated or quality demand, attracting children from higher-income groups or from advantaged social groups.

Many years ago, when Milton Friedman first postulated his concept of vouchers in schools, he was convinced that liberalising the school sector would result in the emergence of a market where none existed, with educational "entrepreneurs" entering the market to take advantage of opportunities offered and in turn, to offer quality school services. While the effectiveness of voucher programmes remains a matter of some debate, it does seem true that the desire of parents to find an alternative to poorly performing government schools may have led in recent years to a growth in the number of available private schools, under both recognised and unrecognised management. It is certainly true that there is greater interest in establishing private schools today than there was earlier; no longer viewed as a purely philanthropic activity, the setting up of private schools is now attracting more and more corporate firms who see this as a potential business. In the case of some real estate developers, it is even being seen as another form of forward integration, making the purchase of apartments in their developments more attractive by virtue of guaranteeing a "good" school in the neighbourhood; a case in point is the recent announcement by a well-known real estate group, of a chain of 150 CBSE schools to be set up all over India. Similarly, the provisions of The Right of Children to Free and Compulsory Education Act, 2009, requiring the earmarking of 25 percent seats for children from disadvantaged families, are being viewed by many in the private sector as an opportunity to invest in setting up schools, in order to take advantage of the "guaranteed" reimbursement of costs by government.

The government's proposal to establish 2500 "model" schools in various districts through the Public Private Partnership (PPP) mode has also generated significant interest in the private sector, with several corporate houses exploring options of investing in the sector. Thus, the creation of educational "entrepreneurs" does appear to be taking place to some degree, even though the numbers remain comparatively small.

When various variables such as family background, income and others are controlled for, the difference in learning levels between government and private schools becomes marginal.

Similarly, Education Initiatives (EI), India's largest private sector testing organisation, found that "any lead that private schools show in their learning outcomes over government schools can be completely explained away by... (a) students' socio-economic background, (b) students' initial levels, (c) rote/procedural nature of learning tested. In other words, if you control for factor 1, look for improvements between say, Grade 3 and Grade 7 (to nullify any initial advantage), and the test is not rote/testing procedural knowledge only, private schools (do not) show any advantage over government schools".

3.3. Initiatives for Rural Education

A plethora of government initiatives to provide access to education may be underway, but issues of equity, quality and access remain areas of concern. Children in rural areas continue to be deprived of quality education owing to factors like lack of competent and committed teachers, lack of textbooks or teaching-learning materials, and so on.

A number of educational NGOs have emerged such as Pratham, Digantar, Azim Premji, MV Foundation and others—and some have acquired substantial stature both in terms of their contributions to educational improvements in a number of dimensions, as well as in terms of their influence, advocacy voice, public/media profile, research capacity and ability to mobilise funds for education both from individual donors in India and abroad and from the Indian corporate sector.

3.3.1. Sarva Shiksha Abhiyan

The *Sarva Shiksha Abhiyan* (SSA)—literally 'Campaign for Universal Education'—is India's flagship programme to universalise elementary education (grades 1 to 8) by the year 2010. It is a scheme sponsored by the Central government that is funded out of a revenues from a new cess, equal to 2 percent of all taxes, which was introduced in 2004. SSA provides additional funding to states to enrol out-of-school children and to improve school quality.

There is no rigorous evaluation of the impact of this massive intervention or its individual components so far. Two recent impact evaluations of the District Primary Education Project the predecessor to SSA and quite similar to it are by Schmid who uses a treatment intensity approach, and Jalan and Glinskaya who use a propensity score matching approach. The treatment intensity of a certain age group in a specific district depended on the years DPEP was in place and on the number of years that the group was in school-going age during this time period.

3.3.2. Mid-day Meal Scheme

Indian Supreme Court in late 2001, directed all states to implement the Mid-Day Meal Scheme by providing every child in every government and government assisted primary school with a prepared mid-day meal with a minimum content of 300 calories and 8-12 grams of protein each day of school for a minimum of 200 days.. By 2006, the MDM scheme was near universal in all states, following public mobilisation efforts to encourage states to act. This is a centrally funded scheme in that the central government provides grains, funds transportation and also pays food preparation costs, though the state government is responsible for providing the physical infrastructure for cooking the meals. Though it is not yet free of problems of quality and corruption, the fact that mid-day meals have become a part of the daily routine in most primary schools across the country is a major achievement. The scheme provides lunch to about 120 million children every school day and, as such, is the largest school meal scheme in the world.

Though there are no rigorous evaluations (e.g. randomised experiment studies) of the impact of this scheme on children's school enrolment and attendance and on nutritional and health status, several micro studies suggest major increases in enrolment immediately after the introduction of mid-day meals, e.g., 23 per cent in Barmer district of Rajasthan, 36 per cent in Madhya Pradesh, and other large increases in Karnataka. However, Deaton and Drèze note that the consumption of mid-day meals in primary schools appears to be heavily under-recorded in the National Sample Survey (NSS) data, making it hard to verify the impact of MDMs on school attendance from NSS surveys.

3.3.3. Para Teacher Schemes

Several states began using low-cost untrained teachers known variously as *Shiksha karmis, Shiksha mitras, Vidya Volunteers*, etc from the mid 1990s. By 2002, about 220,000 such 'para-teachers' had been appointed and by 2004, their number had risen to about 500,000. The schemes have been expanding rapidly since 2002 because from that year states could appoint contract teachers with central government grants. Under these schemes, persons with educational qualification requirements below those of government primary school regular teachers are employed on salaries that are one-fifth to one-half of government teacher salaries, in order to (a) expand schooling in a low cost way to small hamlets which are unserved by regular government schools, (b) to increase the number of instructors in single-teacher schools and (c) to reduce high pupil-teacher ratios. Although the model varies from state to state, the para-teacher jobs are typically tenable for ten months per year, but are annually renewable.

Para teacher schemes have raised a number of concerns about the ethical, legal, and political difficulties of sustaining two different standards of employment between regular teachers and contract teachers. The quality of teaching provided by these less-qualified instructors. Others have pointed that para-teachers may exhibit greater accountability due to closer community involvement in their recruitment and dismissal and because of the impermanence of their job-contracts. The contribution of these low-cost schemes so far is uncertain and that it is premature either to applaud or dismiss them.

3.3.4. Public-Private Partnerships in Education

A substantial public private partnership (PPP) system does operate in India, at least at the secondary and higher levels of education. This is the system of government grant-in-aid to privately managed schools known as 'aided' schools. However, over time, largely due to successive governments conceding teacher union demands, aided schools have become more and more like government schools: their teachers are now paid directly by the state government treasury at the same uniform salary rates as for government school teachers, and are recruited by a government-appointed selection committee rather than by the school. Aided schools also have the same fee policy as in government schools. Perhaps not surprisingly, learning achievements in aided schools are similar to those in government schools and significantly lower than in private schools after controlling for student intake and selection bias.

3.3.5. Empowering the Girl Child

The Kasturba Gandhi Balika Vidyalaya (KGBVs)—a scheme for girls from rural and disadvantaged groups from educationally backward blocks (EBBs) – is aimed at realising the constitutional commitment of providing free and compulsory education to all children in the age group of 6-14 years. The programme also aims to bridge gender and social gaps in education, which is an important objective of SSA.

Currently, the scheme is operational in over 3,000 EBBs in 24 states, where rural female literacy is below the national average and the gender gap in literacy is more than the national average. At present, there are 2,578 KGBVs, of which 2,383 are operational and the total number of girls enrolled is 1,76,713, according to Srivastava.

Similarly, the Mahila Samakhya Programme (MSP), working in the field of women empowerment through education, aims to promote 'skill-development' and 'entrepreurial skills' to make women self-reliant.

Likewise, the 'Pehchaan' project is a model that attempts to ensure that out-of-school girls (9-14 years) are provided with educational opportunities and brought on par with the other children of their age in schools. The project is a collaboration between Unicef, NGOs Digantar and Culp and the community.

3.3.6. NGO's Contribution

NGOs are conducting widespread education-related work in India. Their important contribution has been not only in grassroots educational work but also in terms of successful advocacy for education at the macro level by contributing to national educational debates and helping to make education access and quality prominent public issues. For instance, the role of the NGO *Right to Food Campaign* at both the micro and macro levels was critical in mobilising public opinion and building pressure for the rapid implementation of the school Mid-Day-Meal scheme in Indian states.

Pratham is the largest non governmental organisation working to provide quality education to the underprivileged children of India. Pratham was established in 1994 to provide education to the children in the slums of Mumbai city. Since then, the organisation has grown both in scope and geographical coverage. Today it reach out to millions of children living both in rural and urban areas through a range of interventions.

Pratham's programmes are designed to ensure that:

- Enrollment in schools increases
- Learning in schools and communities increases
- The education net reaches children who are unable to attend school
- Models are replicated and scaled up to serve large numbers of children to achieve a large scale impact.

Pratham has also become a powerful voice in the area of educational reform. The Annual Status of Education Report (ASER) facilitated by *Pratham* is referred to by the Central and State Governments for formulating various plans and policies.

Pratham runs a large scale. Bal Sakhi, a programme which provides an assistant teacher for remedial teaching of weak children in government schools. A randomised evaluation of this scheme in Gujarat and Mumbai by MIT's Poverty Action Lab showed that it dramatically increased learning by focusing on improving basic literacy and numeracy skills and that it was very cost-effective.

Another NGO, *Seva Mandir,* runs primary single-teacher non-formal education centres in tribal villages in Rajasthan and faces the problem of high teacher absenteeism. *Seva Mandir* tried to incentivise teachers by introducing an attendance-contingent bonus which was a function of the number of days the teacher was present in school. It selected 120 schools to participate in an experiment where teachers in 60 schools were given a camera with a tamper-proof date and time function and instructed him to take pictures of himself with his students every day at school opening and closing time, to provide proof of presence.

3.4. Role of Technology

Technology plays an important role in the education of any

country. Now a days, India is also implementing technology in the field of rural education.

The initiatives taken in this area are:

1. Every school in the villages has at least one computer.
2. Group classes are taken by using video conferencing and audio conferencing.
3. The teachers are given tools like Laptops, printers to provide notes and other important notices to the children.
4. Private Institutions like Real, NIIT are opening their centers in the rural areas to provide computer education to the students and the teachers.
5. Private companies like Wipro and others are providing basic infrastructures like computer parts, teachers and technicians for promoting rural education.

Many other initiatives are being taken in order to promote rural education through the use of technology.

The above mentioned initiatives are proving very effective towards the promotion of rural education. Computers in the rural primary schools attract the children and in turn they attend classes.

The computer education brings a feeling of confidence and equality among the village children. They feel like they are no less than those studying in high-fi schools in the cities. This feeling makes them work harder to achieve their goals.

The companies and institutions that provide free computer education are also promoting the talent of the village children in a very productive manner. This all can give a good boost to the slow pace of rural education in India. Also, technologies like video conferencing and audio conferencing and others are proving a very good means of mass education.

Many schools are using the electricity produced by non conventional resources of energy, this helps in the field of effective application of research.

All in all, technology is really helping the promotion of rural education in India. Although there are many productive initiatives taken in the field of promotion of rural education through technology, yet there are many hurdles in the path of progress. They can be mentioned as under:

i) *Corruption*–The computers, laptops, projectors and printers and other hardware that is provided for the village schools hardly reaches to its intended destination. Most of the time these things are swallowed in the path by the people incharge.

ii) *Lack of basic infrascructure* – Even after having a computer and a projector to attend a video conferencing class, we cannot go to school if we do not have roads and means of transport.

iii) *There is a lack of number of schools in the rural areas.* Students have to walk miles to reach their schools. And even if they reach their school, they are not in a condition to study.

iv) *Electricity*–What is the use of having a computer in a schools when we don't have proper electricity supply there?

All these things are very ugly hurdles in the path of promoting rural education in india. Technology has brought and can bring critical changes in any aspect of life. It can do so in the field of education as well. But all it needs is a good and honest implementation.

References

Agarwal, S.P., and N. Kanta. *Child Education in India: Index to Scholarly Writings*. Concept Publishing Co. New Delhi. 1990.

Caldwell, J.C., P.H. Reddy, and P. Caldwell. Educational Transition in Rural South India. *Population and Development Review*, Vol.11. No.1. 1985.

Dreze, Jean and Geeta Kingdon. School Participation in Rural India. *Review of Development Economics*, Vol. 5. (1). 2001.

Duraisamy, Malathy. Children's Schooling in Rural Tamil Nadu: Gender Disparity and the Role of Access, Parental and Household actors. *Journal of Educational Planning and Administration*, 12 (2). 1998.

Govinda, R. (ed). *India Education Report—A Profile of Basic Education*. Oxford University Press. New Delhi. 2002.

Jagannathan, Shanti. *Role of NGOs in Primary Education. A study of NGOís in India*. World Bank Policy Working Paper. August. 2000.

Jaychandaran, Usha. Understanding School Attendance and Children's Work Participation in India. *Journal of Educational Planning and Administration*. Vol. 15.No.1-4. 2001.

Sinha, Amarjeet. *Primary Schooling in India*. Vikas Publication House, New Delhi. 1998.

4

RURAL AGRICULTURE IN CHANGING ERA

After independence, India gave greater priority to agriculture. As a result, this sector achieved record growth during this period. The policy makers adopted a two fold strategy for regenerating agriculture immediately after independence. The first element of this strategy was to implement land reforms in order to remove institutional bottlenecks and the second element was to undertake massive investment in irrigation and other infrastructure in order to update the existing agricultural technology.

Technological innovations are essential to attain higher growth. To maintain a tempo of high growth, huge investments in new technology are essential. It needs to be underlined that without investment in irrigation, roads, electrification and other infrastructure, research and development and extension services, large increments cannot be achieved in agricultural output. It is, therefore, no wonder that the fastest growth has not taken place in states like Kerala and West Bengal where land reforms have been quite radical but in Punjab and Haryana which are not known for any radical land redistribution.

Investment in new technology determines the frontiers of growth where as the nature of growth and sharing of gains of new technology are determined by the institutional structure, in particular the pattern of land ownership. The latter, in turn is a direct consequence of changes brought about through land reforms. It needs to be underlined that technology and institutions are inextricably linked and cannot be easily separated.

Land reforms brought about important changes in most of the states in India during the mid-fifties. The most important contribution of land reforms was abolition of intermediaries and giving land titles to the actual cultivators. This released productive forces and the owner cultivators put in their best to augment production on their holdings. Whereas land reforms were important in increasing agricultural production during the first period, it also needs to be emphasised that during this period major output increases also took place because of large investments in irrigation infrastructure.

However, along with institutional changes, irrigation technology was an important instrument of growth. Further, it is absolutely incorrect to say that this period was characterised by equitable pattern of growth. The most important limitation of land reforms in various states was its failure in implementation of land ceilings enactments. Consequently land ownership distribution continued to be highly skewed. Because of this even during the first period, the interpersonal inequalities continued to be very large. There is evidence to suggest that the major gainers of irrigation technology were the upper middle, the rich and large farmers. It is no doubt true that the extent to which land reforms resulted in abolishing the intermediaries did release production forces by removing institutional barriers and thereby led to increase in output. But since large inequalities in land ownership were legitimised, the pattern of growth was such where the main agents of growth were the upper middle and rich farmers. Another point to be noted is that although green revolution technology did make a qualitative difference in augmenting yields, in a sense, it represented a continuation of the earlier irrigation technology. Given assured irrigation much higher yields became possible because of genetic break through in seeds. Highly accelerated output when superimposed on iniquitous institutional framework has had a far reaching impact on agrarian structure and land relations.

The domestic production of foodgrains in pest independence era of India was not adequate to meet the domestic demand. It was justifiably considered humiliating for a country of the size of India to be going around with a begging bowl. Hence increasing foodgrain output and achieving self sufficiency in foodgrains become a matter of high priority for the policy makers.

During the British rule, Indian agriculture was stagnated. To regenerate this India implemented various development programmes. But these programmes helped to develop only the upper-middle and rich farmers. Looked at in this context, to blame green revolution technology for distorted pattern of agricultural development is totally misconceived and illogical. It could actually be argued that without the introduction of new technology, India could not have recorded high growth in agriculture and could not have achieved near self-sufficiency in foodgrains.

The creation of skewed land structure as a result of halfhearted land reforms was the major reasons for unequal pattern of development. Interpersonal and inter-regional inequalities and poverty were the major characteristics of agrarian scene in India.

All categories of cultivators seem to have recorded substantial increases in their income as a result of adoption of new technology in areas where new technology has been introduced. It is the middle and small farmers rather than the large farmers, who seem to have derived relatively higher benefits out of the initial thrust of green revolution, mainly because of their ability to augment yields by adopting labour intensive methods by utilising their family labour in an optimum manner. With the intensification of new technology, the capitalist farmers are also tending to become as efficient as the small owners through optimum utilisation of capital assets.

In regions where new technology has been introduced it has led to increases in labour productivity. This, in turn, initially led to higher bargaining power of the landless labour and increased incomes and wages for them. However, this has gradually been counteracted by increased mechanisation on the one hand and large rural to rural migration of landless labour on the other. These two factors have tended to dampen the increases in wage rates in the prime green revolution regions.

Rural poverty is inversely correlated with agricultural growth. Notwithstanding the recent data, the extent of rural poverty is extremely high. Although anti-poverty programmes have tended to somewhat alleviate poverty in some parts, the vast amount of corruption and leakages and the incapacity to create permanent assets have made these programmes exorbitantly expensive. Nevertheless these programmes continue to be attractive for political reasons.

To conclude, the agrarian scene is not too comforting. Very large inter personal inequalities have given rise to deep discontent resulting in serious conflicts in many parts of India. With all these conflicts we are sitting on a powder keg. The emergence in this scenario of rich peasant leaders with strong regional affiliations has made the scene even more murky. The important fact to remember is that basically such peasant leadership is bound to be backward looking, non-secular and tyrannical towards the rural poor. Their increasing clout and elevation from the state to national politics is bound to disrupt the national consensus so assiduously built by the national bourgeoisie.

But it is the national bourgeoisie that is primarily responsible for the emergence of present situation—in so far as they failed to build an equitable agrarian structure through radical land reforms during the 'fifties. Now it is too late in the day as the political power fortress of landed interests has become almost impregnable.

However, in India the pace of industrialisation has been relatively slow and halting. This is because industrialisation and modernisation require large amounts of investment. Until recently, the rate of investment has been quite low. The recent increase in investment has been accompanied by sharp increase in capital output ratio. Further, industrialisation in developing countries needs huge investment in research and development for building up their own technologies. Besides capital investment, it requires large outlay on science education. Another important reason for slow industrial growth has been the deficiency of domestic rural demand which in turn has been constrained due to slow growth of agricultural incomes in many parts of the country.

The increasing capital intensity of consumer goods industry has hampered rapid growth in manufacturing employment, despite lip service paid to small scale industries. The recent policy of import liberalisation has on the one hand created serious problem for the domestic capital goods industry, it has simultaneously accelerated the process of capital intensification.

Unemployment is a major problem one cannot forget about the problems posed by increasing inequalities not only within the agricultural sector but also between urban and rural India and between organised and unorganised sectors of the economy. In India for example, the average income of workers in the organised sector was four times that of the unorganised workers. Further, among the unorganised workers, the agricultural worker had one third the income earned by the non-agricultural workers. This level of inequality has created the rural-urban divide along with great deal of tensions. It needs to be underlined that equitable distribution cannot be reconciled with the path of capitalist development. It requires a revolution to abolish the feudal inequalities of land ownership. Since these were not abolished, the capitalist development in India has resulted in further aggravating inequalities because of increasing value of land, property, other assets and because of multiplication of money acquisition opportunities. Urbanisation is a necessary concomitant of industrialisation. The pattern of urbanisation taking place in India is full of distortions. This is because despite Government intervention the land for housing has by and large been appropriated by the colonisers, the merchants and traders and affluent professionals and the migrant labourers from rural areas are forced to live in burgeoning slums.

In a nut shell, the problems of excessive dependence on agriculture, slow process of agricultural and industrial growth and ensuing inequality, unemployment and poverty are much too serious and demand careful thinking by all the enlightened and progressive sections of people in the country.

4.1. Growth of Rural Agriculture

From a nation dependent on food imports to feed its population, India today is not only self-sufficient in grain production, but also has a substantial reserve. The progress made by agriculture in the last four decades has been one of the biggest success stories of free India. Agriculture and allied activities constitute the single largest contributor to the Gross Domestic Product, almost 33 per cent of it. Agriculture is the means of livelihood of about two—thirds of the work force in the country.

This increase in agricultural production has been brought about by bringing additional area under cultivation, extension of irrigation facilities, the use of improved high yielding variety of seeds, better techniques evolved through agricultural research, water management, and plant protection through judicious use of fertilizers, pesticides and cropping practices.

4.1.1. Crops

The 1970s saw a multi-fold increase in wheat production that heralded the Green Revolution. In the next decade rice production rose significantly; in 1995-96, rice production was 79.6 million tons. Total grain production crossed 191 million tons in 1994-95, a big leap from 51 million tons in 1950-51. During the Seventh Plan, the average grain production was 155 million tons, 17 million tons more than the Sixth Plan average.

To carry improved technologies to farmers, a National Pulse Development Programme, covering 13 states, was launched in 1986. The Special Food Production Programme augmented efforts to boost pulse production further. In 1995-96, pulse production was 13.2 million tons. With some States offering more than the statutory minimum price, sugarcane production also received a boost, in 1995-96 a record 283.0 million tons was registered.

4.1.2. Irrigation

As efforts continued to increase the irrigation potential in the country, the last 40 years saw the gross irrigated area reach 8~ million hectares. Flood forecasting has become an important activity over the years. Over 500 hydrological stations collect and transmit data through 400 wireless stations for issuing forecasts for 157 sites. About 5000 forecasts are issued in a year with 94 per cent accuracy. The country also receives international support, with the World Bank as a primary source, for developing the water resources. International cooperation is also envisaged in setting up a National Center for Information on Water and Power. As there is a broad seismic belt in the country, particularly along the Himalayan, the Kutch region and ports of Maharashtra, a scheme is being evolved to collect all data on seismic activity at various dam sites.

4.1.3. Fertilizers

The fertilizer industry in India has grown tremendously in the last 30 years. The Government is keen to see that fertilizer reaches the farmers in the remote and hilly areas. It has been decided to decontrol the prices, distribution and movement of phosphatic and potassic fertilizers. Steps have been taken to ensure an increase in the supply of non-chemical fertilizers at reasonable prices. There are 53 fertilizer quality control laboratories in the country. Since bio—fertilisers are regarded as an effective, cheap and renewable supplement to chemical fertilizers, the Government is implementing a National Project on Development and Use of Bio-fertilisers. Under this scheme, one national and six regional centers for organising training, demonstrating programmes and quality testing of bio-fertilisers has been taken up.

It was a challenging decision of the Government to take Bombay High gas through a 1,700-km pipeline to feed fertilizer plants located in the consumption centers of North India. However, the major policy which has ensured the growth of the fertilizer industry is the thrust on accelerating fertilizer consumption by fixing, on the one hand, low and uniform price for fertilizers, and on the other hand providing the manufacturers adequate compensation through the retention price and subsidy scheme. As expected, fertilizer nutrient demand has gone up from 0.29 million tons in 1960-61 to 13.9 million tons at the end of 1995-96, compared to 12.15MT during 1992-93.

4.1.4. Fisheries

Fish production achieved an all-time high of 4.9 million tons at the end of 1995-96. Programmes that have helped boost production include the National Programme of Developing Fish Seeds, Fish Farmers' Development Agencies and Brackish Water Fish Farmers' Development Agencies. The Central Institute of Fisheries Nautical and Engineering Training trains the necessary manpower. To diversify fishing methods and introduce processed fish products on a semi-commercial scale, an Integrated Fisheries Project has been launched. A National Fisheries Advisory Board has also been established.

4.1.5. Food Processing

A Ministry of Food Processing Industries was established in July 1988 to ensure better utilisation of farmers' output by inducting modem technology into the processing of food products, thus augmenting the income of farmers and generating employment opportunities in rural areas. A new seeds policy has been adopted to provide access to high quality seeds and plant material for vegetables, fruit, flowers, oil-seeds and pulses, without in any way compromising quarantine conditions. Initiatives have been taken to encourage private sector investment in the food processing industry.

4.1.6. Agricultural Research

The apex body for education, research and extension education in the field of agriculture is the Indian Council of Agricultural Research (ICAR), established in 1929. India's transformation from a food deficit to a food surplus country is largely due to ICAR's smooth and rapid transfer of farm technology from the laboratory to the land.

ICAR discharges its responsibilities through 43 research institutes, four national research bureaus, 20 national research centers, nine project directorates, 70 all-India coordinated research projects, and 109 Krishi Vigyan Kendras (farm science centers). Besides, the programme of Agricultural Education is coordinated by ICAR with the curricula and other normative guidance given to the 26 Agricultural Universities and four National Research Institutes.

4.1.7. Oilseeds Production

A Technology Mission on Oilseeds was launched in 1986 to increase production of oilseeds in the country and attain self-sufficiency. Pulses were brought under the Technology Mission in 1990. Before the Mission was launched in 1985-86, oilseed production was 10.83 million tons; during 1995-96, it was estimated at 22.42 million tons, which is a record. Soybean, rapeseed and mustard largely contributed the increase in production. Production of pulses has seen many ups and downs, which is expected to be checked under the Mission. The country grows mainly nine oilseeds, with groundnut, rapeseed and mustard accounting for 62 per cent of total production. Lately, soybean and sunflower have shown major growth potential.

4.1.8. Drinking Water

A Technology Mission on Drinking Water and Related Water Management has been constituted to cover the residual problem villages and provide potable water at 40 liter per capita per day, and 70 liters per capita per day in desert areas inclusive of 30 liters for cattle. The Mission is tackling the problem through 55 mini-missions in project districts and countrywide problem oriented sub-missions. A Village Level Operation and Maintenance (VLOM) pump called India Mark-11 has been developed and is being exported to 40 countries. By March 31, 1993, over 79 per cent of the rural and about 85 per cent of the urban population was provided drinking water facilities.

4.2. Issues and Challenges

Although agriculture contributes only 21 per cent of India's GDP, its importance in the country's economic, social, and political fabric goes well beyond this indicator. The rural areas are still home to some 72 percent of the India's 1.1 billion people, a large number of whom are poor. Most of the rural poor depend on rain-fed agriculture and fragile forests for their livelihoods.

The sharp rise in foodgrain production during India's Green Revolution of the 1970s enabled the country to achieve self-sufficiency in foodgrains and stave off the threat of famine. Agricultural intensification in the 1970s to 1980s saw an increased demand for rural labour that raised rural wages and, together with declining food prices, reduced rural poverty.

Sustained, although much slower, agricultural growth in the 1990s reduced rural poverty to 26.3 percent by 1999/00. Since then, however, the slowdown in agricultural growth has become a major cause for concern. India's rice yields are one-third of China's and about half of those in Vietnam and Indonesia. With the exception of sugarcane, potato and tea, the same is true for most other agricultural commodities.

The Government of India places high priority on reducing poverty by raising agricultural productivity. However, bold action from policymakers will be required to shift away from the existing subsidy-based regime that is no longer sustainable, to build a solid foundation for a highly productive, internationally competitive, and diversified agricultural sector.

4.2.1. Slow Down in Agricultural Growth

Both the poorest as well as the more prosperous 'Green Revolution' states of Punjab, Haryana and Uttar Pradesh have recently witnessed a slow-down in agricultural growth. Some of the factors hampering the revival of growth are:

– *Poor composition of public expenditures*: Public spending on agricultural subsidies is crowding out productivity-enhancing investments such as agricultural research and extension, as well as investments in rural infrastructure, and the health and education of the rural people. In 1999/2000, agricultural subsidies amounted to 3 percent of GDP and were over 7 times the public investments in the sector.

– *Over-regulation of domestic agricultural trade:* While economic and trade reforms in the 1990s helped to improve the incentive framework, over-regulation of domestic trade has increased costs, price risks and uncertainty, undermining the sector's competitiveness.

– *Government interventions in labour, land, and credit markets:* More rapid growth of the rural non-farm sector is constrained by government interventions in factor markets — labour, land, and credit — and in output markets, such as the small-scale reservation of enterprises.

– Inadequate infrastructure and services in rural areas.

4.2.2. Weak Framework for Irrigation

Many states lack the incentives, policy, regulatory, and institutional framework for the efficient, sustainable, and equitable allocation of water.

Public spending in irrigation is spread over many uncompleted projects. In addition, existing infrastructure has rapidly deteriorated as operations and maintenance is given lower priority.

4.2.3. Inadequate Access to Land and Finance

Stringent land regulations discourage rural investments: While land distribution has become less skewed, land policy and regulations to increase security of tenure (including restrictions or bans on renting land or converting it to other uses) have had the unintended effect of reducing access by the landless and discouraging rural investments.

Computerisation of land records has brought to light institutional weaknesses: State government initiatives to computerise land records have reduced transaction costs and increased transparency, but also brought to light institutional weaknesses.

Rural poor have little access to credit: While India has a wide network of rural finance institutions, many of the rural poor remain excluded, due to inefficiencies in the formal finance institutions, the weak regulatory framework, high transaction costs, and risks associated with lending to agriculture.

4.2.4. Weak Natural Resources Management

One quarter of India's population depends on forests for at least part of their livelihoods. A purely conservation approach to forests is ineffective: Experience in India shows that a purely conservation approach to natural resources management does not work effectively and does little to reduce poverty. Weak resource rights for forest communities: The forest sector is also faced with weak resource rights and economic incentives for communities, an inefficient legal framework and participatory management, and poor access to markets.

4.2.5. Weak Delivery of Basic Services

Despite large expenditures in rural development, a highly centralised bureaucracy with low accountability and inefficient use of public funds limit their impact on poverty. In 1992, India amended its Constitution to create three tiers of democratically elected rural local governments bringing governance down to the villages. However, the transfer of authority, funds, and functionaries to these local bodies is progressing slowly, in part due to political vested interests. The poor are not empowered to contribute to shaping public programmes or to hold local governments accountable.

4.3. Agrarian Distress

Agriculture, the backbone of Indian economy is passing through a critical conditions. It is not at all a profitable business now. The condition of farmers is also very pathatic unable to face the miseries, suicides among farmers is also very high.

As the number of suicides in farmers spreading like an epidemic, it would be easy to identify the recent agrarian distress as an 'epidemic of suicides'. Yet identifying these suicides as an epidemic would be to naturalise the incidents and to be as dismissive of the suicides as have been the many governments and most policy makers and the media. To go beyond the simplistic and dismissive diagnoses that most government-nominated committees have made, it is imperative that we see the incidents of suicides by agriculturists as signalling 'distress' in as much the problems which have triggered such a response are widespread and affect a large number of rural citizens.

Some of the factors leads to agrarian distress are the impact of neo-liberal economic policies including the integration of Indian agriculture into the world market; increasing costs of production; inadequate institutional support including lack of availability of credit; deceleration in rural growth; decline in wages, growing indebtedness and unemployment, frequent loss of production, and as the results of a triple crisis of economy, society, and ecology.

The economic reasons which leads to the suicide of farmers are, most of the victims were undertaking commercial agriculture and were struggling with a range of new risks (of production, credit, marketing, climate) associated with commercial agriculture. Although cultivating these commercial crops, most of the victims lacked the economic and social wherewithal to be strong players in the Green Revolution game. All the reports indicate that most of the victims from the different states were marginal cultivators (less than 1 hectare) and small (1 to 2 hectares) cultivators, followed by semi-medium (2 to 4 hectares) cultivators. Compounding such economic marginality is the fact that a significant proportion of the victims were from the 'Backward Classes' or from lower ranked caste groups.

To gain a foothold in agriculture the non-cultivating groups also entered in farming. So, the number of suicides in such caste is also very high. They entered in agriculture because of the loss of their traditional occupation by the integration of agriculture into the market economy and the displacement of rural products by industrial products. Members of artisan, service and craft groups such as potters, wheel-makers, smiths, basket makers and others have particularly been impacted by such trends. Until recently such groups have had to perforce resort to becoming agricultural labourers or to migrating to urban areas. In some cases where artisan caste groups have taken to agriculture, they face problems as they are unable to practice agriculture without incurring large losses. While several studies have indicated the increasing popularisation and de-peasantisation processes which impact small and medium cultivators, these cases of suicides underscore the ways in which families from the low-ranked caste strata are attempting to stall or overcome such conditions of impoverishment or are seeking to enhance their incomes and standards of living. In their attempts to sustain or enhance their livelihoods, many of these marginal agriculturists attempt to shift from predominantly non-commercial cultivation and gain entry into commercial production with a focus on marketing their produce.

Huge debt, together destruction of agriculture was the key reason for distress. Since the key sources of non-institutional creditors have been agri-business agencies (who provide both inputs at deferred credit to agriculturists and loans), and the new money lenders and creditors, including relatives and friends who draw on their urban salaries, these debts pose a double burden on agriculturists. For one, interest rates are exorbitant and secondly they are linked to their personal and social networks. Inability to pay is often met with ridicule, ostracism or public humiliation.

4.3.1. Agricultural Knowledge Dissonance

Range of risks of resource and credit availability and the unreliable quality of seeds is the problem of agricultural knowledge and the increasing dissonance among agriculturists as to what knowledge is to be drawn upon to use their land. Local agricultural patterns and practices drew from a shared repository of knowledge much of which were transmitted and reproduced through the social and cultural structures of agricultural transactions and practices. However, the new agricultural regimes, from the Green Revolution model's use of hybrid seeds and external inputs to the new regime of using genetically modified (GM) seeds, induce increasing dissonance in the knowledge and know-how of agriculturists. Such a dissonance indicates a significant shift from not only the locally focused knowledge systems or the combining of both local and 'modern' ways in the Green Revolution model.

In the context of increasing commercialisation of agriculture, the intensity of competition among agri-business players and the growing distance of State extension service personnel have meant that agricultural practices are increasingly dictated by market-led fads. The result is intense competition among agriculturists to out compete each other by using new commercial varieties of seeds, fertilisers, and pesticides. Such absorption and adaptation of fads, while displacing their own local knowledge systems, has also led to increasing 'agricultural deskilling', that is the inability to use appropriate and relevant knowledge and practices.

The absence of public agencies in rural India and the lack of knowledge dissemination to a significant proportion of people. The inability of the cultivators to have used appropriate knowledge and skills of the new commercial inputs, especially that of pesticides, as a reason for their problems in agriculture.

The range of unsafe ways in which pesticides are applied and the ways in which pesticide containers are used for domestic and cooking purposes, thereby leading to a range of pesticide related health hazards and deaths. In addition, the lack of knowiedge about the use of appropriate amounts of pesticides was a leading cause for increasing debts as agriculturists purchased and sprayed large amounts of pesticides on their fields.

To sum, the increasing commercialisation of agriculture, the subscription to the dominant Green Revolution model, the range of risks, and the knowledge dissonance indicate the impact of the Green Revolution for marginal areas and for marginalised agriculturists. Increasing indebtedness, lack of marketing support, unviable parcels of land and the inability to provide basic support to cater to the family's requirements mark the lives of those attempting to sustain themselves within this dominant model. This is specially so for those who have inadequate capital, knowledge, and social support and who consider this to be the only route to enhancing their livelihoods, economic mobility and social status. Compounding such conditions and trends are the social and cultural contexts of the agrarian world in which the individual agriculturist's position in the world of risks is also linked to the social contexts, pressures and burdens s/he bears.

4.3.2. Agricultural Individualisation

The agrarian system was largely hierarchical with caste-based allocation of rights over land and its resources, agriculture was conducted on a pattern that was based on collectively shared knowledge forms and a common rhythm.

The caste-based social bases of production have been largely retained while the support and sustenance that could have been provided during times of crisis under the patron-client systems have disintegrated. As interdependence based on customary structures has declined, dependence on external structures and agencies has increased. While the disintegration of the customary forms of support has also liberated the working, low-ranked caste groups and enabled them to escape from caste prescribed subservience and debt servicing, the provisioning mechanisms of the moral economy have not been adequately replaced by State mechanisms of provisioning. Most government programmes that seek to provision the poor with food grains, housing or employment are also subject to rent-seeking behaviour which in the form of commissions, bribes and misallocation mean that the benefits barely reach the most deserving.

Moreover, the "autonomisation from the 'traditional' rural economy and structures of patronage and loyalty" and the continued prejudice of the upper castes against the former Untouchables increases the isolation of the low ranking, new agriculturists. If taking to the new forms of agriculture lead to knowledge dissonance, then for those taking to agriculture itself as a new occupation is doubly hazardous. Mohanty has highlighted, from his studies in the districts of Yavatwal and Amaravati in Maharashtra, that as new entrants into agriculture, members of low ranked communities are marginalised and face hostility from the dominant landed castes. Not only is knowledge not shared by the upper castes with the new entrants but there is also intense competition between agriculturists. This competition among themselves and the lack of adequate understanding of the new knowledge gleaned from marketing agencies has led to disastrous consequences. The details about agriculturists using excess fertilisers and pesticides in their fields and of not knowing how to deal with outbreaks of pests are indicative of this.

Besides, the fissioning of joint families into nuclear households. In such contexts, the head of the household and in most cases a single person bears the burden of having to eke out a satisfactory livelihood. Bearing risks that arise from debts, growing new crops, or ensuring good sale prices are all burdens on a single individual. Many of the reports highlight this; young men who having become heads of households, taking to economic strategies on their own, and negotiating the demands of the market with little or no support. Individualised decisions made in the context of recently divided families place an unduly large burden on individuals leading them to commit suicide in the face of large debts, loss of crops and loss of face. All of these; the separation of agriculturists from each other, the loss of a shared body of knowledge and practices, the onerous burden of risks that agriculturists bear without adequate support from institutions and State, the risks borne by heads of households and enterprising individuals and the double burdens of the low-ranked, new agriculturists can be identified as leading to the individualisation of agriculture. In the individualisation of agriculture is the disembedding of the shared social and cultural basis of agriculture and the integration of the individual agriculturist as an individual player into the market economy.

Agriculturists are often unable to gauge the risk involved in engaging with an unpredictable market, varying and unreliable climatic conditions, unreliable quality of seeds, fertilisers and pesticides, and unsure and untested forms of new agricultural practices. A marked impact of this is the inability of individual agriculturists to socially and psychologically bear the risks that comes with such atomised practices of agriculture. Loss of production, especially in the context of the risks or burdens of debts, means that it becomes a deeply personalised loss of self.

Agriculturists with marginal landholdings had borrowed large sums at exorbitant interest rates to purchase pumpsets, seeds, fertilisers and pesticides or to have wells dug. In the face of loss of crops from either pests or diseases or the lack of remunerative prices and the subsequent inability to repay the debts compounded their conditions of desperation. And in many cases, the humiliation in front of others when they were unable to repay the loans was the last straw that subsequently led to the act of committing suicide. The various reports provide poignant portrayals of such conditions.

The practice of agriculture is then longer either a 'social performance' conducted by drawing on social relations and networks or a planned set of strategies with which agriculturists make decisions, choices, and activities. As individual players, agriculturists must seek knowledge, credit, and access the market for the range of inputs on an individual basis thereby individually bearing a larger burden of the risks than they would have in the context of agriculture as socially embedded. But the individualisation of agriculture is not met with a concomitant individualisation of the private, social sphere.

Social obligations including new demands to subscribe to consumer defined life-styles and the increasing commercialisation of social lives, including life cycle rituals, leaves many an agriculturist with multiple burdens. Each person bears in the context of this dual burden of new economic pressures and risks, the social burdens of subscribing to pre-existing and new collective norms and obligations. Such consumerism is linked to the pervasive impact of sanskritisation and to the unusual consolidation of rituals as lifestyles in even rural societies. In the larger cultural frame in which economic modernisation is retained within an intensification of social traditionalisation, the individual bears the load of both worlds; risk and isolation at the economic level, where s/he must act as an individual and yet must subscribe collectively to social pressure and stigma at the social and cultural level. The result is the intense stress in which suicide seems to be the way out.

4.3.3. Marginalisation of Agriculturists

The crisis in Indian agriculture at the end of the twentieth century and marking the beginning of the new century encapsulates the social, economic and political position of agriculturists in which they remain vulnerable subjects and whose position and rights as citizens are recognised and reckoned with only during elections. The post 1991 period has witnessed the growing marginalisation of agriculturists and of agrarian issues in the public sphere of the nation. No longer is even the lip service of 'farmers are the backbone of the economy', or 'villages are the microcosm of India' being made. The inability of the central and state governments, once considered to be 'an embodiment' of development and 'an engine of agricultural progress', to have reviewed the situation in a comprehensive manner and to have adequately addressed the problems, linked to the recurring suicides, testify to the marginal position that agriculturists now occupy in the nation's social sensibilities and political economy.

The key issues that pertain to them; redistribution of resources, rights to basic education, health care and housing, policies that could provide remunerative prices, and State support in periods of crises are no longer central to the planning or budgetary agendas, and the poverty line is increasingly politically determined. Such neglect and oversight have in some cases led to situations where desperate village residents in the Punjab have gone to the extreme of putting up their whole villages for sale and have invited the President and Prime Minister of India to conduct a 'human market' for the sale of their kidneys. The development and legitimisation of Special Economic Zones, now emblematic in the standoff in West Bengal's Nandigram and Singur, in which the rural must make way for new manufacturing sectors, or what is fashionably being referred to as India's second wave of industrialisation, are only some cases in which agrarian issues are continuously bypassed.

Agriculturists are now in a state of 'advanced marginality' which Wacquant has identified as that of a group being isolated from the larger society and the oversight of their needs and rights by the State and the leading economic players. In fact, many governments have attempted to understand the crisis as a sign of personal weakness among agriculturists or indicative of their dependency.

Recently the Maharashtra government has sought the help of popular, 'hugging guru', Amritanandamayi and other spiritual leaders, to assist in addressing the crisis in the Vidharbha region and to set up spiritual guidance and rehabilitation centres. Such strategies and discourses have only further legitimised the role of the market with an emphasis on entrepreneurship and productivity rather than on resource distribution, sustainable agriculture, and equity. Subsequently, the focus on the market and the individual makes it all the more legitimate to lay the blame for failure on individuals. All these forces and processes are then coalescing against small and marginal agriculturists.

The oversight and negligence of agricultural issues by the State is compounded by the invisibilisation of agricultural issues by the popular media. Despite the spread, frequency and gravity of the distress, many mainstream media have neglected providing detailed and on-going news of the suicides.

The inability or failure of agriculturists to mobilise around these issues and to demand and gain policies that could assure their sustenance and survival indicates the problem of political mobilisation among agriculturists. Mobilisation, if any, in most rural areas continues to be centred around the interests of the dominant class or upper caste farmers who do not recognise the heterogeneity of agriculturists and hence do not often represent the interest of the small and medium agriculturists.

The aftermath of negligence has led to widespread disenchantment with agriculture as a livelihood and as a way of life. Contrary to until recent expressions of the close bonding between agriculturists and the land and of the village as a way of life, many rural residents seek to have alternative livelihoods that are distanced from that of agriculture. The need to be out of agricultural and caste-based occupations is linked to both: the largely un-remunerative bases of agriculture and the sense of deep futility and frustration it seems to bring. In now becoming widespread acts, either emulating others or as meaningful acts in which to state their frustration and disappointment, suicides are indexical of this disenchantment with agriculture.

4.3.4. Suicide of Farmers

Agriculture, long embedded with the caste system and its key source of reproduction, is now the site of economic modernity bringing with it the individualisation of actors, the introduction of new technologies, marketisation, and alien knowledge. For those economically and socially marginal in the system, the games of the new agricultural modernity induce and indict them into new risks. But the individualised economic actor remains embedded within the social and cultural fabric of his or her society and is therefore circumscribed by its norms and values of honour, shame, and responsibility.

The miseries of most of India's agriculturists seems to be precisely this, the 'disappearance of what gives meaning to everything' they know. The current predicament is one of intense anomie, which in a true Durkheimian way is represented in the conditions of loss of meaning, confusion and disorientation among marginal cultivators. That most victims choose to end their lives by consuming pesticides symbolises the key source of distress; agriculture itself and its new inputs, engaging with which has led to their ruination.

In gaining epidemic proportions the suicides have become both private and public acts that seek to call attention to the intense distress of the marginal and marginalised agriculturist. If such trends continue, unaddressed and seen as part of the inevitable 'grand transformation' that India must make to becoming a post-agricultural nation, then perhaps what Eric Hobsbawn noted as the most significant change of the twentieth century, that of the 'passing of the peasants', will in India be played out fully in the twenty-first century with the beginning of the death of its myriad forms of agricultures. Embedded in an unsustainable model of production, in which the significant symbols and meanings of agriculture and land itself are fast altering, and in which the State remains a distant actor, the mass of rural subjects, marginalised and overlooked, will probably provide the labour on which the nation will march towards its urban shift and for which agriculturists will be largely unremunerated and unremembered.

The beginning of agrarian crisis requires to be located much earlier to the beginning of suicide, which goes back to the 1980s when the terms of trade were going against agriculture, urban-biased policies were dominating the state policies, and farming was becoming a loosing proposition. Nonetheless, the crisis of agrarian economy during the decade of 1980s was expressed in different forms.

The protest was largely led by the farmers' movements in different parts of India such as *Shetkari Sangathana in* Maharashtra, *Vyavasayigal Sangam* in Tamil Nadu, and *Rajya Raitha Sangh* in Karnataka. Nowhere their protests were translated into a form of suicide, because the organisational form of farmers' struggle or movement provided them a sense of identity and belongingness. It also brought newer areas of discourses to the farmers to deal with. In the process, the opposition was translated into vibrant discourses on major issues such as development paradigm that the Indian state was following, the politics of denial, the third world development, the urban-biased policies, marginalisation of peasantry/farmers etc. However, a shift in the discourse came during the time when Indian state was succumbing to the pressure of global capital.

During the decade of globalisation, no activist from the Indian side committed suicide protesting against globalisation. Lee Kyung-Hae, a South Korean farmer and lawmaker in Cancun who was holding a banner that read, "WTO Kills Farmers", committed the first suicide against Globalisation. Lee was the former president of the Korean National Future Farmer's and Fisherman's Association, an agricultural lobbying group. Thus, one could discern that farmers' suicide was the result of deep or sharpening agrarian crisis emanating from the capitalist development in agriculture, although there are five important debates, which attempt to look at the issue of suicide differently.

The suicide is a part of multiple crises, such as ecological, economic, and social, each inter-linked with the other. The ecological crisis is the result of intense use of hybrid seeds, chemical fertilisers and pesticides, causing the erosion of soil fertility and increasing crop-susceptibility to pests and diseases. Heavy indebtedness led to the economic crisis. In the final analysis, this debate attempts to understand suicide through anthropological tools.

Secondly the crisis or the suicide is the negative growth of agrarian economy.

Again, the reasons for the suicide is in adapting the World Bank model of agriculture or what is called McKinsey Model of development that created spaces for industry-driven agriculture which ultimately translated into agri-business development including Information Technology. This model of development has not only exacerbated the crisis leading to an environmental catastrophe but also destroyed millions of rural livelihoods.

Next is suicide exclusively to one phenomenon, that is, the increasing indebtedness or the debt trap. As a corollary, one more discourse attempts to locate suicide in the wrong policies pursued by the central as well as the state governments over the past two decades, even while there is hardly any substantial investment in agriculture.

Finally, there are multiple issues such as incessant floods, manipulation of prices by traders, supply of spurious pesticides and seeds, decline in prices of agricultural produce, increase in the cost of agricultural inputs, successive drought in recent years, and of course, the neglect of farmers by the previous state government.

In the Indian context, the agrarian capitalism was introduced or juxtaposed on the existing social structure. In the process, it allowed different social structures to coexist along with the capitalism-it allowed the presence of different social structures along with agrarian capitalism. This does not mean that the state intervention was limited: its intervention was conditioned by such other factors as increasing the productivity, interlinking the local with the international market, bringing in large amount of land under capitalist development, remove the social categories who are "drag on the economy", and finally create new social categories such as rich peasantry who can partake in the capitalist development.

Green Revolution created surplus food, but allowed global capitalist to enter into the domain of agriculture through the means of seeds, fertilisers, etc. Land reforms was only partially successful, and that too, only in some states including Karnataka. This helped in bringing new social categories into the market, and also created spaces for them to operate at local/regional/national level. The introduction of co-operatives and other financial institutions tended to cater to the needs of large farmers, especially those who had land and other properties. However, the intervention of the state in the capitalist development of agriculture, including the ambiguous path that it resorted to, ultimately led to larger consequences on agriculture. Here lies the failure of Indian State too.

This is also the reason why the crisis began to emerge within one or two decades of the introduction of Green Revolution, when a series of farmers' movements came to emerge in different parts of India. Their demand mainly centred on the issues of remunerative prices or support prices, writing off loans, declaring agriculture as an industry, increased subsidies to agriculture produce, etc. Thus, the crisis brought the Indian State, including the Indian industrial classes to the focus. While analysing the crisis, loosing the class identity of the farmers' movements also assumed the centrality of debate. Further, the farmers' movements employed newer theoretical discourses.

Capitalism mediating through the process of globalisation became the immediate reason for the sharpening of the crisis. However, this too did not carry new agenda of overcoming ambiguous path that the Indian State all these years pursued, nor it attempted to create absolutely autonomous categories, which are not dependent on global capital.

Loosing the identity becomes most important at a time when the crisis was becoming too sharp. Secondly, the loss of identity emanated from the fact that new autonomous categories who derived their identity through leasing in land or market, began to view the crisis engulfing their own identity. To retain their distinct identity as "Market Oriented Autonomous Farmer" (MOAF), suicide became the last resort; it was but to escape from the intense crisis as well as to retain their social identity as "Market Oriented Autonomous Farmer". It is here that the attempt to retain the identity; as well as to protest against the growing crisis needs to be located.

Growing crisis is not the result of ambiguous path of capitalist development that the Indian state pursued over the past couple of years alone, but also due to the global capitalism pursuing the same path. It is also due to the way the global capitalism brought in or introduced new methodology to link the autonomous farmers or the social categories with the larger market.

The path of development has increased the disparity between the urban and rural areas. It is true that the poverty percentage over the past two decades has declined considerably between the urban and rural areas, while the disparity has increased or widened.

It has not made the farmers a debt-free category; rather it has trapped the farmers in the vicious circle of debt-trap. There is no farmer who is not indebted to financial institutions, co-operatives etc. Interestingly two types moneylenders have emerged in those areas where farmers have committed suicide. One type of moneylenders comes from within the rural side, who are either big farmers or capitalist farmers, and the second type of the moneylenders comes from the urban areas. In both the cases, the moneylenders use different techniques to extract the interest. Unlike earlier decades, the moneylenders in the globalisation context are not interested to appropriate the land in the event the farmers failed to pay the rent. This is because of uncertainty involved in the agrarian economy; secondly, agrarian economy requires the physical presence or physical Labour of the moneylenders, which the latter always sought to avoid it. This is the reason why the moneylender demands the interest rather than attaching the property.

Moneylender also uses other techniques like advancing the loan so that the farmers submit their agricultural produce to them. During this process, the prices of agricultural commodities are pegged to the lowest level. Interestingly it is true that indebtedness of rural household has not completely come to an end in recent years.

The cost of production also increased uncontrollability without a corresponding increase in the prices of agricultural produce. The increase in the cost of input prices lies in such issues as "withdrawal of subsidy" whether it is given for power or for fertilisers. This is nothing but the reinforcement of the argument that the terms of trade have gone once again against the agriculture. This has created a situation of negative growth in agricultural sector. In the process, the farmers lost heavily.

Negative growth has further accentuated the people living below the poverty line. It has not been able to create any job opportunities in the agrarian sector, either it is ending up in pushing large number of rural population to urban sector or increasing the pressure on the land. It is further fragmenting the land as well as increasing the people living below the poverty line.

The crisis has further fuelled by the external linkages, particularly the way the global capitalists resort to the strategy of subsidising the commodities at the cost of Indian farmers. They pursue a policy of duplicity: subsidising their domestic economy on the one hand, forcing the third world to withdraw the subsidies and in the process forcing the farmers to pay the accumulated debt to the regimes concerned.

4.4. Agriculture—Changing Scenario

Steady globalisation of trade has profound implications for future agricultural development. The diversity of India's agro-ecological setting, high bio-diversity and relatively low cost of labour provide potential for agricultural competitiveness in a globalised economy. It is expected that with increasing globalisation of markets over the years there will be demands for agricultural intensification. This will also be favoured because of greater backward and forward linkages between agriculture and food industry. Therefore, increase in production and productivity are bound to be strategically important to economy. Intensification will not only favour alleviation of rural poverty but will also improve resource conservation particularly in the small farming sector where farmers can be encouraged to take up organised production of high value crops such as fruits, specialty vegetables, flowers medicinal and aromatic herbs etc. Stronger demands for crops of the small farmers' will not only improve incomes and welfare but will also make investments in technology and resource conservation more attractive.

The General Agreement on Tariff and Trade (GATT) and liberalisation of global trade is bound to have impact on future land use and production pattern. Understanding the local, national and international environment under which agricultural production is taking shape will be crucial in developing our own strategies.

4.4.1. Extension Strategies

Since early fifties a number of public by funded agricultural development programmes have been sponsored. These have included programmes like the National Extension Service (NES) Blocks in 1953, the Intensive Agricultural District Programme (IADP) in 1961-62, the Intensive Agricultural Area Programme (IAAP) 1964-65, the High Yielding Variety (HYV) programme

1966-67 and the Small and Marginal Farmers' Development Programmes (SMFDP) in 1969-70. Though these programmes had a perceptible impact the efforts did not get replicated over different areas and categories of farmers. In mid seventies based on pilot level project in Rajasthan Canal and Chambal command area a 'Training and Visit' (T&V) system of extension was promoted in different states. Extension efforts of the Indian Council of Agricultural Research through its research Institutes and the State Agricultural University were largely limited to demonstration of new technologies through such programmes as National Demonstration Project, Operational Research Project, the Lab to Land Programme and the Krishi Vigyan Kendras. However, there appears much to be desired in the way that extension programmes are conceived and implemented.

At present extension programmes are implemented in largely a top-down fashion leaving little scope for localised planning and action. Farmers are almost passive receivers and their involvement in the process of technology generation and adoption is almost absent. Extension services, at present, are almost exclusively in the public sector domain and there is no effort or institutional support for other operators e.g. the NGOs, the corporate bodies etc.

Extension programmes sponsored by the government operate largely in isolation and there appears a strong need to view the extension programmes as an integral part of the research and development process.

The challenges facing agricultural development call for fundamental changes in our approach to technology transfer/ extension programmes. Changes are necessary in the context of changing economic environment following policy adjustments in relation to privatisation, deregulation and globalisation calling for greater efficiency and effectiveness of the extension system. More importantly there is need for

- Greater emphasis on providing producers with knowledge and understanding needed to overcome the problems or to exploit opportunities of their own specific production systems. Correspondingly there will be a need to de-emphasise 'package of practices' or the blanket recommendations, top down approach followed thus far.

- Shift in the focus of public extension systems from promoting inputs use to one on sustainable management of resources and improvements in the production system as a whole.
- Closer interaction between farmers, extension scientists and production system researchers in diagnosing problems and identifying location specific recommendations emphasising participation and education rather than being prescriptive.
- Widening the range of extension delivering agencies. While the publicly operated extension systems will continue to be important, there will appear a greater role for NGOs, farmers' associations and corporate sectors in particular situations. Role of commercial suppliers of seeds, agrochemicals, machinery, vaccines and medicines in providing advisories, as is already being done in a limited way, will need to be encouraged and factored into public system's own priorities.
- Wider and more creative use of mass media in tune with current developments in information technology to get information across to the farming community whose ability to overcome constrains at farm level will increasingly depend on access to reliable and up-to-date information.

The need for agricultural and rural information and advisory services is likely to intensify in the foreseeable future. In much of the world, agriculture faces the challenge of keeping pace with rapidly increasing population with few reserves of potentially cultivable land. Farmers will have to become more efficient and specialised.

From government perspectives, whatever priority is given to production, extension will remain a key policy tool for promoting ecologically and socially sustainable farming practices.

Some of the most promising recent developments in extension methodology have occurred where the key agenda is environmental or is concerned with equity, for example in the need for the joint management of forests by professionals and local forest users and in integrated pest management. A consistent theme running through the innovative approaches being used, such as participatory rural appraisal, is a fundamental change in what are the respective roles of extension agent and clients. The agent is no longer seen as the expert who has all the useful information and technical solutions; the clients' own knowledge and ingenuity, individually and collectively, are recognised as a major resource; solutions to local problems are to be developed in partnership between agent and clients. Since the scale at which extension support is required is thus often larger than the individual farm, extension workers need new skills of negotiation, conflict resolution, and the nurturing of emerging community organisations.

The future is also likely to witness a reversal of recent trends towards bureaucratisation within hierarchical extension services and a reduction in their levels of public funding. Moreover, a rapid increase can be expected in the use of information technology in support of extension. The forces for change in these areas will come from four main directions.

With the collapse during the past decade of socialist forms of economic organisation, the (dominant) role of the public sector in national economies has become questionable, with a strengthening trend to reduce levels of public spending. Thus government extension services and those which are largely publicly financed are, and will continue to be, under pressure to become more efficient, to reduce their expenditure and staff, and to pass on (some of) the costs of provision to their clients who directly benefit financially. This is particularly the case in countries where the farm population forms a small minority and agricultural production is in surplus. The case is weaker, but not absent, in less developed countries where farming households form a high proportion of the total population and where increasing food production is still important. Thus charging clients for services is likely to become more widespread, while governments will find it attractive to contract out the operation of services to the private or the voluntary sector.

In the future, rural populations will undoubtedly be progressively better educated, while their exposure to the mass media will continue to reduce their isolation and detachment from information, ideas, and an awareness of their situation within a national and international context. However, this exposure will not reduce the need for extension. Rather, given the changing demands on agricultural producers from population growth, increasing urbanisation, legislative changes, and market requirements, the more knowledgeable farming population will require different kinds of extension services. Social and economic trends within rural areas will therefore necessitate more highly trained, specialised, and technically competent workers, who also know where to obtain relevant information and problem solutions and various provision and organisational forms to replace monolithic government extension agencies. These agencies will need to recognise and serve different types of clients defined not in terms of "adopter categories" but of access to markets, degree of commercialisation, and relative dependence on agriculture for family income and welfare.

A recognition of the locale-specific nature of farming systems and the agricultural information systems which support them is an important source of the pressure towards the debureaucratisation and devolution of extension services. This recognition also implies that extension workers and farmers be jointly involved in the verification and adaptation of new technology, and thus that the extension workers respect farmers as experimenters, developers, and adapters of technology and devote more energy on communication within their local areas. The devolution of extension services to become local organisations is a reasonable corollary of this. Developments in mass media technology, already apparent over a decade ago, will continue to support this localisation of extension effort.

The continuing rapid development of telecommunications and computer-based information technology (IT) is probably the biggest factor for change in extension, one which will facilitate and reinforce other changes. There are many possibilities for the potential applications of the technology in agricultural extension. IT will bring new information services to rural areas over which farmers, as users, will have much greater control than over current information channels. Even if every farmer does not have a computer terminal, these could become readily available at local information resource centres, with computers carrying expert systems to help farmers to make decisions. However, it will not make extension workers redundant. Rather, they will be able to concentrate on tasks and services where human interaction is essential—in helping farmers individually and in small groups to diagnose problems, to interpret data, and to apply their meaning. The future will call for more able, more independent, more client-oriented extension workers. The emphasis will be on the quality of interaction between agent and client rather than on the movement of "messages" through a hierarchical system.

Flexibility and adaptability will be seen as virtues rather than aberrations. Paradoxically, these trends will bring us full circle to the early manifestations of modem extension in Europe. The itinerant agricultural teachers, unencumbered by large bureaucracies and tall hierarchies, will find their modem counterparts in the computer-carrying extension workers who are at ease helping farmers to identify the information they need in order to realise the potential of their farming operations. Looking back, we can regard the period from 1970 to 1995 as a necessary but expensive stage in the evolution of extension systems, after which extension agents were able to settle down to their main task—bringing together the expertise of farmers and the best available scientific knowledge to develop farms and local agricultural economies.

4.4.2. Technological Needs

It is apparent that the tasks of meeting the consumption needs of the projected population are going to be more difficult given the higher productivity base than in 1960s. There is also a growing realisation that previous strategies of generating and promoting technologies have contributed to serious and widespread problems of environmental and natural resource degradation. This implies that in future the technologies that are developed and promoted must result not only in increased productivity level but also ensure that the quality of natural resource base is preserved and enhanced. In short, they lead to sustainable improvements in agricultural production.

Productivity gains during the 'Green Revolution' era were largely confined to relatively well endowed areas. Given the wide range of agroecological setting and producers, Indian agriculture is faced with a great diversity of needs, opportunities and prospects. Future growth needs to be more rapid, more widely distributed and better targeted. Responding to these challenges will call for more efficient and sustainable use of increasingly scarce land water and germplasm resources.

Technical solutions required to solve problems will be increasingly location-specific and matched to the huge agroecological/climatic diversity. Detailed indigenous knowledge and greater skills in blending modern and traditional technologies to enhance productive efficiency will be more than ever before, key to the farming success and sectoral growth. Most technological solutions will have to be generated and adapted locally to make them compatible with socio-economic conditions of farming community.

New technologies are needed to push the yield frontiers further, utilise inputs more efficiently and diversify to more sustainable and higher value cropping patterns. These are all knowledge intensive technologies that require both a strong research and extension system and skilled farmers but also a reinvigorated interface where the emphasis is on mutual exchange information bringing advantages to all. At the same time potential of less favoured areas must be better exploited to meet the targets of growth and poverty alleviation.

These challenges have profound implications for products of agricultural research. The way they are transferred to the farmers and indeed the way research is organised and conducted. One thing is, however, clear—the new generation of technologies will have to be much more site specific, based on high quality science and a heightened opportunity for end user participation in the identification of targets. These must be not only aimed at increasing farmers' technical knowledge and understanding of science based agriculture but also taking advantage of opportunities for full integration with indigenous knowledge. It will also need to take on the challenges of incorporating the socio-economic context and role of markets.

With the passage of time and accelerated by macro-economic reforms undertaken in recent years, the Institutional arrangements as well as the mode of functions of bodies responsible for providing technical underpinning to agricultural growth are proving increasingly inadequate. Changes are needed urgently to respond to new demands for agricultural technologies from several directions. Increasing pressure to maintain and enhance the integrity of degrading natural resources, changes in demands and opportunities arising from economic liberalisation, unprecedented opportunities arising from advances in biotechnology, information revolution and most importantly the need and urgency to reach the poor and disadvantaged who have been by passed by the green revolution technologies.

Another important implication of increasing globalisation relates to the need for greater attention to the quality of produce and products both for the domestic and the foreign markets. This would imply that production must be tuned to actual rapidly changing product demand. Such adaptation to global markets would require state of the art research, which can be achieved only by setting global standards of research, focus on well defined priorities and mechanisms which permit close interaction of farmers with researchers, the private sector and markets.

4.4.3. Priority Areas

4.4.3.1. Enhancing Productivity

Creating a more productive, internationally competitive and diversified agricultural sector would require a shift in public expenditures away from subsidies towards productivity enhancing investments. Second it will require removing the restrictions on domestic private trade to improve the investment climate and meet expanding market opportunities. Third, the agricultural research and extension systems need to be strengthened to improve access to productivity enhancing technologies. The diverse conditions across India suggests the importance of regionally differentiated strategies, with a strong focus on the lagging states.

4.4.3.2.Improving Water Resource and Irrigation Management

Increase in multi-sectoral competition for water highlights the need to formulate water policies and unbundle water resources management from irrigation service delivery. Other key priorities include: (i) modernising Irrigation and Drainage Departments to integrate the participation of farmers and other agencies in irrigation management; (ii) improving cost recovery; (iii) rationalising public expenditures, with priority to completing schemes with the highest returns; and (iv) allocating sufficient resources for operations and maintenance for the sustainability of investments.

4.4.3.3.Strengthening rural non-farm sector growth

Rising incomes are fueling demand for higher-value fresh and processed agricultural products in domestic markets and globally, which open new opportunities for agricultural diversification to higher value products, agro-processing and related services. The government needs to shift its role from direct intervention and overregulation to creating the enabling environment for private sector participation and competition for agribusiness and more broadly, the rural non-farm sector growth. Improving the rural investment climate includes removing trade controls, rationalising labour regulations and the tax regime and improving access to credit and key infrastructure.

4.4.3.4.Improving Access to Sustainable Natural Resource Use

Balancing poverty reduction and conservation priorities: Finding win-win combinations for conservation and poverty reduction will be critical to sustainable natural resource management. This will involve addressing legal, policy and institutional constraints to devolving resource rights, and transferring responsibilities to local communities.

Improving access to land: States can build on the growing consensus to reform land policy, particularly land tenancy policy and land administration system. States that do not have tenancy restrictions can provide useful lessons in this regard. Over the longer term, a more holistic approach to land administration policies, regulations and institutions is necessary to ensure tenure security, reduce costs, and ensure fairness and sustainability of the system.

Improving access to rural finance: It would require improving the performance of regional rural banks and rural credit cooperatives by enhancing regulatory oversight, removing government control and ownership, and strengthening the legal framework for loan recovery and the use of land as collateral. It would also involve creating an enabling environment for the development of micro-finance institutions in rural areas.

4.4.3.5.Strengthening Institutions

State Government efforts in scaling up livelihood and community-driven development approaches will be critical to build social capital in the poorest areas as well as to expand savings mobilisation, promote productive investments, income generating opportunities and sustainable natural resource management. Direct support to self-help groups, village committees, user's associations, savings and loans groups and others can provide the initial 'push' to move organisations to higher level and access to new economic opportunities. Moreover, social mobilisation and particularly the empowerment of women's groups, through increased capacity for collective action will provide communities with greater "voice" and bargaining power in dealing with the private sector, markets and financial services.

As decentralisation efforts are pursued and local governments are given more prominence in the basic service delivery, the establishment of accountability mechanisms becomes critical. Local governments' capacity to identify local priorities through participatory budgeting and planning needs to be strengthened. This, in turn, would improve the rural investment climate, facilitating the involvement of the private sector, creating employment opportunities and linkages between farm and non-farm sectors.

References

FAO. *The potentials of microcomputers in support of agricultural extension, education and training*. Rome: FAO. 1993.

Government of India. *Report of the Expert Group on Agricultural Indebtedness*, Ministry of Finance. 2007.

Jodha, N. "Effectiveness of Farmers' Adjustment to Risk", *Economic and Political Weekly*, Vol. 13, No. 25, pp. A38-A48. 1978.

Mishra, S. *Agrarian Scenario in Post-reform India: A Story of Distress, Despair and Death*, WP-2007-001, Indira Gandhi Institute of Development Research, Mumbai. 2007.

Paroda, R. "Sustaining the Green Revolution: New Paradigms", Lecture delivered at the 2nd International Crop Science Congress, New Delhi. 1996.

Sampath, R.K. and C. Gopinath. "Land Distribution in India: Its Nature and Economic Implications". *Margin*, Vol.2 (3): 43-70. 1979

Sinha, Basawan and Ramesh Bhatia.*Economic Appraisal of irrigation projects in India*. Agricole Publishing Academy, New Delhi. 1982.

World Bank.*India: Sustaining Rapid Economic Growth*, A World Bank Country Study, and The World Bank, Washington, D.C.1997.

5

CHANGING RURAL EMPLOYMENT PATTERNS

During in the last decade, the Indian economy grew at an impressive rate and demographic pressure also slowed. However, the incidence of unemployment towards the end of the 1990s was more than seven percent. The situation is especially disconcerting in the rural sector. Employment in rural sector, which is associated mostly with agriculture, has stagnated during the 90s.

The agriculture sector shoulders the major responsibility of releasing material resources, necessary for meeting the capital and current expenditures of the modern sectors that generally provide the lead in the growth process. It is also supposed to sustain the process of urban industrial development by meeting the costs of shifting of workers from rural to urban areas, finding a shelter and sustenance at least during the period of transition. Further, able-bodied male labour required in the upcoming activities in towns and cities are also made available through release of workforce from within the agrarian system. More importantly, workforce displaced in industrial sector when it comes under slump due to fluctuations in global market, technological shifts or other socio-political disturbances, often seek absorption within agriculture in the short run.

Indian agriculture has been a major provider of surpluses and investable funds, during the colonial regime. Terms of trade were to the disadvantage of rural population, which helped in operationalising a "suction mechanism" for expropriating resources from the country. Internally, these resulted in a high disparity between agriculture and non-agricultural sectors and between rural and urban areas in per capita earnings as also in other dimensions of economic and social wellbeing.

In India, 1990's was the period of liberalisation. During this period, inequalities in the economy widened further. Launching of the programmes of globalisation and structural reform in the country has led to emergence and rapid growth of a few industries. Entrepreneurs from the global market have brought in capital in the select industries. Most of these have come up in and around large cities that are or in the process of being linked to tne global market. Globalisation, unfortunately, has brought little relief to agrarian economy, as the latter has no capacity to provide incentive to attract the global players. Instead, the import of agriculture and related products from international market has impacted negatively on the primary sector by lowering down the prices of its products. Sluggish growth in production, near stagnation in productivity and high regional variation have characterised agriculture, leading to phenomenal rise in unemployment. The negative impact of liberalisation are much more thus significant and visible in the rural than in urban economy, at least during its initial years.

Agriculture and low productive non-farm activities have come under serious stress as these have become a sink for the surplus labour, sharing the limited income among larger number of workers. Rural households have, thus, been forced to bear the cost of unstable growth process in globalising world of today and this needs to be understood in some depth by analysing the changing employment structure in the agrarian economy.

Increase in inequality induced through globalisation would accelerate rural urban migration. The pull factors operating through the highly productive sectors in urban centres would attract labour force from rural areas. Many among rural poor would move to urban areas in any case as a part of their survival strategy and supplement their family income in their villages.

Rural areas in the immediate periphery of large cities often act as dormitories for long distance poor migrants who commute on daily basis, as they are unable to find a foothold in the cities. Providing housing and basic amenities to these people is another mechanism through which the rural economy contributes to social viability of the region. The rural periphery, which absorbs these migrants has to deal with various socio-economic problems, due to deficiency of basic amenities and social fragmentation. These often lead to outbreak of epidemics, social tensions as also group conflicts, as the residents struggle to access or share the limited employment opportunities and basic amenities. This process helps the cities in reducing their infrastructural costs and pass on the responsibility and costs of social transition to peripheral villages.

The landed peasants in villages around a few manufacturing cities have successfully organised private financing institutions and are able to provide loans to local industries at low interest rates, without imposing any other administrative costs. Further, large sections of poor migrant workers have organised themselves into region or community-based-groups. They, thereby, bring down their cost of survival by sharing their dwelling units, other basic facilities and even their earnings on a monthly or weekly basis. The members of these groups jointly plan their vacations or going to the villages to meet exigencies in a manner that the total demand for labour in the local industry is met without any shortfall.

5.1. Impact of Economic Liberalisation

Policies of globalisation in the initial stage enable only the urban centres attract investment from within as well as outside the country although the growth process, through its forward and backward linkages, would ultimately transform the entire rural economy. The process of economic development in India, and more recently, the measures of liberalisation are also expected firstly to give a boost to urban economy but would then help in promoting growth of commercial and other service activities in rural areas, ushering in a process of sectoral diversification.

Rural economy here has indeed experienced a process of diversification. Information from various rounds of NSS suggests that there has been a modest and fluctuating process of sectoral diversification in rural areas during 1973–93 with the share of non-farm sector in employment (principal and subsidiary status) showing an increasing trend.

However, certain structural rigidities in Indian socio-political system have inhibited major shifts in workforce across sectors. Compared with the significant decline in the share of income of the primary sector and a corresponding increase in that of tertiary activities, their employment shifts can be described as modest.

Women and the rural population were the victims of the slow down of the sectoral diversification and decline in over all employment. Furthermore, one observes a decline in the percentage of subsidiary employment as also self-employment in rural areas, jobs that arguably help the poor households in finding a survival strategy. Yet another important dimension of change in the labour market in recent years is the process of casualisation.

However, the share of the unorganised sector in the total value added by manufacturing in has remained about the same, despite its significantly higher growth in employment. This implies that productivity in unorganised manufacturing has declined in relation to that of the organised sector. This reinforces the argument that the growth of nonfarm employment at a slightly higher rate that in agriculture in the nineties is not necessarily a healthy manifestation in the Indian economy.

This growth rate can, at least partly, be attributed to lack of productive opportunities anywhere else in the economy, and unorgnised activities constituting the proverbial "residual sector". It is to be noted that workforce dependent on agriculture has gone down only marginally in 1990s, although its share in the GDP has declined significantly, implying a decline in labour productivity and economic well-being of the rural population. It is important that the growth of demand for food-grains has been slow, much below what was predicted by policymakers. Per capita cereal consumption has gone down systematically over the past few decades, both in rural and urban areas.

The decline in rural consumption is indeed very substantial. The problems of serious malnutrition and hunger in the countryside can be attributed in no small measure to the worsening of the employment situation and lack of purchasing power. Importantly, agricultural production was stable during the first three years of the 1990s but thereafter has shown significant fluctuations. All these have led to a paradoxical situation when the country is forced to build a huge buffer stock and maintain it at enormous cost, despite serious nutritional deficiency.

5.2. Pattern of Interdependencies

The lack of productive opportunities with in the primary sector is the reason behind the deceleration in the growth of Non-farm Employment (NFE) during the 1990s. It would, indeed, be erroneous to encourage NFE in rural areas or be complacent about its growth, unless the wages, labour productivity and working conditions productivity of the workforce are resonably high or have prospects of improvement.

Incidence of NFE in rural areas is generally seen as a manifestation of sectoral diversification and the setting in motion of a process resulting in overall development in a region through inter-sectoral linkages. It is, therefore, surprising that the percentage of workers in rural NFE in 1993–4 shows no positive correlation with the overall employment level captured through WPR for the 15+ age group. The absence of employment opportunities forces people to go into trading, transport and industrial activities that possibly have low productivity. This hypothesis is supported by the positive correlation of NFE with the unemployment rate both by daily status. It is, therefore, difficult to argue that the growth of non-farm employment in rural areas has promoted economic development and generated employment opportunities for the masses.

NFE and poverty is negatively correlated. This is not very surprising, since one associates higher levels of NFE with higher economic opportunities, leading to a reduction in poverty. The disturbing point is that the relationship is extremely weak and statistically insignificant. The correlation of the former with per capita (state) income, is also insignificant. There is thus no evidence to suggest that the states reporting higher levels of income or low levels of poverty have experienced a high incidence of employment outside agriculture in rural areas or vice versa.

Nonetheless, the percentage of non-farm employment exhibits a strong and positive relationship with indicators of social development. The states with a high incidence of NFE report high levels of literacy and also low infant mortality. It may, therefore, be argued that the success of non-farm activities ensures or is dependent on a certain minimum level of infrastructural facilities and the social environment. The growth of non-farm employment may not have a positive impact on employment or income opportunities for the poor but appears to be increasing their access to educational and health facilities. The growth of NFE can not, thus, be dismissed as an insignificant phenomenon in the agrarian society of India.

The level and growth in urbanisation is expected to have a positive impact on the level of NFE in rural areas. Similarly, the level of NFE in rural areas has no significant relationship with the growth of the urban population during the 1980s. The 1990s, however, witness a strong negative correlation, which implies that the states with higher growth of urban population report lower levels of NFE. During the 1990s, many of the developed and highly urbanised states reported high urban growth, unlike the pattern observed earlier. Unfortunately, however, this process of urbanisation has not resulted in higher non-farm job opportunities for the rural labour force. Moreover, the persons engaged in traditional occupations, such as artisans, craftsmen, carpenters, goldsmiths, blacksmiths, etc. have been badly hit by the state-of-the-art technological innovations during the postreform era and forced to leave their profession. The incremental labour force, thus, seem to be switching over to the farm activities not by choice but by compulsion. Therefore, rural NFE has become more of a residual sector with an increase in urbanisation.

The level of NFE in rural areas reports a negative and significant relationship with the share of small towns (class IV to VI) in the total urban population in 1991. This suggests that the states with a high share of urban population in small and medium towns tend to have low incidence of NFE in rural areas. In 1999–2000, the relationship between rural NFE and the level of urban population in small towns is statistically insignificant. Furthermore, the correlations between the growth of small towns and level of rural NFE are not significant at all for the 1980s and 1990s. There is thus no evidence that small and medium towns help in promoting non-agricultural activities in the rural hinterland.

The correlation of urban growth with rural NFE shows a similar pattern. Further, the correlations between the growth of large cities and the growth of the overall urban population, across the states, are positive and significant. It is, therefore, not surprising that rapid growth in class I cities should be associated with low levels of NFE. One can conclude that the process of urbanisation during the 1990s, which has been strongly linked with the growth of class I cities that have attracted much of the infrastructural and industrial investment, has failed in disseminating growth, resulting in low levels of employment outside agriculture in rural areas.

5.3. Migration and Regional Disparity

Migration and regional disparity are strongly interrelated phenomenon, which leads to differential growth in population in different regions, which is expected to bring about some kind of equilibrium in labour market. There seems to be a general agreement among planners and researchers that regional disparity in India has gone up since the mid sixties, after a slight decline in the fifties and early sixties. The inequality can be noted to be going up in terms of per capita income as also various other socio-economic indicators. The disparity in per capita income across states, measured in terms of coefficient of variation (CV) has gone up.

Inequality in agricultural development has gone up very sharply in the nineties on the face of dismal performance in this sector. Similar increases in disparity can be noted in case of other sectors as also infrastructural facilities and basic amenities like power, transport system, sanitation and health services etc. In some of the social dimensions like access to elementary education, drinking water supply and toilet facilities, the regional disparity has, however, registered a decline. But when we consider higher order amenities like high school or college education, flush toilets, per capita water consumption etc. the disparity has gone up.

The interstate inequality has reported a rising trend in several other social dimensions like incidence of poverty, population growth, infant mortality rates etc. Spatial disparity in development should, ceteris paribus, encourage migration towards the developed states and regions, as per the neo-classical models of growth and labour mobility. Interestingly the migration pattern in India, as observed through the data since 1961, fits well in these models that assume that optimality in the spatial distribution of economic activities in the long run would be brought about through free movement of the factors of production. Indeed, the backward states had high rates of outmigration while the developed states were absorbing these migrants.

However, migration in general and interstate migration in particular, shows a different pattern in recent decades. Despite significant increase in regional disparity, migration has gone down. The outstanding feature of the changing pattern of migration is a clear shift from the colonial pattern wherein people moved from the impoverished hinterland to a few developed regions or to their large cities. As a result of this change, the developed states in the nineties report a much lower percentage of immigrants than in the previous decades. As a corollary to that, outmigration from the backward states has gone down.

Persons who used to migrate out of the backward areas in search of jobs are now generally able to find means of livelihood at their own places. Availability of education, health and other services has also stabilised the population in backward regions. Similarly, better communication and transport facilities have alleviated the need to move for employment, education etc., since people can now commute to distant cities, providing employment. Thus, the mobility of the factors of production, operationalised through the market, would automatically ensure optimal distribution of economic activities in space.

The problem of decline in the rate of outmigration from the rural areas in backward states namely, Bihar, Madhya Pradesh, Rajasthan and Uttar Pradesh and their seeking absorption within the rural economy itself would pose a serious since these have high rates of natural growth. Indeed, absorbing the growing labour force productively within the rural economy has become more difficult in the backward states due to the fall in their rate of outmigration in recent years.

A "suction mechanism" is in operation within the Indian agrarian system whereby the regions with high and growing land productivity are able to attract migrant workers from other regions. This, results in equalisation of labour productivity in space. Analysing the data on land productivity and labour absorption, Alagh, Bhaduri and Bhalla have come to a similar conclusion. It is possible to use their stipulation to build up a rationale for adopting a development strategy in agriculture, focusing on only a select regions having a high growth potential, as often proposed under the liberalisation policy. However, with a sluggish growth in rural immigration, the possibility of making migrant workers—coming from across districts and state—share the benefits of concentrated agricultural development in a few districts, seems rather bleak. On the otherhand, the growth of manufacturing sector in the nineties has drawn the rural migrants in and around a few large cities in a few developed states. With the restrictions on locating industries within certain stipulated distance of the large cities being gradually withdrawn and incentives available for setting up units in backward regions being phased out, city peripheries are emerging as the major areas of attraction.

5.4. Degenerated Peripheralisation

The urban processes in India seems to operate in a manner so as to pass on a part of the cost of urbanisation to the immediate periphery, manifested in strong backwash effect on the welfare of rural households (HH). A number of indicators, pertaining to socio-economic dimensions of development, have been built by aggregating HH data at the village level, giving equal weights to all the HH. These have been plotted against the distance of the villages from their nearest town which has been ascertained from the 1991 Population Census.

Wages paid to male and female agricultural workers, non-agricultural workers and child workers have been included separately for males and females. Average size of HH is obtained as the number of persons per HH, averaged at the village level.

Infant and child mortality rates have been included in the health dimension. These are calculated as the number of deaths among children of less than a year and the number of deaths in the age group of 1–5 years, per 1,000 live births. Information on major diseases such as epilepsy, hypertension, diabetes mellitus, heart diseases, mental illness, tuberculosis, leprosy, etc. are available from the survey. Information has also been gathered on short duration sicknesses, e.g. diarrhoea, coughs, colds and fevers. The cost incurred by HH for consulting physicians, buying medicines, travel, hospitalisation, etc. have been disaggregated by the nature of illness, namely short- and long-term. Expenditures incurred in treating short and long-term ailments have been considered separately.

In educational dimension, the literacy rate has been calculated as the percentage of persons who can read and write in the age group of 7 years and above to the total population in the village. The percentage of children (in the age group 6–14 years) enrolled in a formal school to the total children in the concerned age group has been taken in as the primary enrolment rate. Expenditure on books, stationary, uniforms, private coaching, transport, boarding and lodging and school examination have been included to articulate private expenditure.

The values of socio-economic indicators tend to decline linearly with distance in the rural hinterland. It may nonetheless be argued that space incorporates imperfection, leading to a departure from linearity. In view of this, the relationships among the selected indicators have been analysed using rudimentary non-parametric plots known as cubic splines, as given in the figures below. This has been done to see if there exists a non-linear relationship between the indicators and distance and whether it changes at different intervals.

Per capita income falls drastically in the immediate vicinity of the town but the fall becomes smooth thereafter. The steep decline could be due to migration of people from distant rural areas and their absorption in the immediate rural periphery. Many among the migrants, coming to urban centres in search of jobs, seem to be pushed to this periphery which acts as a dormitory for the city or town. Fast increasing HH sizes in the immediate peripheries, is also an indication of the absorption of large number of migrants in the peripheral region.

Long duration morbidity shows a negative correlation with distance, implying that the incidence of sickness closer to the urban centres is higher than in villages away from them. Certain diseases, such as hypertension, heart diseases, etc. would possibly have a higher toll in urban centres, due to the tensions of an urban environment. Further, a large number of poor migrants who cannot afford shelter in the city/town reside in villages just outside the urban limits. Their nutrition and health status would be low which partly explains the high morbidity near the urban centres.

The distributional pattern in the case of the indicators of educational development confirms the thesis of degenerated peripheralisation, built on the basis of the analysis of economic and health related indicators. The literacy rate (7+ age group) declines sharply in the immediate periphery of the cities/towns, but tends to stabilise thereafter. This obviously is due to the absorption of a large number of poor and illiterate migrants in the immediate hinterland.

The same is true for enrolment rates wherein the decline is sharper still. In fact, after the initial decline, the enrolment rate tends increase slightly after 15 km and thereafter it stabilises. The percentage of school going children in the periphery villages is less than even that of the distant villages. This is possibly due to a high incidence of child labour and/or the incapacity of poor migrants residing in the peripheral villages to send their children to formal educational institutions. The decline thereafter is marginal. All these reflect an absence of a continuum in space around the urban centres in the country.

5.5. Absorption of Market Shocks

Recent developments in labour and capital market bring out various informal and semiformal institutional arrangements made by peasants and migrant labourers that absorb, a part of the cost of uncertainty in capital and labour market. Many of the industrialists and large traders in all the four towns get finances from private financers to meet their requirements of working capital. This institutional arrangement makes it possible for them to avail loans without much delay and at a cheaper rate. The interest rate becomes comparable to that of the formal banking system at the time of glut in the market and even lower than the latter, when all transaction costs are taken into consideration. Importantly, the interest of the financiers here has not been to see that their borrowers fail in their business so that the former can use their powers in usurping the property or business of the latter, as often described in the traditional literature pertaining to usurious capital in India.

There is no "unholy nexus" between traders and money-lenders that led to ruining of the borrowers in rural areas during the colonial period or as it happens even now in the backward states in the country such as Bihar, Uttar Pradesh and Orissa. There is no interlocking of credit, land and product markets, which often leads to a conflict of interest between the entrepreneur and his/her financier. The latter's sole interest, as observed in the towns under consideration, is to get back the instalments of interest along with the principle amount. It is seldom that the financier does anything to make the borrowers default in the payment or even wishes a calamity on him. This is because, if the entrepreneur fails in his business, there is a risk that the financier would not get his money back, due to the informality of arrangement.

The informal credit system functions well and the codes or behaviour are respected by one and all. Importantly, a number of these finance companies have been set up, directly or indirectly, by the landed peasantry. Many of the farmers find it more productive to put their surplus funds in private finance companies. The profitability of these companies, thus, gets determined by that of the industries and other business that take loan from the former.

Surpluses generated within rural economy are, thus, transferred to the urban sectors and creates productive assets. Furthermore, the process makes the peasants risk bearers in industrial sector. Loans are often given within known circles, caste or community groups etc. whereby informal pressures are brought in for loan recovery. Also, in case of individuals refusing to pay back, physical force is exercised by the groups running the finance companies or their hired workers. However, if there is a large-scale failure of business in the town, informal nature of the borrowings makes loan recovery extremely difficult since monetary transactions take place mostly without proper documentation or following legal procedures. Also, legal battles to recover the dues are mostly long drawn and not very rewarding. Consequently, dip in profitability in urban industries often depresses the income in rural economy due to the risk sharing mechanism, institutionalised through the informal capital market. It is this institution of risk sharing which has enabled many of the entrepreneurs, financiers and contractors in the city to remain in business during the period of slump in recent years.

5.6. Changing Employment Structure

With differential growth of employment among different sectors of the economy, there have obviously been changes in the structure of employment. Among the three major sectors by broad division of economic activity, namely, agriculture, industry and services, there has been a decline, as expected, in the share of agriculture and increase in the share of industry and services in total employment. The structural changes have, however, been slow. In a period of 27 years, from 1973 to 2000, the share of agriculture has declined by 17 percentage points only from 74 to 57 per cent. Share of industry increased from 11 to 18 per cent and that of services rose faster from 15 per cent in 1972-73 to 26 per cent in 1999-2000, growing particularly fast during 1987-88 to 1999-2000.

Table 5.1. Employment Shares of Major Sectors (per cent)

	1972-73	1977-78	1983	1987-88	1993-94	1999-2000
Agriculture	74.0	72.3	68.4	65.5	60.38	56.70
Industry	11.4	12.3	13.7	15.5	15.82	17.56
Services	14.6	15.4	17.5	18.4	23.80	25.74

The slow change in employment structure assumes the nature of a problem particularly when seen along with the change in the structure of the national gross domestic product. During the period when the share of employment in agriculture declined from 74 per cent to 57 per cent, its contribution in GDP declined from over 40 per cent to 22 per cent; and, when the share of services sector in employment increased from 15 to 26 per cent, its contribution to GDP increased much faster from around 30 per cent to 52 per cent. As a result the asymmetry between the income and employment shares among different sectors has sharply increased, particularly between the agricultural and non-agricultural sectors. A sharper decline in contribution of agriculture in GDP than in its share in employment implies a decline in its relative productivity and increase in income differentials between agriculture and non-agricultural sectors. An opposite trend is seen in the services, where the increase in GDP share has been faster than of employment, while industry has retained its position in respect of relative productivity. That there would be a decline in the share of agriculture in GDP was expected, but a continuance of heavy dependence of workers and population on agriculture as source of income and livelihood is a matter of concern from the viewpoints of poverty and inequality. One hopes that a relatively higher employment growth in manufacturing, construction, transport and services like trade, as experienced in recent years will lead to some correction in this increasing imbalance.

Another aspect of employment trends and structure that is of interest in a developmental context is the distribution of workers by employment category in terms of self-employed, regular wage and salaried workers and casual wage earners. It has been generally expected that with shift of workers from agriculture to non-agricultural activities and from footloose to enterprise based employment, there will be an increase in the proportion of workers employed on a regular wage and salary basis. There has been a decline, albeit slow, in the share of self-employed, from 61 per cent in 1972-1973 to 53 per cent in 1999-2000. The share of regular wage-salaried workers has, however, stagnated at around 14 per cent, while that of casual workers has increased from 23 to 33 per cent.

Table 5.2. Employment Status by Category of Employment

	1972-73	1977-78	1983	1987-88	1993-94	1999-2000
Self Employed	61.4	58.9	57.4	56.0	54.8	52.9
Regular Wage/ Salary Workers	15.3	13.9	13.9	14.4	13.2	13.9
Casual Wage Workers	23.3	27.2	28.7	29.6	32.0	33.2

This situation has generally been interpreted to mean an increasing 'casualisation' of workforce. In so far as the term describes an increase in the share of casual workers, it is factually true. But if it is meant to imply a process of 'regular' workers turning 'casual', or a decline in employment and earnings, the trend needs to be carefully analysed. The shift is seen from self-employed to casual workers category and most of it has taken place in rural areas, from agriculture to non-agricultural activities, such as construction, trade and services. There has, no doubt, been displacement of workers from large industries in urban areas, rendering the regular workers to the status of casual workers. But the magnitude of such change in status of workers has not been very significant in relation to the total numbers involved.

The phenomenon of casualisation, therefore, needs to be seen in the overall perspective of employment trends in the economy. Agriculture is increasingly unable to productively absorb the growing rural labour force. At the same time, there has been some growth of non-agricultural activities in rural areas in construction, trade and services which have generally offered better earnings than agriculture. Most of these employment opportunities have been of temporary and casual nature. But they have provided either full-time or supplementary employment adding to the incomes of the rural households. On the other hand, regular jobs have hardly increased in he urban areas; in fact, there is evidence to show that such jobs have declined due to redundancy caused by technological and competitive compulsions in the larger industrial enterprises. So, part of the regular workforce has been rendered casual and most new jobs have been in the casual category.

Increasing proportion of casual workers in the total employment is thus mostly a result of structural shifts taking place in the rural areas. To some extent, it is distress-driven, the small and marginal landholders and the landless not finding gainful work in agriculture and taking up whatever work they find in the non-agricultural activities, irrespective of earnings from them. But there is evidence to suggest that many are opting for non-farm work due to more regular employment and better earnings. This has been possible partly on account of various state sponsored employment programmes, and partly because of an increase in the demand for labour in expanding construction, trade and service activities in rural areas. In other words, 'casualisation' of the nature observed does not necessarily imply a deterioration in the quality of employment. A small part of the real casualisation that has taken place due to displacement of regular workers from large enterprise in the urban areas, no doubt, indicates such a deterioration.

Slow growth of employment in the organised sector has been a major factor in the stagnancy in the proportion of regular wage and salary earners. This sector consisting of public services and enterprises and large private firms, is the one that offers regular jobs. Employment growth in this sector has been just about 0.5 per cent during 1994-2000. In the post-2000 period, organised sector employment has, infact, shown an absolute decline; it declined by about one million from around 28 million to 27 million during 2000-2003.

Of around 21 million new employment opportunities generated during 1994-2000 only about 4 per cent has been in the organised sector, and the rest 96 per cent in the unorganised sector. As a result, the share of the unorganised sector in total employment has increased from around 92 per cent to 93 per cent. The high and increasing preponderance of the unorganised sector has been a matter of anxiety from the viewpoint of quality of employment as workers in this sector suffer from poor conditions of work, low earnings and lack of employment and social security.

5.7. Employment Prospects

The fact that a high rate of economic growth has not been able to generate high employment growth, and it has, in fact, been accompanied by a slow down in employment growth in recent years, has led many economists and others concerned to portray the recent experience as one of 'jobless growth'. A brief account of the performance of different sectors as attempted earlier, however, shows that but for the almost negligible growth in agriculture, employment growth in non-agricultural sector has not really been jobless. Yet, employment elasticities have declined in most sectors, though in some sectors like construction, trade and transport, they continue to be relatively high. And a faster growth of these sectors will lead to an increase in overall employment growth. Their share in employment, however, is still small as compared to manufacturing which have shown a relatively low employment growth and low and declining employment elasticity. Yet, manufacturing still has an employment elasticity of around 0.3 and there are indications to suggest that it may improve. For example, its export-oriented sub-sectors have recently experienced higher employment growth and employment elasticity. During the 1990's employment in the export-oriented industries grew at 3.36 per cent per annum and showed an employment elasticity of 0.48. A faster growth of manufactured exports, which now constitute over 75 per cent of total exports, as compared to 58 per cent in 1980, therefore, promises to be an important factor in reversing the declining trend in employment growth.

Employment growth is a function of growth of GDP and employment elasticity. Indian economy has sustained a relatively high growth of over 6 per cent for about two decades and is expected to grow at that, if not a higher, rate in coming years. There are indications towards reversal of the declining trend in elasticities, particularly in manufacturing and expectations of a growth structure in which sectors with higher employment elasticity will grow faster. Thus overall employment elasticity is likely to increase from the low of 0.15 experienced during 1994-2000. There is, therefore, a strong likelihood of growth rate of employment getting restored to over 2 per cent during the first decade of this century. In fact, the evidence from the limited sample survey of the NSSO suggests a reversal of the trend already during the 2000-2004 when employment growth is estimated to be around 2.70 per cent. This, however, is still to be validated by the results of the larger sample survey.

The recent experience, however, suggests that most of the new employment opportunities are likely to be generated in the unorganised sector and will be characterised by poor conditions of work, and lack of employment and social security. Even within the organised sector an increasing number of workers are being employed in a 'flexible' manner on casual or contract basis, without the social security benefits available to regular workers. And, also, the problem of the 'working poor', namely, of those fully engaged in work, but earning less than the poverty line income, will persist. Thus the challenge of quality of work, in terms of earnings and social security will continue. Tightening of the labour market with increase in the demand for labour may lead to improved earnings over time, but a vast majority of workers will continue to have no social protection against the risks of work related hazards, unemployment, sickness and maternity and old age. A measure of security against these risks is currently available to the workers in the organised sector. With a decline in its share and increase in that of the unorganised sector, the share of the unprotected workers will increase. Provision of a minimum social protection to this large mass of workers is, therefore, likely to emerge as a much greater challenge than of expanding employment opportunities. It will require special attention of the state and society at large in coming years, as the market-driven high growth even if accompanied by an expansion in employment opportunities may not by itself be adequate to address the issue of social protection.

REFERENCES

Goldar, B.N. *Trade Libe.alisation and Manufacturing Employment: The Case of India*, Employment Paper 2002/3,4, Geneva. International Labour Office. 2003.

GOI. *Employment and Unemployment Situation in India: January-June, 2004*, Government of India. National Sample Survey Organisation. Report No. 506. 2005.

Papola, T.S.'The Question of Unemployment', in Bimal Jalan (ed.) *The Indian Economy: Problems and Prospects*. New Delhi. Viking, Penguin Books India (P) Ltd. 1992.

Planning Commission. *Second Five Year Plan*, New Delhi. Government of India. 1956.

Planning Commission. *Report of the Special Group on Targeting Ten Million Employment Opportunities*. New Delhi. Government of India. 2002.

6

PANCHAYATI RAJ AND RURAL DEVELOPMENT

The Government of India passed a series of constitutional reforms in 1993, which were intended to empower and democratise India's rural representative bodies—the Panchayats. The 73rd Amendment to the Constitution formally recognised a third tier of government at the sub-State level, thereby creating the legal conditions for local self-rule—or Panchayati Raj. Since this time, the process of decentralisation has been highly variable. Early experiences have also revealed considerable uncertainty and confusion about the precise political, administrative and fiscal powers Panchayats have in relation to the States, line ministries, and local user groups. This, in part, reflects the fact that the 73rd Amendment gave the State governments considerable autonomy to interpret and implement the constitutional reforms.

The central state-led development produces systems of governance that undermine national economic performance and effective public policy. The decentralisation of public administration and the introduction of locally elected bodies will produce systems of governance that are better able to meet the needs of poor and politically marginal groups in society. Democratic decentralisation is a political strategy that national élites have used to maintain legitimacy and control in the face of political disintegration. However, economic liberalisation, political regionalism and the rise of powerful inter- and sub-national actors have weakened the traditional nation state and created the conditions under which more local identities could emerge.

Large and centrally-administered bureaucracies represent an inefficient and potentially destructive means of allocating resources (and generating wealth) within society. However, central state agencies lack the 'time and place knowledge' to implement policies and programmes that reflect people's 'real' needs and preferences.

Besides, time and place gaps give local officials unlimited ability to distribute resources and extract 'rent' as they see fit. Such outcomes are believed to be particularly prone in poor countries, where government represents a vital source of wealth, and mechanisms to ensure accountable governance are often poorly enforced. In theory, decentralisation would undermine these opportunities by creating institutional arrangements that formalise the relationship between citizens and the state, giving the former the authority to impose sanctions (such as voting, recourse to higher-level authorities) on the latter. Decentralisation is also thought to create the conditions for a more pluralist political arrangement, in which competing groups can voice and institutionalise their interests in local democratic forums. Finally, it is argued that decentralisation creates institutions that are more amenable to local needs and preferences. However, a problem that is well-recognised in the literature on decentralisation is that the devolution of power will not necessarily improve the performance and accountability of local government.

Decentralisation has simply empowered local élites to capture a larger share of public resources, often at the expense of the poor. Reflecting on these relatively long-standing problems, an important strand of scholarship in the decentralisation literature has argued that the underlying distribution of assets and entitlements will have an important bearing on the extent to which marginal groups are able to take advantage of the mechanisms and opportunities created by decentralisation, and improve their ability to gain access to the (various) resources provided by the bureaucratic state. Within rural areas (which are often the central focus of decentralisation), such assets and entitlements would include land, land tenure, formal property rights, and full rights of citizenship. An important hypothesis that emerges from this scholarship is that societies in which the distribution of assets and entitlements is relatively equal will produce more effective and accountable forms of governance.

Nevertheless, decentralisation is not free from criticisms. First of all, formal processes, such as decentralisation, representation and democracy, matter less than informal processes of power and change in rural societies. In India, for instance, it has been argued that subordinate groups—backward castes, agricultural labourers, women—will only begin to use and benefit from decentralisation when there is a genuine redistribution of land and other agrarian assets. In other words, the formal mechanisms matter less than the informal institutions that underpin local political economies.

6.1. Aims of Decentralisation

Democratic decentralisation can be defined as meaningful authority devolved to local units of governance that are accessible and accountable to the local citizenry, who enjoy full political rights and liberty. It thus differs from the vast majority of earlier efforts at decentralisation in developing areas, which go back to the 1950s, and which were largely initiatives in public administration without any serious democratic component.

Decentralisation can be usefully understood as a political process whereby administrative authority, public resources and responsibilities are transferred from central government agencies to lower-level organs of government or to non-governmental bodies, such as community-based organisations (CBOs), 'third party' non-governmental organisations (NGOs) or private sector actors. Conceptually, important distinctions can be made among:

- deconcentration, in which political, administrative and fiscal responsibilities are transferred to lower units within central line ministries or agencies;
- devolution, in which sub-national units of government are either created or strengthened in terms of political, administrative and fiscal power;
- delegation, in which responsibilities are transferred to organisations that are outside the regular bureaucratic structure and are only indirectly controlled by the central government;
- privatisation, in which all responsibility for government functions is transferred to nongovernmental organisations (NGOs) or private enterprises independent of government.

This kind of transfers can involve the power to decide the allocation and distribution of public resources, the power to implement programmes and policies and the power to raise and spend public revenues for these and other purposes. These three powers can be classified broadly as political, administrative and fiscal decentralisation.

Anyway, democratic decentralisation implies more than the downward delegation of authority. Crucially, it entails a system of governance in which citizens possess the right to hold local public officials to account through the use of elections, grievance meetings and other democratic means.

But the decision-makers are under the 'effective popular control' of the people they are meant to govern. How this is accomplished, of course, constitutes a major dilemma for theorists and proponents of democratic development.

Democracy implies a wide range of rules, norms and customs through which citizens can exercise 'effective popular control' over public officials. Included here would be an independent judiciary, a free press, systems of transparency, and freedom of association and speech.

Greater participation in local political affairs will improve the quality and reach of government services, particularly ones aimed at improving the lives of poor and politically marginal groups in society. For proponents of democratic decentralisation, a central challenge of improving the delivery of public services becomes one of 'crafting' institutions which can maximise participation in political life. In the context of poverty reduction, access to the (myriad) resources and benefits that governments provide is associated with systems of governance that empower poor and vulnerable groups in society.

Devolution of authority can enhance systems of local governance in a number of ways. The establishment and empowerment of local resource user groups (delegation or privatisation) can improve the ways in which local people manage and use natural resources, thereby improving the resource base on which poor people are often disproportionately dependent. Such arguments are generally made in relation to the provision of local public goods, such as common pool resources or local credit organisations.Collaboration between public agencies and local resource users can produce 'synergistic' outcomes, in which citizens and civil servants cooperate to provide goods that would be unobtainable were they acting alone.

The democratisation and empowerment of local administrative bodies can enhance participation in decision-making fora, particularly among groups that have traditionally been marginalised by local political processes. The introduction of elections, systems of transparency and rights of association can empower poor people, enhancing their ability to participate in local decision making and (crucially) encouraging them to hold public officials to account. Increased representation offers significant benefits in itself. Framed in this way, participation in local, democratically elected bodies can lead to improvements in self-identity and worth, which can help to break down customs of inequality and discrimination. Membership of local administrative bodies can provide important skills that can be transferred to other walks of life. However, the notion that improving participation through decentralisation will necessarily lead to improvements in people's wellbeing is not entirely consistent with documented evidence. A recurring theme that emerges from a sizeable body of literature is the relatively weak correlation that exists between democratic decentralisation and poverty reduction.

This reflects the difficulty of establishing a clear and rigorous link between changes in governance and improvements in well-being. It also suggests a more sober conclusion about the ways in which democratic decentralisation is thought to affect the quality and availability of local economic opportunity.

Even the most successful forms of democratic decentralisation have been unable to overcome economic and political disparities, both within and among regions. This, in part, highlights the problem of raising public revenue in rural areas, in which economic surplus is typically poor.

Decentralisation can also pose new problems of co-ordination and planning. As the Kerala experience has shown, too much devolution can lead to major duplications of effort and gaps among different government agencies. Without adequate training and support, the devolution of large sums of money can also over-burden local bodies whose members lack the resources and expertise to spend large and complex budgets.

One of the dangers of devolving authority is that it simply empowers local élites and, worse, perpetuates existing poverty and inequality. Whether the introduction of democratic principles—on its own—would overcome the historical and cultural factors that perpetuate political inequality is somewhat doubtful. This, in turn, highlights the challenge of encouraging democracy in rural areas in which large numbers of people are dependent upon small numbers of local, powerful élites. It also highlights the challenge of encouraging 'empowerment' without addressing the rights and entitlements that underlie political structures in rural areas.

Where the spoils of government intervention are particularly good, one can predict with reasonable confidence that the costs of ensuring equitable distribution and of discouraging local corruption will be high. This is notoriously true of rural infrastructure projects, such as road building or irrigation, in which markets for primary inputs, labour and public regulation are strong.

The establishment of strong and accountable systems of governance will encourage a more equitable distribution of state provided resources, which can be directed towards poor and vulnerable groups. An underlying hypothesis here is that democratic participation will yield strong mechanisms of accountability, which in turn, will improve the distribution of benefits to groups that are traditionally marginalised by market and state.

Accountability implies a more formalised set of expectations and responsibilities, on which the performance of public officials can be judged. Here the existence of clear and explicit rules, governing the duties, jurisdictions and standards of public officials is an essential part of accountability. Accountability works best when rewards (for good performance) depend directly on the quality of service provided –failures occur when there is no direct relationship between the two.

The most ambitious forms of decentralisation (i.e. devolution) constitute a substantive shift in power from national or regional levels to more local spheres of political life. Decentralisation empowers new actors (at local and non-local levels), and (in theory) creates conditions for new lines of participation and accountability. However, the notion that decentralisation will lead to improvements in poverty reduction is not well-supported. Moreover, decentralisation—on its own—will necessarily produce systems of governance that are more effective or accountable to local needs and interests. In other words, local forms of accountability are dependent on more than just the devolution of political, administrative and fiscal power.

6.2. Features Panchayati Raj System

The 73rd Amendment Act of constitution describes the importance of local governance. It envisages Gramsabha as the foundation of the PRI system to perform the functions of and powers entrusted to it by the state legislatures. The amendment provides for a three-tier PRI system at the village, intermediate and district levels. Small states with population below 20 lakh have been given the option to not to constitute the intermediate level. The Act provides that the Panchayat bodies will have an assured duration of 5 years with mandatory elections after this period.

However it might be noted that under the Act the establishment of Panchayat and the devolution of necessary powers and authority on the PRIs are vested in state governments. In view of this it may be said that the success of the PRIs as a unit of democracy and thereby ushering an all round development of rural areas will much depend on the intention and support of the state governments. Without sincere intention and political will these institutions would be misused by rural elites and the poor and illiterate masses will remain as mute supporters. The following are the basic elements of the PRI system introduced through 73rd Amendment Act.

6.2.1. Gramsabha

Gram Sabha" means a body consisting of persons registered in the electoral rolls relating to a village comprised within the area of Panchayat at the village level. It may exercise such powers and perform such functions at the village level as the Legislature of a State may, by law, provide. Thus 73rd Amendment makes Gramsabha as the foundation of PRI system.

6.2.2. Powers and Functions of Panchayats

Subject to the provisions of this Constitution, the Legislature of a State may, endow the Panchayats with such powers and authority as may be necessary to enable them to function as institutions of self-government and such law may contain provisions for the devolution of powers and responsibilities upon Panchayats at the appropriate level, subject to such conditions as may be specified therein.

Although, Panchayati Raj was one of the most remarkable social and political reforms since independence. PRIs today face a number of daunting challenges. Across all states there is a lack of genuine devolution of funds, functions and functionaries in Panchayati Raj. Added to that are social challenges that work against the emergence of leadership from marginalised sections of society, such as women, Dalits and tribals. Further, there is a lack of role clarity among Gram Panchayats, Block Panchayats and District Panchayats.

The objectives like social equality, gender equity and the change at grass-root level leadership envisaged as the main among the objectives of Panchayati Raj were not fulfilled in a meaningful manner. In this regard it was felt that the marginalised groups like the women and other backward castes in the society continue to face many hurdles and found it difficult to participate at the grass-root level developmental process.

The PRI system has many positive features. However, the elite control over the system, apprehensions of state level leaders of challenge to their power and the lukewarm attitude of the bureaucracy have not yet allowed the PRIs to function as real democratic institutions with people's participation. Studies from different states in India clearly proves that even though some states have shown political activism to implement PRIs the unequal social structure and rigid caste system prevalent in Indian villages coupled with power-hungry local bureaucracy kill the spirit of the system.

All states in India initiated the process of radical democratic decentralisation after the 73rd Constitutional Amendment Act. However the experience of PRIs shows that success of PRIs in India is not uniform throughout the country. In some states the system has played a vital role in changing traditional power structure dominated by local elitebureaucratic network. In other states the new system has lead to empowerment of hitherto marginalised sections of society like women, SC and SC. Unfortunately in some other states lack of political will and administrative apathy killed the real devolution of power. Using the conventional classification of 'political, administrative and fiscal decentralisation,' the World Bank's three-volume study of Indian decentralisation ranks India 'among the best performers' internationally in terms of political decentralisation, but 'close to the last' in terms of administrative decentralisation.

The three important limitations, which are commonly associated with Indian decentralisation are:

i) The government bodies that operate within their jurisdiction are part of a federal system, in which powers are defined by a written Constitution, and divided among Union, State and sub-State bodies.

ii) The institutions empowered by Indian decentralisation are situated in a longstanding structure of public administration, whose interests and nature are not necessarily consistent with the provisions outlined in the 73rd Amendment.

iii) Finally, this process has happened in a context of political transition, in which customs of discrimination and inequality in rural areas are thought to have been challenged by forces arising from the green revolution and other forms of guided intervention.

6.3. Functioning of Panchayats

In the thirteen years following the enactment of 73rd Constitutional Amendment Act, in nearly all States and Union Territories to which Part IX of the Constitution applies except Jharkhand, two rounds of elections have been completed and in several of them, three. Today, more than 27 lakh representatives stand elected to the three levels of Panchayats, of whom more than 36.5 percent are women, 16 percent belong to Scheduled Castes and 11 percent to the Scheduled Tribes. The Panchayats today provide a diverse, widespread and strong political foundation for inclusive and participative growth. However, beyond being instruments for political empowerment, if they are to function as institutions of self-government in rural areas in keeping with the letter and spirit of Part IX of the Constitution, the Panchayats will require clear functions and responsibilities, matching financial transfers, powers to raise their own finances and their own functionaries. Finally, a framework will also be needed for holding Panchayats accountable to their constituents for the performance of functions that have been devolved to them.

In compliance with the Constitutional pattern, while all States and UTs to which Part IX applies have passed strong and sweeping enabling legislations for the devolution of powers and functions listed in the Eleventh Schedule to Panchayats, formal transfer of functions has not been matched by the concomitant transfer of funds and functionaries for effectively performing these devolved functions. There has also been very little change in the first decade after the 73rd Amendment in the design of Central ministries programmes dealing with the mandates of Panchayats. When Central ministries, which send down substantial funds for implementation of Centrally Sponsored Schemes, ignore Panchayats, it leaves very little incentive for States to go ahead with real devolution.

6.3.1.Functioning of Gram Sabha

Article 243A of the Constitution provides for the establishment of Gram Sabhas to exercise such powers and perform such functions at the village level as the Legislature of a State may, by law provide. Powers assigned to the Gram Sabha will therefore vary from State to State. Examination of State legislations indicate that functions assigned to the Gram Sabhas in most States include reviewing all development programmes of the village, selection of beneficiaries for beneficiary oriented programmes transferred to the Panchayati Raj Institutions (PRIs) and preparing plans for local development including minimum needs, welfare and production oriented programmes. In some States, Gram Sabhas also prepare lists of all able bodied persons to whom employment is to be provided under locally taken up wage employment schemes. In few States, Gram Sabhas consider annual statements of accounts, administration reports, audit notes and replies of Gram Panchayats. Gram Sabhas also monitor report submitted by GPs in respect of ongoing development programmes and approve programmes proposed to be undertaken. In some States, if the GP fails to convene the Gram Sabha, the Executive Officer of the intermediate Panchayat is mandated to convene the Gram Sabha.

At the First Round Table of State Ministers of Panchayati Raj held in Kolkata in July 2004, it was decided that State Governments may identify steps needed to be taken to ensure that the powers and functions mentioned in Article 243A are adequately incorporated in State Panchayati Raj laws. These include constitution of Sabhas below the Gram level such as Gram Sansad or Ward Sabha, periodicity of meetings of Gram Sabhas and Ward Sabhas, full consultation with special or disadvantaged categories of the population such as women, Scheduled Castes, Scheduled Tribes, landless labourers, provision for Mahila Sabha Meetings comprising the adult women of the ward/ Gram Panchayat Area and empowering the Gram Sabha with measures such as right to all information required to make the Panchayats truly answerable to the Gram Sabha, approval of plans prepared by the gram Panchayat, issue of utilisation certificates of funds allocated for the plans, programmes of the Panchayat and identification of beneficiaries.

Though Gram Sabhas are mandated since over a decade in India, sample studies of the system show that their functioning is uneven. Gram Sabhas may not meet at all, may be thinly attended or may be vibrant and active. Commonly heard complaints are that attendance is thin, agendas are not circulated in advance and several activities, such as social audit etc. are only nominally carried out. Another common complaint heard is that officials concerned rarely attend Gram Sabhas. Disillusionment with Gram Sabhas also tends to snowball, with office bearers of Gram Panchayats also not keen to convene meetings as they find it inconvenient to face people without meeting their earlier demands.

While levels of Panchayats are organs of representative democracy, the Gram Sabha is an important forum for participatory democracy. On the matter if the constitutional and legal structure of the Gram Sabha, Article 243(b), defines a Gram Sabha as consisting of all persons registered as voters in the electoral roll relating to the village comprised within the area of the Panchayat at the village level. Panchayati Raj legislations will need to comply with this definition strictly. In order to deepen the opportunity for more participation, States may seriously consider establishing Ward Sabhas at the level of each Ward, through appropriate legislative changes. In this regard, the provisions of the Panchayats (Extension to Scheduled Areas) Act, 1996 extending the provisions of Part IX of the Constitution relating to the Panchayats to the Scheduled Areas provide that a village shall ordinarily consist of a habitation or a group of habitations or a hamlet or a group of hamlets comprising a community and managing its affairs in accordance with traditions and customs and that every village shall have a Gram Sabha consisting of persons whose names are included in the electoral rolls for the Panchayat at the village level.

6.4. Role of Civil Society Organisations

Effective and responsive governments require strong and vibrant civil societies to keep them in check. Civil society sits between the family and the state. The 'third-party' organisations (such as domestic and international NGOs), membership organisations (such as trade unions, farmers' associations, credit groups, water-user associations, etc.), political parties, Mafia arrangements, religious affiliations (formal and informal) and firms (i.e. organisations that engage in competitive economic exchange). The value of defining civil society in this way is that it attempts to differentiate between groups and relations that are organised on principles of hierarchy and control and ones that are based on the relatively altruistic motivations of the nuclear and extended family unit. The drawback, of course, is that it underplays the normative and ideological terms on which people join and establish social groups in the first place.

Civil society organisations fostered strong accountability in peripheral rural areas. Accountability is strengthened when people outside the state organise to ensure that public officials are acting in accordance with formal and informal norms of performance. External civil society organisations (i.e. organisations that exist outside of the affected communities) can empower poor and marginal groups in society. NGOs, for instance, have been shown to empower poor people by connecting them with a wider circle of allies, with whom they can mount a more effective political lobby. They can absorb some of the costs of engaging in political action (e.g. transportation, communication and so forth).

After the Seventh five-year plan officially recognised the contribution of No-Government Organisations (NGOs) in various development programmes, their involvement has burgeoned. However, the reaction of the NGO community to the Panchayati Raj system, has been mixed. While some have seized the opportunity to work with Panchayats on local development, others consider them as competitors.

The Second Round Table Conference of Ministers in charge of Panchayati Raj held at Mysore in August 2004 agreed that parallel bodies, which are set up to plan and execute development projects in areas that are in the functional domain of local Governments, should be brought into an organic, symbiotic relationship with Panchayats at the appropriate level. Thus must (a) be set up if at all, in consultation and with the collaboration of Panchayats at the appropriate level, (b) report periodically to the Gram Sabha and (c) should not undermine the constitutional authority of Panchayats, but work together with them.

There are several roles that NGOs could play in Panchayati Raj. First, NGOs can help in building voter awareness for Panchayat elections. Second, they can take a lead role in capacity building of Panchayats, through training, exchange programmes, visits to successful panchayats, building networks and lobby bodies and information sharing. Third, NGOs can assist District Planning Committees established under Article 243ZD and Panchayats in undertaking village planning, resource mapping and identification of development schemes. Fourth, they can take up evaluation studies on panchayat performance and educate people periodically so that they can better hold their Panchayats to account. As a continuation of this approach, NGOs have a big role to plan in mass movements and campaigns to ensure effective use of empowering legislations such as the Right to Information Act.

Panchayats, in turn can undertake several initiatives to ensure a good NGO movement:

i) They can identify and nurture good local NGOs, and encourage them to directly disclose information to Gram Sabha meetings.

ii) Panchayats could also entrust implementation of some of their development programmes and plans to NGOs. This is particularly useful in those areas where Panchayat involvement so far has been tentative, such as credit, agricultural marketing, dairy development etc.

iii) Panchayats can provide sustainability to NGOs initiatives, by being associated with project plans from the very beginning and taking over maintenance of the assets created.

Development strategies of the immediate past have created and relied on a multiplicity of institutions such as watershed development teams, water supply and sanitation committees, village education committees and joint forest management committees to implement them.

However, there is a clear distinction between Community Based Organisations (CBOs), Self-Help Groups (SHGs) and User Groups existing as autonomous social groups, augmenting social capital and deepening democracy and government-organised groups for implementation of specific programmes like water supply, irrigation, watershed management or poverty reduction. The former are entitled to absolute freedom of action and can even challenge Panchayats through public action.

But the latter, organised for specific purposes around using public development funds, have to be considered differently. These groups cannot be considered as substitutes for Panchayats, which are local governments performing a range of governance and development functions accountable to the entire population of a Panchayat and not just responsible to a small circle of beneficiaries for project implementation.

The myth that these bodies are in some way more efficient than Panchayats also needs to be addressed. There is little hard evidence to show that such groups are free of all the evils that are supposed to bedevil PRIs, such as politics, sharing of spoils, corruption and elite capture. There are also serious questions about the sustainability of such groups. People may be very active when there is fund flow and capacity building support, but tend to lose interest when faced with the more mundane tasks of maintenance of assets and collection of user charges.

6.5. Reforms in Fiscal Devolution

Efficient Panchayati Raj involves devolution of functions, functionaries and finances. The ambit of functional assignments is indicated in the 11th schedule to the constitution. Accordingly States have undertaken varying degrees of devolution through their Panchayati Raj legislations. In addition all of them are in varying degrees engaged in activity mapping, which is absolutely necessary to estimate expenditure requirements of local governments.

To improve the provision of public services at the local level, there needs to be:

i) a clear activity mapping based on comparative advantage in implementing expenditures and devolution of functions to the panchayats on that basis;

ii) provision of appropriate revenue handles to Panchayats;

iii) guidance of Panchayats to raise taxes, particularly on land and property, and efficiently provide public services,

iv) unbundling of state sector schemes and consolidating central sector schemes to enable greater flexibility and autonomy to panchayats in implementation;

v) professionalisation of State Financial Corporations (SFCs) and reforms in the state transfers to make them adequate, rule based, equitable and incentive compatible;

vi) an up to date information system comprising of fiscal, demographic, geographical and economic data for the village, block and district panchayat jurisdictions.

Effective fiscal decentralisation demands that finances should follow functional assignments. This necessitates looking at both (a) raising of ones own revenue and (b) devolution of funds from higher levels of government by local bodies. Ideally speaking, revenues raised locally ought to cover the provisioning of services by Panchayats—only this can fully ensure efficiency as well as direct accountability in the provision of local services. However, in practice, revenue bases assigned to Panchayats for collection and appropriation are inadequate to meet their expenditure requirements, for two reasons. First, while Panchayats may have a comparative advantage in implementing local service delivery due to their lower transaction costs, they have a comparative disadvantage in raising revenues as all broad based, mobile and redistributive taxes can be effectively levied only by higher-level governments. Second, there are significant differences between different local bodies in their capacity to raise revenues and costs of providing public services. Therefore, it is essential that such vertical and horizontal fiscal imbalances are offset through a system of intergovernmental transfers.

Ideally, the design of an inter-governmental fiscal transfer system must work at the margin, by first estimating the fiscal requirements that cannot be covered by Panchayats with their own sources of revenue. However, the approach so far has been completely the opposite – the endeavour being, to get to transfer more funds to Panchayats, with hardly any emphasis on local revenues. Apart from establishing the importance of own revenues, a sound and well-designed system of fiscal decentralisation must ensure a clear linkage between revenue and expenditure decisions at the local level and in particular address the following imperatives:

i) Such transfers have to be ideally unconditional to enable Panchayats to provide a normative standard of public services at a stipulated revenue raising effort.

ii) Additionally, in order to ensure prescribed standards of basic services to nationally set standards in essential activities of national concern such as poverty alleviation, basic education, healthcare, housing, water supply, sanitation, nutrition and child development, specific purpose grants will have to be provided to Panchayats, which have comparative advantage in implementing all these services at lower transaction costs.

While creating an appropriate mix of unconditional and specific purpose transfers as described above, two pitfalls will also need to be avoided:

i) Unconditional transfers must not create disincentives for resource mobilisation nor encourage fiscal profligacy.

ii) Conditional transfers should not constrain the capacity and initiative of local governments and deny them flexibility to enable efficient service provision.

Seen from the perspective of these cardinal principles of good design, the prevailing system of fiscal transfers is in urgent need of reform. The following ought to be the areas of focus during the Eleventh Plan:

i) Own revenues of Panchayats should begin to contribute much more to Panchayati Raj finances,

ii) The design of specific purpose fiscal transfers must be simple and create the right incentives for good local expenditure,

iii) There must be a substantial corpus of untied block transfers in the fiscal transfer system.

6.5.1. Improving Revenues of Panchayats

Assigning revenue bases to Panchayats and providing them adequate powers to effectively enforce powers to tax has been neglected immensely, resulting in abysmally low volume of revenues raised by Panchayats at all three levels – just 0.07 per cent of GDP or 0.36 per cent of the total revenues collected in the country in 2002-03, as noted by the Twelfth Finance Commission (TFC). Panchayats alone are not to blame for this pathetic situation. In fact, the onus is on States to undertake policy reform and other steps to vitalise own revenue collection at the Panchayat level.

The common pattern of revenue assignments made by States to Panchayats is as follows:

i) Tax assignments systems are weighted heavily in favour of Village Panchayats. District and Intermediate Panchayats are generally not assigned worthwhile own revenue sources and at best, can only raise meagre revenues from rents on their own buildings.

ii) Major revenue raising powers assigned to the village panchayats comprise of (a) tax on land and buildings not subject to agricultural assessment; (b) entertainment taxes excluding those on cinematograph shows, (c) vehicle taxes on non-motorised vehicles, (d) advertisement and hoarding taxes, (e) pilgrim fees, (f) market fees; (g) cattle registration fees (h) parking fees, (i) grazing fee. None of these, except property tax is significant as either the tax base is negligible or local bodies do not have the capacity to administer them.

iii) In respect of taxes on land and buildings too, States often impose ceiling rates, restricting flexibility,

iv) States, sometime give tax concessions without consulting Panchayats exempting otherwise lucrative tax sources, such as large industries in rural areas, from being taxed by Panchayats.

v) States hardly invest anything in training of Panchayat elected representatives or staff s in tax estimation or tax collection.

vi) Worse, in some States, Panchayats do not have unrestricted freedom to utilise the taxes they collect – they are compelled to obtain hierarchical approvals to spend money that is their own, which is a strong disincentive for tax collection.

vii) Most local governments do not have enforcement capacity. Providing guidance in the design and implementation of property tax which is presumptive yet realistic and buoyant and building capacity and powers to enforce the tax are critical for enhancing own revenues of Panchayats.

viii) Finally, recommendations by State Finance Commissions to strongly incentivise tax collections are routinely ignored by States.

Most such policy shortcomings arise from persistent wrong attitudes and notions. First, local taxation is not considered a priority for reform. Second, there is a feeling that this is politically inadvisable – that the poor would suffer. Moreover, the fact that they have been given taxation powers does not stir in Panchayats any constructive response – all but the most active among them would much rather spend funds devolved from above than collect their own, particularly from ignorance and partly the apprehension that own revenues would impose upon them greater demands for accountability.

6.6. Panchayats and Rural Development

The term rural development connotes overall development of rural areas to improve the quality of life of rural people. In this sense, it is a comprehensive and multidimensional concept, and encompasses the development of agriculture and allied activities, village and cottage industries and crafts, socio-economic infrastructure, community services and facilities and, above all, human resources in rural areas. As a phenomenon, rural development is the end-result of interactions between various physical, technological, economic, social, cultural and institutional factors. As a strategy, it is designed to improve the economic and social well-being of a specific group of people – the rural poor.

In the Indian context rural development assumes greater significance as 72.22 per cent (according to the 2001 census) of its population still live in rural areas. Most of the people living in rural areas draw their livelihood from agriculture and allied sectors and poverty mostly persists here. At the time of independence around 83 per cent of the Indian population were living in rural areas. Accordingly, from the very beginning, our planned strategy emphasised rural development and will continue to do so in future. Strategically, the focus of our planning was to improve the economic and social conditions of the underprivileged sections of rural society. Thus, economic growth with social justice became the proclaimed objective of the planning process under rural development. It began with an emphasis on agricultural production and consequently expanded to promote productive employment opportunities for rural masses, especially the poor, by integrating production, infrastructure, human resource and institutional development measures.

The spread of the green revolution has considerably changed the profile of the farmer from the old traditional farming to an aggressive and commercialised modern farming system. The green revolution not only brought prosperity to the farmers, but also changed their psyche, mindset and pattern of living. Structural changes started taking place in the villages. Majority of farmers now view agriculture as a commercial enterprise and seek more and more facilities and infrastructure support from the government for improving living conditions in the villages. Considering the overall development that has taken place so far, much more remains to be done for improving the quality of life of rural farmers, which has a large deprived population, consisting of marginal farmers, landless labourers, besides Scheduled Castes and Backward Classes. This component of the population has to be brought into focus for their upliftment, with special emphasis on their skill upgradation, removal of unemployment and poverty and vertical growth to acquire productive assets for better living on a sustainable basis.

Development of physical as well as social infrastructure plays an important in the overall advance of the rural economy, role by directly contributing to employment generation and asset creation. Improved network of physical infrastructure facilities such as well-built roads, irrigation, rail links, power and telecommunications, information technology, food storage, cold chains, market-growth centres, processing of produce and social infrastructure support, viz., health and education, water and sanitation, and veterinary services and co-operatives are essential for the development of the rural economy, especially in the era of liberalisation, privatisation and globalisation (LPG).

In the present policy environment of LPG, agriculture and rural development are now poised for a paradigm shift. The core factors that can bring forth a tangible transformation are the following:

i) Reduction of rural-urban disparities in terms of economic development, employment and infrastructure.

ii) Development of industry in rural areas related to agricultural development, cottage industry and allied sectors.

iii) All-round skill upgradation through research and extension and information technology, so that rural people can design means for the improvement of their own links own betterment.

v) Minimising social differences through collective participation in rural developmental activities; developing common programmes for village improvement and to make combined efforts for eliminating or minimising gender disparities and social evils within rural society, through the decentralised Panchayati Raj System.

To meet the incoming challenges, the above-mentioned points assume greater significance today. It is now expected that the transformation can be hastened through the effective implementation of the Panchayati Raj System, which has the constitutional authority to plan and implement programmes for rural development.

6.6.1. Development Rural Non Farm Sector

Out-migration of the rural population in search of jobs has not only resulted in overburdening urban resources but has also forced the labourforce (displaced from the rural economy) to live in slum-like situations in urban centres. It is necessary to create better socially acceptable employment opportunities by developing the non-farm sector in rural areas, to stop the migration of the rural unemployed to urban areas. For this, minimum basic facilities, such as availability of safe drinking water, proper sanitation and sewerage, better rural health and education and community social assets, wherever existing, have to be utilised effectively and developed where non-existent. The need is to mobilise and involve the community for the proper maintenance of the facilities available at the local level, preferably under Panchayati Raj Institutions. The corporate sector can play a major role by bringing resources, new technology, modern management and extension services to the local people, which can facilitate provision of employment opportunities for the rural unemployed in secondary and tertiary sectors, by training them for the required jobs.

6.6.2. Development of Agro-based Industries

Development of agro-based industries has a significant role in rural development. These industries not only provide input services but also gainful employment opportunities to rural people. Agroprocessing basically involves value addition to farm produce. Current agro-processing activities are based on the crops produced, which have very limited scope for secondary processing. However, there are some secondary processing units engaged in the production of bread and biscuits, juice and jam, wood and paper in the private sector.

In the past, almosc one-fourth of the horticulture and vegetables were lost through wastage and spoilage, because of inadequate arrangements for cold storage transport and dehydration. Efforts of some private units to establish fruit- and vegetableprocessing units could not succeed because of lack of facilities such as good roads, regular power supply, and the license-quota system, poor information networking, shortage of technical labour and supply of quality raw material. Given the present structure of crop production, some important technologies for small and cottage processing units are: mini rice mills, mini grain mills, mini dal mills, mini wheat mills. It provides atta, suji, maida and grain, which can further be used for value addition in bigger units.

6.6.3. Rural Development Programmes

India has a long history of government intervention in the rural sector of its economy. India's development strategies have accorded high priority to agriculture and rural development. The Community Development Programme (CDP) reflected India's concern for nation-building and equity. The Intensive Agriculture Development Programme (IADP) employed the selective principle in deploying resources for achieving rapid production gains, ensuring thereby the equity concern of the CDP. Its main objective was to achieve rapid increase in agricultural production through the use of complementary inputs and services at the farm level.

A number of programmes, such as the Intensive Agricultural Area Programme (IAAP), the High Yielding Varieties Programme (HYVP) and the Intensive Cattle Development Programme (ICPD) had been patterned like the IADP. The lesson learnt from these programmes was that a rising economic growth rate was no guarantee against poverty and unemployment. The growing inter-regional and inter-personal disparities that surfaced from these selective growth-oriented programmes led to a re-examination of the development strategies. As a consequence, special programmes, such as Small Farmer Development Agency (SFDA), Marginal Farmers and Agricultural Labourers Schemes (MFALS), Drought Prone Area Programme (DPAP) and Tribal Area Development Programme (TADP) were introduced for the weaker sections and the economically depressed areas in the seventies. These programmes were aimed at tackling the problems of poverty and backwardness by helping the weaker sections to increase their incomes through selfemployment and wage-paid employment.

A Minimum Needs Programme (MNP) was also launched, to supplement the income-increasing effect of these programmes in order to provide civic amenities and community facilities in rural areas. In 1978-79, the principal contents of Community Area Development (CAD), DPAD, MFAL, SFDA were all integrated into a new programme, Integrated Rural Development Programme (IRDP) for providing income generating assets and self-employment opportunities to the rural poor.

A series of special employment programmes were also initiated in the seventies, namely, Rural Works Programme (RWP), Crash Scheme of Rural Employment (CSRE), Pilot Intensive Rural Employment Projects (PIREP), Employment Guarantee Schemes (EGS), Food for Work Progarmmes (FFWP), National Rural Employment Progarmme (NREP) and Rural Landless Employment Guarantee Programme (RLEGP), to address the acute unemployment situation in rural areas.

The experiences of these progarmmes indicated the need for more concentrated efforts to tackle the problems of rural unemployment and construction of public works under the schemes. Keeping this in view, the Jawahar Rojgar Yojana (JRY) was launched in April 1989 by merging the two ongoing NREP and RLEGP into a single rural employment programme. Consequently, on 1 April 1999 the Jawahar Gram Samridhi Yojana (JGSY) was started to ensure development of rural infrastructure at the village level by restructuring the erstwhile JRY. The Employment Assurance Scheme (EAS) was launched on 2 October 1993 to make larger and efficient use of available human resources for alleviation of poverty, reduction in inequalities and sustenance of a reasonable high pace of economic growth. Subsequently, the Jawahar Rozgar Yojana (JRY) has been merged with the EAS since 1 January 1996. It now covers all the rural blocks of the country. The scheme aims at providing assured employment of 100 days of unskilled manual work in a year to the rural poor, who are in need of employment and seek it. The second objective is the creation of economic infrastructure and community assets for sustained production and employment generation. The programme is restricted to males and females above 18 years and below 60 years of age. A maximum of two adults per family are to be provided assured employment for 100 days under the scheme.

The newly launched centrally sponsored Swarn Jayanti Gram Swayrozgar Yojana (SGSY) has been revised keeping in view experiences of the strength and weaknesses of earlier self-employment programmes, viz., IRDP, Training of Rural Youth for Self-Employment (TRYSEM), Development of Women and Children in Rural Areas (DWCRA), Supply of Improved Toolkits to Rural Artisans (SITRA), Ganga Kalyan Yojana (GKY) and Million Wells Schemes (MWS), which are no longer in operation. SSGY has been started from 1 April 1999. It is a comprehensive self-employment, programme for the rural poor and is conceived as a holistic scheme of micro-enterprises covering various aspects of self-employment, viz., organisation of the rural poor in Self Help Groups (SHG), capacity building, training, planning of activities clusters, infrastructure buildup, technology, credit and marketing. Thus emphasis in rural development has progressively shifted from growth to welfare and then from a responsive to an integrated approach.

References

Riddell, Rogar and Mark, C and Robinson. "*Non Government Organisations and Rural Poverty Alleviation*. Clarendon Press. Oxford. 1995.

Roul Chhabilendra. *Bitter to Better Harvest*. Northern Book Centre. New Delhi. 2001.

Sarkar, K. Gautam. *Agriculture and Rural Transformation in India*. Oxford University Press. Delhi. 1995.

Singh Katar. *Rural Development: Principles Policies and Management*. Sage Publications. New Delhi. 1999.

Malhotra Rashpal. *Impact of 73rd Constitutional Amendment on Rural Industrialisation in India: Issues and Policies*. paper presented at expert group seminar on Rural industrialisation – Issues and Policies, organised by South Asia Multi Disciplinary Advisory Team (SAAT) ILO at Gurgaon. 25-26 August 2000.

India Panchayati Raj Report-2001 Volume I & II. National Institute of Rural Development. Hyderabad. January 2002.

India: Human Development Report. National Council for Applied Economic Research. Oxford University Press. New Delhi, 1999.

7

ROLE OF ICTS IN RURAL DEVELOPMENT

Development is a multi-dimensional exercise that seeks to transform society by addressing the entire complex of interwoven strands, living impulses, which are part of an organic whole. Development, as a process meant to empower the poor, reduce exploitation, and oppression by those having economic, social, and political power. It also means an equitable sharing of resources, improved health care and education for all.

Communication is one of the major components and driving force of rural development. Conventionally, communication includes electronic media, human communication and now information technology (IT). All forms of communications have dominated the development scene in which its persuasive role has been most dominant within the democratic political framework of the country. Persuasive communication for rural development has been given highest priority for bringing about desirable social and behavioural change among the most vulnerable rural poor and women. Initially, the approach lacked gender sensitivity and empathy of the communicators and development agents who came from urban elite homes. Added to these constraints is political will that still influences the pace and progress of rural development.

Technological changes further compounded the direction of rural development as information and communication technology (ICT) has been thought by communication and development workers as a panacea for other ills that obstructs the development process. It has lead to indiscriminate applications and use of ICT in every aspect of information dissemination, management and governance of development. While there are few shining examples of achievements of ICT in development, there are a large number of failures and unauthenticated claims. A view has also been advanced that "totalitarianism is latent in (information and communication) technology". Also communication technology is always expressions of socio-economic, geographical and political interests, partialities, alignments and commitments. In brief the will to technical knowledge is the will to technical power. The relationship between democracy and communication technology is quite tenuous and transient. In order to understand and appreciate the implications of communication technology for rural development, it would be essential to describe the current communication scenario of the country.

The last decade of twentieth century witnessed enormous and unprecedented changes in every aspect of communications technologies, policies, infrastructure development and services. Political leaders of India have begun abandoning archaic government control over communication that has lately moved from government to national and international private players. Finally, airwaves and electronic signals have achieved their freedom from centuries old colonial bondage to reach out and connect people through a privately owned and operated communication network and infrastructure.

Both international and national private players have taken a dominant role in redefining, reshaping and providing telecommunication, broadcasting and information services for national development. It has initiated an era of partnership of public and private entrepreneurial skills and abilities to bring about unlimited connectivity. It has already started reshaping the life of a number of elites in India.

The Indian civilisation is one of the world's oldest and ancient civilisations that evolved, matured and decayed over several millennia. After independence we have been experimenting and carving a path of revitalisation for development through democracy. The existing sharp divide between the small but economically, politically and socially "rich elite ruling class" and a very big but "economically poor and socially deprived" continue to persist as a legacy of the past. While the rich elite has had access to knowledge, both oral and written, the economically poor remained confined only to oral knowledge. The imposition of British educational system for over two centuries help add another layer of social barrier though on surface it gives an impression of equitable access to education. Privatisation of education has further helped the rich elite to dominate the contemporary social and political scene at the cost of the poor who remain oblivious of communication technology for any improvement in their existing miserable life.

Communication has been seen by a large number of development planners as a panacea for solving major social ills and problems. Apart from development, the introduction of communication in the educational process for open and distance learning is seen as step towards improving the quality of education and bridging the social and educational gap. However, experience indicates that those rich who could afford to have access to private resources have hogged the advantage whether development or education. In this respect, it seems that communication technology has, in no way has helped the poor for improving their socio-economic condition.

In the post economic liberalisation period, rural development projects added information and communication technology (ICT) to provide individual need-based information in broad development areas through Internet. In the post economic liberalisation phase without abandoning the extension model "social marketing approach" to rural development has been adopted.

7.1. Possibilities Digitally-oriented development

Digitally-oriented development is as powerful and seductive as the technology upon which it is based. No single technological revolution has changed the lives of current generations in the way that the internet has. No cultural-technological innovation since Television has had this kind of impact on the world's economy, its politics and its globalising popular cultures, or even on our cultural conceptions of distance and time. The promise of digital development is that it might have the same reach as the original internet boom of the mid 1990s—only this time, the most disprivileged communities, those who had missed out on earlier waves of technology, might be able to 'leapfrog' over their more developed competitors. The greatest obstacles to rural development—large distances and inadequate infrastructure—might be obviated by instant access to virtual institutions that provide banking, education, health care, neonatal information, agricultural advice, and so forth.

However, a computer cannot benefit someone earning less than a dollar a day, remains a serious challenge to any attempt to ameliorate social and economic disparities through Information and Communications Technologies (ICTs). In South Asia, where most rural populations lack running water and sanitation systems, where electricity is still a scarce and intermittent resource, where roads are poor and education a luxury, these technologies truly appear to be far removed from the everyday concerns of the poorest sections of the countryside.

India's IT sector took off in the early 1980s with the establishment of off-shore development centres. Relatively cheap English-speaking engineering and technical talent were employed at centres in Bangalore and Chennai, then Hyderabad, and now in the suburbs of New Delhi (NOIDA). Since the liberalisation of the Indian economy in the early 1990s, the Indian government has relentlessly promoted the IT sector as the harbinger of the nation's economic aspirations.

The initial euphoria surrounding India's successful software export industry has given way to a new introspection into the reasons why these intellectual and human resources have not driven improvements in India's public and private institutions, education systems, and infrastructure. These reasons are not hard to find: (i) the Indian software industry solves small components of larger problems for international clients; (ii) this work is usually protected by confidentiality agreements; (iii) many Indian software professionals and companies compete for the same international contracts; (iv) the opportunity costs of working for Indian versus international clients is very high; and finally (v) low teledensity, computer usage, literacy, the inadequacies of regional language software interfaces, and other obstacles of India's developing infrastructure, coupled with regulatory hurdles have inhibited such ventures. None of this prevented Andhra Pradesh's Chief Minister Chandrababu Naidu from crafting an aggressive state policy to attract IT-oriented investments, simultaneously claiming that this sector served the larger public interest.

Lack of electoral politics in India's largely rural society have meant that economically liberal and technologically sophisticated leaders could not afford to leave themselves open to the charge of promoting IT at the expense of rural development, and this is a fine line to walk: Even as he invited Microsoft to set up a software center in the Hyderabad's technology park, Naidu also installed a highly sophisticated network of communications systems in his home constituency of Kuppam, as a model for other regions of the state. Beginning in 1996, he was the first Indian politician to advocate E-governance for making the state machinery more responsive and sensitive to citizen needs at the district and panchayat level.

These policies are being emulated at the national level through an 'IT for the Masses' policy statement, as well as a forthcoming policy statement on Egovernance. Neighbouring Karnataka is one among many other states of India to have issued an IT policy statement directed towards the 'common man.' Naidu's solution to the political dilemma of promoting high-tech alongside rural empowerment, therefore, long anticipated current international debates on 'digital divide.' Despite the on-going deregulation of India's telecommunications sector, its national teledensity (telephones per hundred persons) has improved very slowly.

However, the export-oriented software industry has yet to take full advantage of the opportunities presented by the newly networking home market. A new synergy between the Infotech and Telecom sectors in India could create a profound social and economic revolution in rural communities across South Asia.

7.1.1. Technology-driven Social Change

South Asia hosts an extraordinary concentration of new technology driven companies, tech-savvy administrators and managers, a political class newly sophisticated to the possibilities of IT, social entrepreneurs and NGO institutional structures that could all come together to bring the benefits of networked technologies to rural and disprivileged groups. And yet, we must face the frustrations of intermittent, inconsistent electrical power, archaic, scarce and unreliable telephony and net-connectivity, neo-feudal politico-business consortia that hinder or hijack developmental efforts, deeply ingrained ideologies of caste hierarchy, gender inequality, and religious communal difference, as well as significant deprivations of basic human needs. These limitations cast grave doubt over the optimism of those attempting to use emerging technologies for developmental purposes.

The IT initiatives in South Asia are premature because as much as electricity, telephony, and connectivity are highly erratic and variable in many parts of South Asia. Moreover, more basic kinds of infrastructure including schools, healthcare centres, balanced nutrition, gender equity, employment, and transportation are lacking.

Post-colonial societies in Asia, Africa and the Americas have repeatedly shown that they can be successful in one or another dimension of human, social, and economic achievement, without necessarily replicating a normative European trajectory of industrial development. Diverse social and infrastructural needs must be addressed more or less *simultaneously* to ensure a nation's future growth and prosperity.

Information networks can become conduits that allow money to flow into the village through new kinds of non-discriminatory, clean and relatively unoppressive industries. Information and communications technologies can also compensate for other kinds of infrastructure limitations.

PCs remain expensive, fragile, quickly obsolete, English-centric, complex and difficult to master, and therefore almost entirely elite in their scope and operation. Nevertheless, *networks* of human-mediated computer kiosks, shared among *multiple users* of a rural community, could in fact prove to be the most inexpensive and inclusive form of rural infrastructure possible today.

Rural information networks can allow knowledge, services, money, and certain kinds of products to more easily flow from node to node across long distances. Each village node can also serve as a range of virtual institutions, such as a community center, a bank, a medical center, a government information center, a matrimonial office, a public telephone booth, a public library and educational resource center, all at a fraction of the cost of corresponding 'real' institutions. By making these resources available in villages, information centres can alleviate the asymmetry between urban and rural environments. In order to accelerate rural growth, it is essential that we learn new ways of integrating social and human infrastructure development into the installation of basic information and communications infrastructure.

7.1.2. ICTs and Rural Infrastructure

There are three basic infrastructural requirements needed for rural ICT initiatives. They are, of course, (i) Electricity, (ii) Telephony (or its equivalent), and (iii) Network Connectivity. The problems associated with these inputs must be recognised as inherent features of the landscape, and tackled as an integral part of the implementation process.

i) *Electricity*: In many rural areas, electrical supply may be restricted to only 6 or 8 hours a day. When electrical power is available, its voltage and frequency may vary far outside the acceptable limits of most hardware. Finally, there is often no earthing provided.

ii) *Telephony*: Landline telephones are still not available in many villages in South Asia. Where they do exist they may be down for weeks at a time, and there may be other kinds of incompatibilities, which prevent data transfer.

iii) *Connectivity*: Internet subscription is not always available in rural and underdeveloped sections of South Asia. Even when it should, in theory, be available, long distance calls to nearby towns may be required in order to achieve true connectivity. Poor telephony ensures that modem speeds are often restricted to 28.8 kbps or slower. The wireless-fax system in Pondicherry runs even slower, at under 14.4 kbps.

Both urban and rural citizen consumers may benefit from ICT projects by receiving: (i) enhanced access to information and communication across large distances, (ii) improved access to governmental and quasi-governmental resources and services, (iii) opportunities to trade or bank online through kiosks, (iv) opportunities to design, manufacture and market their products through internet or intranet systems, (v) education through computers or about computers or both, and (vi) superior medical advice, diagnosis or knowledge in their own locality.

Inappropriate software, expensive hardware and weak telecommunications infrastructure are the three major hurdles to the use of information technology in rural areas of South Asia. In each of these fields, however, the landscape is slowly changing.

The cost of hardware is continuously falling, such that computers that were state-of-the-art 3 or 4 years ago, are now available for a fraction of their original cost. Those computers—or, indeed, new computers configured just like them—are still good for basic text-processing, email, and browsing functions. In addition, however, new entrants into the basic computing market such as the Simputer and the iStation have been specifically designed for a mass market, including both urban and rural users.

Wireless-in-Local-Loop and related technologies have emerged as a cheaper, smarter form of telecom infrastructure, in comparison with traditional wire telephony. The TeNet Group at the IIT-Madras has been at the frontline in developing technology solutions designed to improve telecommunications infrastructure in rural areas. The group has incubated several companies that work up and down the value chain in this sector, including, most recently, n-Logue Communications, which is working as a rural internet service provider.

Though human mediated intranet systems, several projects are now attempting to provide information and services to rural citizen consumers. The Village Knowledge Centres Project run by M.S. Swaminathan Research Foundation in Pondicherry represents an early experiment in providing information and knowledge resources to rural communities. The project uses wireless radios for data and analog voice transmissions between a semi-urban hub center and eight village centres. At each village center, offline content is updated through routine transmissions using fax protocols. Although the project displays outstanding sensitivity to context, as well as gender and social equity, and has conducted pioneering participatory experimentation and documentation, it has not developed a strong economic model to ensure the financial sustainability of the project. For this reason, it is also inhibited from scaling up its experiment to include a larger section of the countryside.

Young boys and girls from the settlement became highly proficient at using the graphic interface, and in surfing parts of the web, notwithstanding limitations of language and training. The social and economic returns of setting up such unattended systems are yet to be fully comprehended. While these initiatives represent diverse approaches to the question of wiring rural India, several trends can now be observed: First, economically responsible projects are already proving more successful than charitable or free models. Second, projects that identify and cost the services they provide are also more successful. Third, an intimate understanding of the social and economic parameters of rural India gives connectivity providers a significant advantage. Fourth, WLL systems appear to be emerging as the infrastructure solution of choice.

7.1.3. E-Governance

The introduction of e-governance speed up the proceedings in government offices. Previously, the Govt. offices worked in a snail pace. But now, everything has been changed with the computerisation in Govt. offices.

The Andhra Pradesh government is responsible for some early initiatives that sought to use networked technologies to improve citizen services. A series of catchily-acronymed services including CARD, TWINS, FAST, etc. provide licenses and certificates, allow the registration of deeds, and various kinds of payments at a single counter, in certain urban and rural areas of the state.

'Bhoomi' is a major Government of Karnataka initiative to computerise land records across the state. About a *quarter of the state's* talukas, or sub-*districts, have* now been computerised. At specified government offices in these districts, citizen-consumers may receive printouts of their land holdings with a schematic plan of their property on the obverse face. The computerisation of these land records is an expensive, laborious and time-intensive process, as the online system must (i) aggregate several different types of traditional village record-keeping, and (ii) provide a realtime record of landholdings, so that they may have unimpeachable legal standing.

7.1.4. Computerisation of Microfinance

The computerisation of microfinance and microcredit records

could result in savings of time and effort, and generally facilitate the maintenance of these accounts. However, the real transformative effect of this technology will be seen only once microcredit accounts come to be used for online or distance transactions amongst or within village communities at the grass-roots. This will allow rural entrepreneurs and craftspersons the same savings of time, travel, and effort, that the Internet has afforded individuals and institutions in the industrialised world. These possibilities have not yet been charted in any rural ICT project.

The Swayam Krishi Sangam project is recording transactional information on optical ID cards for microfinance, as well as for education and healthcare. Dr. Mohammed Yunus, Founder of the Grameen Bank of Bangladesh has notably called for the establishment of an 'International Center for Information Technology for the Elimination of Global Poverty'. A related agency, Grameen Telecom has attempted to provide mobile telephones to rural consumers through existing MFI / MCI networks.

7.1.5. IT-enabled Artisanal Industries

Besides facilitating the flow of capital across rural areas, online financial and commercial systems could also provide the capital and infrastructure for new kinds of IT-enabled industries, in fields such as regional language data entry, Computer-Aided Design (CAD), and Computer-Aided Manufacture (CAM). These applications of information technology, of course, will only become possible on a large-scale once rural ICT projects are better established in the landscape. The Asian Center for Entrepreneurial Initiatives has made an early attempt to introduce CAD / CAM technologies to artisans in north Karnataka, alongside online advertising and sales.

7.1.6. Computer Training and IT-Enabled Education

Till now, computer-training and IT-enabled education has been distressingly conflated and confused in the understanding of administrators and policy makers as well as the general public. Most commercial providers, moreover, are involved in both sectors, and aggressively crossmarket themselves.

Pratham, Akshara and The e-Learning Center together represent the most important attempt to create IT-enabled learning software for disprivileged children. They have developed educational games, which are now being tested in several rural areas through the Center for Knowledge Societies. Bangalore.

Interactive Learning Systems represent commercial attempts to provide online educational resources coupled with products ranging from in-class instruction to interactive CDROMs, to cable-TV programmes. These products are predominately in English, although regional language translations could become widely available in future.

7.1.7.Telecentre

Telecentre is a generic term for all kinds of arrangement seeking to provide shared and mediated access to information and ICT-enabled services in rural areas through new technologies especially computers and Internet. The concept of shared access emerged as response to the perceived constraint that individual household in rural area cannot afford such technologies. Access is mediated because a telecentre operator mediates between information, technology and the people to overcome the barriers of low literacy, awareness about technology and availability of required skills. In the broad context of ICTs for Development, telecentres have emerged as a popular strategy for bridging the digital divide, providing access to information/technology and delivering a host of applications and services directed towards poverty alleviation and rural development.

The conceptual framework puts forth that the telecentre located in a village is embedded within the external macro policy environment and the local contextual characteristics of the village. Further the organisational characteristics associated with a particular model shape some of the characteristics of the particular instance of the model in the village and the pattern of its access, use and impact.

The policy environment related to telecentres at the international, national and state levels. It is shaped by the policies and plans of the various types of governmental and non-governmental (both for-profit and nonprofit) agencies at each different level. Broadly they set the directions of the developmental programmes, influences issues like research and development of technology, provision of funds etc. The response at the national and state level to the macro policy environment especially in terms of allocated resources, programmes/projects initiated and other support also influences how the telecentres are deployed in rural areas.

The local context is the environment immediate to where the telecentre is located. It is described in terms of both village level features and household level characteristics. The parameters considered under various dimensions are infrastructure, economic, social, cultural, institutional and political. These dimensions and the parameters are not independent of each other, but have categorised for conceptualisation and data collection. Along with the characteristics of the telecentre, the local context determines the short-term impact and the long-term developmental implications of telecentres in general and the specific model in particular. The telecentre depending on members' need, available resources and capabilities which in turn is shaped by interplay of various contextual level characteristics.

The developmental implication of the telecentre within a local context is assessed in terms of the pattern of access and use of its services by households belonging to different socio-economic groups and individuals living in the village. Access itself has multiple meanings. Apart from the implied technological connotation, access is also a physical, social and structured construct. The telecentre has to be located at a place that is physically accessible to all, including women.

7.1.8. Tele-Health

Computer-based and Online expert diagnostic systems could enhance the quality of healthcare and diagnosis available to rural citizen-consumers in many remote parts of South Asia. The real benefits of these systems, however, may be the collation of more comprehensive public health information.

7.2. Impact of ICTs in Rural Societies

ICTs have been largely understood as a new kind of media or telecommunications infrastructure, which allows the dissemination of information, commands, or even education across distances. Developmental ICT projects, therefore, have attempted to assist rural communities by providing them news, information, advice, and knowledge which has hitherto been inaccessible to them. These kinds of inputs have allowed rural citizen-consumers to make more informed economic decisions: farmers can decide whether to sell there produce locally or transport it themselves further afield; landless labourers have been able to negotiate their daily wage more effectively; tractors, threshers, old television sets, cattle and motorcycles have all been traded across towns and villages thanks to online advertisements.

Nevertheless rural ICT projects are yet to effectively position themselves as a vehicle for online commerce and a mechanism of employment for village communities. The first step in this direction would be to put rural Self-Help Groups (SHGs) and other Micro-Credit / Micro-Finance Initiatives (MCIs / MFIs) online. This abstraction of cash money onto an online financial system would lay the groundwork for a new kind of rural ecommerce, which could prove extremely enabling for many communities, especially non-agricultural artisanal groups. Entrepreneurs and small-scale industries might then be able to regularise existing off-line trade relationships into online systems that track raw materials, designs, quality control, and delivery mechanisms. New kinds of banking and finance systems in rural areas would make capital more easily available for investment into new businesses and rural infrastructure.

Persons making less than a dollar a day might immediately benefit only by having access to a more efficient and easily accessible form of banking. So, in the long run unemployed and underemployed poor would experience the significant secondary benefits of actually having access to a far better developed economy and the range of education, employment, and self-empowerment opportunities available therein.

These possibilities can only be actualised once significant sections of rural South Asia achieve connectivity with one another and with the world at large. Despite the economic promise of ICTs, their social benefits may not emerge immediately. According to a preliminary estimate prepared by the Center for Knowledge Societies—Bangalore, the immediate impact of ICT projects upon their rural contexts will be far from equitable.

Rather, ICT access is likely to increase socioeconomic opportunities for dominant caste landholding elites, relatively disprivileging non-elite nonlandholding artisanal communities. There are several reasons for this:

i) *Access to Capital Resources:* Landholding groups always have access to capital in the form of land, which they can sell to start a business, move to the city, rent, etc. Even if they keep the land, their agricultural incomes will always be higher than the non-agricultural incomes of landless groups.

ii) *Literacy and Education:* Dominant caste agricultural communities tend to have higher literacy and education levels relative to disprivileged artisanal groups.

iii) *Social and Educational Access:* Dominant caste landholding communities are often organised through their caste associations and other socioreligious institutions. These institutions have sometimes founded schools, hospitals, hostels, colleges and even professional schools. Non-elite rural communities lack these kinds of social networks and access to social, intellectual or financial capital, and will therefore find it more difficult to take advantage of rural ICT networks.

iv) *Agricultural Technologies*: States like Karnataka and Andhra Pradesh are racing to develop Agribiotech and Agri-infotech policies and projects, in order to demonstrate that emerging technologies can actually help rural communities.

The net effect of all these factors will be that most of the new entrants into South Asia's middle classes will come from rural landowning communities. Artisanal groups, Dalits, Adivasis and other disprivileged groups will be relatively disabled from taking advantage of the opportunities offered by rural connectivity. In fact, these groups may be further discriminated against (i) directly, through harassment or impeded access to networked facilities, (ii) indirectly, on account of the cultural, institutional or otherwise embedded prejudices of the hardware, software, or services offered.

Indirect social discrimination is more difficult to address, as the elite and urbane personalities who often design rural ICT

Projects are likely to encounter and work with rural elites when they visit the field. This can result in a skewing of priorities in favour or rural elites and semi-elites and against artisanal and adivasi communities in the same area. In one project, members of adivasi communities rarely visited information centers, even though they comprised upto 40 per cent of the project population. This was not only due to their relative economic impoverishment, but also because the available services were more precisely calibrated with the cultural assumptions and economic needs of local Dominant Caste and Bahujan communities. No immediate solution presents itself for asymmetries caused by economic disprivilege. Nevertheless, it is possible first of all to ensure that these are not compounded by sociocultural discrimination, and secondly to plan for the expanded use of rural networked resources by lowering costs as soon as economies of scale and network effects emerge from an increasing subscriber base.

Rural ICT projects be carefully designed with a view to enabling and including the very rural non-elite non-agricultural communities which are most likely to be left out. Information Design, which encompasses everything from the pattern of the sweater worn by the kiosk operator, to the architectural space of the information center, to the hardware and software design, to the content, language, accent and fontography of audiovisual interfaces, to the very services which are available at the center, together make the critical difference between inclusivist, empowering projects and exclusivist, elitist information centers. Funding organisations and policy makers can encourage innovations in Information Design by stipulating that their projects routinely undergo socioeconomic impact analyses by specialist external agencies that have demonstrated their understanding of rural socioeconomic relations, and the potential impact that ICTs may have upon them.

7.3. Virtual Education for Rural Communities

In this technically advanced era, the method of teaching is going through a drastic change. Education and Training traditionally involve learning from teachers and other pedagogical standards. The role of the teacher is to impart knowledge to those who do not possess them. Teachers talk in front of the class, and the pupils have to listen and write down what the "knowing" teacher says.

This top-down method is not only used in the formal education system, also training staff uses this method to train the people. Even though this way of teaching and learning is part of our culture, the changing scenarios demand people to adapt new ways to update their skills and knowledge for making their identity in this competitive world.

Advances in ICTs, and specifically in Multimedia, Networking, and Software Engineering have promoted the enormous amount of learning resources and Learning Management Systems (LMSs). During the last years, thousands of electronic texts, images, movies, or Java applet based learning resources have been developed for learning purposes in Internet environments. To take advantage of this situation, new services were developed for creating synchronous and asynchronous learning environments. With the help of these contemporary Information and Communication Technology based services, the search, classification, organisation, and peer-to-peer exchange of learning resources by learners, instructors, and course developers are becoming commonplace. However most of these technologies are accessible to academic institutions, research organisations, multi national corporate companies and elite urban groups. None or very few above discussed technologies are accessible to rural communities that too not for education, training or other learning purposes.

The technological divide has been becoming an important factor in enlarging the rich-poor divide both among and within nations. Therefore, the M S Swaminathan Research Foundation chose to impart a pro-nature, pro-poor and pro-women orientation to technology development and dissemination as its main mandate when it started functioning in Chennai in 1989. This main mandate has given birth to the Information Village Research Project (IVRP) in 1992, and started implementing from 1997 onwards by establishing Village Resource Centres (VRCs) and Village Knowledge Centres (VKCs) in the Union Territory of Puducherry, with financial support from the International Development Research centre (IDRC) of Canada. After receiving successful results from the IVRP pilot experiment, the initiative was further strengthened into the Jamsetji Tata National Virtual Academy in the year 2003 by bringing various International and National partners, with an objective to empower the vulnerable remote rural Indian communities by building the skills and capacities through the Open and Distance Learning (ODL) mode. This education should reach every home and hut, and gives them a better control on their own development i.e., to make better choices, to take better decisions, and to create better livelihood opportunities.

For providing life long learning opportunities to the NVA fellows, and to the needy people who discontinued their education in early stages of life and interested to pursue the same in the later stages for satisfying their information and knowledge needs and to create livelihood opportunities, the MSSRF-NVA has started a school—Jamsetji Tata Training School (JTS) for Leadership in rural knowledge connectivity—on 17 February 2007 with an aim to use contemporary ICTs and ODL principles to educate and train vulnerable rural communities and intermediaries about improved agricultural technologies, health, governance, water management, environment, biodiversity and livelihood opportunities.

The goal of JTS is to bring the knowledge revolution by enabling knowledge transfers between and across rural communities, scientists, educators, administrators, health care providers, technology enablers on local agro-ecological and socio-cultural conditions of each village, and also relating to various farming methods and techniques. The JTS focuses on creating decentralised learning environments with a central knowledge base (blend of traditional and modern knowledge) through a network of VRCs, VKCs and consortium of potential GGA partners, and uses contemporary ICTs and ODL principles for information and knowledge empowerment to achieve the proposed goal.

The government of India has accepted the recommendation of the National Commission of Farmers that knowledge connectivity should become an integral part of the Bharat Nirman (i.e., New Deal for Rural India) programme. The Bharat Nirman document contains the following commitment.

> "The Government is committed to expanding rural connectivity through a slew of measures, so that rural users can access information of value and transact business. This will include connecting block headquarters with fiber optic

> network, using wireless technology to achieve last mile connectivity and operating information kiosks through a partnership of Citizens, Panchayats, Civil Society Organisations, the Private Sector and Government".

The stage is thus set for ushering in a knowledge revolution in rural India. The Green Revolution in rural India. The Green Revolution helped to improve the production of wheat, rice and other crops, and the Knowledge Revolution can lead to the enhancement of human productivity and creativity in every area of human endeavour.

Computers and Internet are important for facilitating the rural knowledge revolution, only rural women and men can help to shape the direction and relevance of this revolution. This is where the Jamsetji Tata National Virtual Academy for Rural prosperity and Jamsetji Tata Training School for Leadership in Rural Knowledge Connectivity is playing such a critical role. NVA-JTS is the largest capacity building and human resource development organisation in the areas of ICT for villages in the country. Its Fellows are grassroots workers in villages who have mastered modern ICT procedures and are devoting their time and talent to training rural women, men and children in the use of the new tools of knowledge and skill empowerment. The ultimate goal is to enlist one woman and one man from every village as Fellows –they will be master trainers, training others in the village. They will also be in charge of the care and management of the VKC in the respective villages.

7.3.1. Experience of IGNOU

IGNOU was established as a National Open University in 1985 blazing a new trail in higher education. The launching of this university is the culmination of the concern and desire to democratise higher education to large segments of population, specially the disadvantaged groups and individuals and bring higher education to the doorsteps of all those who look for it and to maintain standards in education by offering a wide variety of academic programmes using innovative technology and diversity of means with uniform curriculum throughout the country.

IGNOU has been introduced a wide variety of programmes in the areas of Humanities, Social Sciences, and Sciences. In addition, it has also introduced programmes in Women Studies, Rural development, Health Sciences, Education and Distance Education. Professional programmes such as Management, Computer, Engineering, Health and Nursing and Library Sciences have also been added into its fold. Large number of non-formal programmes in the areas of Women Studies, Construction, Tannery, Computer Literacy, Disaster Management, Participatory Forestry Management, etc. has been added. The university is giving more and more emphasis to nonformal programmes keeping in view the large number of unskilled workers engaged in different sectors across the country.

Distance education focuses on people who have missed their education early in life, economically, socially and physically disadvantaged groups, rural youth, women and those living in backward, hilly and remote areas. Thus IGNOU has emerged as one of the mega open universities in the world. The pattern of academic programmes and student enrolment reveals that there is a gradual shift from traditional programmes and diplomas to professional and vocational degrees and diplomas.

IGNOU has adopted a multimedia approach to instruction since its inception. The learning (instruction) package consists of print (self-learning materials), audios and video programmes, assignments. In some programmes practical manuals (for practical and lab based courses) and project guidelines are also supplied. In addition, the learner is supported in various ways through study centres and other centres in the form of face to face counselling sessions, practicals and hands on experience through laboratories/skill based centres (through specialised institutions).

To give more weightage to the component of interactivity in the learning process, IGNOU had introduced interactive radio counselling, interactive tele-counselling and teleconference, voice mail, email and internet based learning. In addition IGNOU uses television broadcasts (limited) and radio and cable television from few places. Even the printed selflearning materials are designed to be interactive. The style is that of guided didactic conversation, with the teacher in-built in the text.

The university began supporting learners through its Study Centres (ground level) and Regional Centre (Middle level) under the Regional Services (Hqrs.). As the enrolment increased, programmes and courses multiplied and specialised nature of facilities required got diversified. Hence, Study Centre approach alone could not meet demands of scattered students across the vast nation. It was felt, therefore, necessary to rationalise and diversity existing centres and add new channels of delivery to reach out all sections and parts of the country.

7.3.1.1. Virtual Campus

The University has introduced 3 programmes through virtual campus concept in July 1998 for the first time under the pilot project. They are Certificate in Computing (CIC), Bachelor Degree in Computer Application (BCA), and Master Degree in Computer Application. However, the University could not continue these programmes due to non-availability of adequate access points to Internet and PCs in the interiors and was thus unable to cope up with huge enrolments in providing web based support and other support required. Hence, the University gave an option to all these students to join in the regular stream called as "Integrated Mode", Thus temporarily shifting students to Regular stream. Many of these students are urban based, working professionals and may be having access to Internet and PC either at their working places/ home/cyber café. In the changing requirements of the Information Technology (IT) sector, IGNOU has launched the Bachelor in Information Technology (BIT) and Advanced Diploma in Information Technology (ADIT) in the month of September 1999 under the Virtual Campus initiative.

7.3.1.2. Teaching Learning Methodology

The components of teaching methods include: Live satellite based Teleconferencing lecturers through Gyan Darshan; recorded video lectures. The teacher takes online counselling of a course by hosting on the web, materials for about a week's study and informing the learners about what materials would be hosted during which week. This schedule will also be available on the website. The learners would then pursue the materials, do self-check exercises, and interact with the peer group as well as the mentor/ instructor through e-mail. A learners can access the course material through website. The learner can also access through the internet, Frequently Asked Questions and their

Answers, which have been organised and structured for each course. If learners need to ask a question on a portion of the course which is not covered in the database of Frequently Asked Questions and their Answers, the learner could ask such a question by submitting a form through e-mail. This could in some sense be the equivalent of an electronic post card. The learners are being assessed periodically through both traditional and innovative methods, which include case studies, assignments, time-constrained assessments and workbased projects and final examinations.

7.3.2. Rural Knowledge Centres (RKC)

A large number of Indian population dependent on agriculture and allied activities. Ecologically sound agriculture is knowledge intensive. Farm women and men need dynamic information relating to meteorological, management and marketing factors as related to crops and animal husbandry, fisheries, agro-forestry and agro-processing. The new approach to productivity improvement and employment generation is also information and knowledge intensive. In the context of globalisation of trade, there is need for launching a genetic (i.e. relating to genetically modified farm products), legal (i.e. IPR and Farmers' and Breeders' Rights), quality (i.e. sanitary and phytosanitary measures and codex alimentarius standards), and trade (i.e. prices in home and external markets) literacy movement. There is presently a disconnect between what farm families need by way of generic and dynamic information and what the conventional extension agencies are able to provide.

So, the need for demand driven and value added information should also be addressed, which is time and location specific. There is also need for technology enablers on local agro-ecological and socio-cultural conditions of each village, and also relating to various farming methods and techniques. Apart from information related to farming, rural women and men urgently need access to healthcare information. Increased health expenditure is an important cause of farmers' indebtedness, leading occasionally to suicides. Information on the health status of livestock and poultry, on-farm and off-farm livelihoods and market-led entrepreneurship opportunities for the poor and the marginalised in rural India need attention. There is also need for promoting functional literacy among the adult illiterate and making learning joyful for the young through interactive pedagogic methodologies. All this can be effectively done through a network of Rural Knowledge Cen.res (RKCs) across the country that focus on skill building at the local level and information empowerment with the help of contemporary Information and Communication Technology (ICT) tools.

Prior to set-up RKCs, the staff and volunteers of the implementing agency should get accepted by the people. Unless the local people accept the implementing agency and are ready to work with them, the programme cannot take off. The people should be ready to work with them. Once the implementing team establishes a good rapport with a wide cross section of the local community, it should carry out largescale consultations with the local people. Information needs of the community and the people's familiarity with different technologies and communication channels should be assessed through PRA. A bottom-up approach of involving the users themselves in assessing their needs is necessary to make the programme more effective. Implementing agency should collect information on district and village profiles, household details, economic activity of the village, maps, existing infrastructure like government institutions, primary health centres, educational institutions, libraries, extension centres, etc. Implementing agency should collect information on people living below the poverty line. The needs of different people could be classified into needs of women, men, children, the poor, landless etc.

In all rural, community-based projects community participation is vital. The right community champions often play a critical role in ensuring the project's success. They are the prime movers in the community. Community participation should be broad based and representative, and cut across social and economic status. Local community participation should start from the conceptualisation stage and be sustained throughout.

7.4. Integrating Technology into Development: Government Initiatives

The government, after independence, took upon itself the major responsibility of development. Hence, the central and state governments carried out development projects. Such projects are radio for rural development and satellite instructional television experiment. The phase of post media liberalisation phase, communication has been further re-emphasised and recognised as "missing link" in achieving development objectives. Almost all healthcare projects for rural poor, especially women and children have used demand driven social marketing approach for rural the development. United States of America, World Bank and other donor agencies have been advocating for such an approach for rural development. At the same time, communication convergence, especially of media and Internet, opened up the possibility of individualised non-broadcast communication. Launch of "Kisan Call Centres" and an exclusive "Farmer Television Channel" are examples of social marketing approach for rural development. Let us look at few examples of social marketing approach of communication for rural development.

7.4.1. Community Radio Initiative

In post media liberalisation phase, Government of India, announced the policy for community radio broadcasting. "Community radio is expected to focus on issues relating to education, health, environment, agriculture, rural and community development".

"Cable" community radio station, named as Namma Dhwani or Our Voices' was set up earlier in Boodikote, Karnataka. The villagers believe that "This radio station is ours because it speaks about us—in our language and in our accent". Community radio in Boodikote, according to Seema Nair, helps the villagers run the radio station "it is a new source of strength for poor people because it addresses their most basic development needs".

7.4.2. Kunjal Panje Kutchji

'Kunjal Panje Kutchji' is an interactive and participative development communication project. It is also the first time that a voluntary organisation, the Bhuj-based Kutch Mahila Vikas Sansthan (KMVS), has bought airtime on the radio as part of its communication strategy. A feedback exercise was planned for continuous improvement and to ensure listener-ship not only decide what issues are taken up but also shape the script of the dramatised serial.

'Kunjal Paṇje Kutchji' has also focused on capacity building for elected women in *panchayats* on development issues. No feedback is available to assess the effectiveness of the project.

7.4.3. Community Television

Since the inception of INSAT satellite television system, Doordarshan achieved a kind of world record in setting up over 1000 low powered television transmission stations in the country. Each station in theory was supposed to telecast local television programme for rural development. A large number of television professional were trained for this purpose. Doordarshan has been planning to introduce local television for rural poor and farmers to achieve the goals of rural development. Earlier similar attempts have been made to set up local television stations for rural development like in Nagpur.

Today, local stations have been largely subsumed in the maize of urban national television. The advertisers have used the television time for selling consumer products that are not of any use to rural poor. Hopefully, small town neighbourhood restaurants, shopkeepers and television dealers will have a new venue for cheap advertisements.

7.4.4. TANUVAS Project

The Tamil Nadu Veterinary and Animal Sciences University (TANUVAS) project has been experimenting as to how Internet can be used and combined with other technologies to benefit farmers and rural communities. Personal discussions with the project leader indicated that there are positive gains. At present and no evaluation is available to base future decisions for expansion of the project.

Communication technology is not culture-neutral. It is no accident that not a single communication projects for rural development discussed here can be an unqualified success. This calls for a serious re-examination and reflection of what we have learnt from the past and before getting fully committed to social marketing.

The "pro-poor" development issues have been pushed aside in favour of urban upcoming rich after media privatisation—leading to proliferation of private and public broadcasting and

ICT in favour of consumerism and entertainment. The current communication policy of the country, which on the face of it is proactive for rural development, but remains urban "pro-rich" in effect. Besides, forces of market economy, focused towards profits, have begun to shape broadcasting and information technology programming philosophy, content and programme schedule.

7.5. Future of ICT-based Development

Non-elite, rural, artisanal and adivasi communities of South Asia do not and will not use information and communication in exactly the same ways as industrialised nations elsewhere in the world. In order to find ways for emerging technologies to truly benefit these groups we must invent and innovate from the ground up, working always in partnership and dialogue with local communities. Far from replicating the online behaviour of highly connected and cosmopolitan societies in North America, Europe, or South East Asia, therefore, digital development in India requires us to design products, services, and technologies that solve very local problems and ameliorate local socioeconomic conditions.

Digital development affords a new perspective from which to imagine the future direction of India's political economy. Rather than remaining locked in the paradigm of an eternally developing nation, it now seems possible to aspire to becoming a knowledge society. Should India become successful in achieving such an empirical and epistemic shift, this could eventually serve as a model for other emerging economies around the world. Before this can begin to happen, however, mutual realignments among the major estates of society—the state, private enterprise, academia, civil society organisations and global state agencies. Moreover, public discourse and policy debate must proceed from a new perspective, which recognises emerging technologies as a profoundly important resource for public practice.

The elite class oppose information oriented development because of their fear and anxiety. Many recoil against the idea of digital development not only because the technology remains alien and intimidating to them, but also because they cannot abide the thought of their social inferiors achieving a literacy that they have not. While there are only a few who would openly oppose empowering information resources because of the threat to their social privilege, such hierarchical ideologies sometimes lurk under the surface of apparently utilitarian objections to information-oriented development.

At every public conference, trade show and media opportunity, scions of major Indian corporate houses dilate on the empowering effects of IT and its role in alleviating poverty. These homilies are rarely, if ever, backed up either by profit-driven infrastructure projects in rural areas, or by indirect philanthropic contributions. India's social sector and grassroots activists will therefore be forgiven for doubting the commitment of the IT sector, and large corporates in general, to actually achieving rural development and economic empowerment. Nevertheless, venture capital can be invested for the creation of social infrastructure that can drive further growth. In this way, the corporate sector can serve the public good while also developing large markets for hardware, software, and connectivity in rural India. It is more and more plausible that social investment projects—which seek financial as well as social returns on their investment—are the swiftest way to create economic prosperity and social empowerment across rural India.

While the three southern states are better prepared to attract multinational investment, some of the progressive states in the Hindi belt have produced excellent policy documents that very effectively outline the governments' plans for rural connectivity, e-governance, e-ducation, and all round e-development. It is not all that difficult to explain this conundrum: the work profile of the IT-Secretariat, in an IT-rich state is very different from its counterpart in an IT-poor state. The former must attract investment, sell the state at road-shows in the US and Europe, liaise with CII, TIE, NASSCOM and other industry groups, plan and host tradeshows, and even promote Biotech as the next wave.

The latter, on the other hand, has only one mandate for the moment: computerise the state machinery and leverage IT to the political advantage of the incumbent government. Civil servants at every level are actually more curious and engaged with the possibilities of e-governance than is commonly believed. As with any other social sample, of course, particular members of the bureaucracy display far greater ability to respond and adapt to changing technology than others. Any developmental ICT project that involves the state apparatus will therefore be subject to not only to the variable aptitudes of the officers concerned, but also to the vicissitudes of cadre politics that rattles officers around into wildly disparate job descriptions without warning.

Rajiv Gandhi's flawed solution to the problem of computer illiteracy in the bureaucracy was to post District Information Officers (DIOs) in every district and State Information Officers (SIOs) in every state, all reporting directly to the centrally controlled National Informatics Center. This had the effect of creating a new caste of officers who are effectively outside the control of the state administration, who sometimes seek to monopolise information access within their office, rather than disseminating it more widely into the administrative machinery of their district.

The DIO is still the only government officer at the district level with an official email address. The various state Infotech PSUs that IAS officers lead also lack any certain mandate: they are expected to firefight every problem pertaining to IT, from rewiring the computers in the Chief Minister's house, to reviewing technology purchases for every department of the bureaucracy, to negotiating networking infrastructure with corporate entities. They are riven by hierarchical striations, union cliques and political interference, all of which inhibits the minimal creativity and initiative that is necessary to keep pace with current rates of technological obsolescence.

These Public Sector Undertakings (PSUs) urgently need to be reorganised as financially responsible corporate entities run by non-cadre executive officers with a clear mandate to build information and communications infrastructure for India's people and their governments. Although administrators and bureaucrats remain generalists, almost by definition, whether in South Asia or in any other part of the world, the difference here lies in the assumption of executive infallibility, and the lack of institutional relations with scholars, intellectuals, and knowledge workers.

To conclude, effectively drive digital development in India, therefore, we need a new pattern of interaction between the different estates of our society, so as to maximally utilise their respective expertise and abilities. We will need: (i) well funded centers of research into technology, media and the social sciences, where new ideas and new models of development, governance, and business can be generated, (ii) venture capital funds and new hybrid public-private corporate entities directed towards the development of social and human infrastructure, (iii) authoritative and responsible civil society organisations that work with, rather than either against or in parallel with the state and private sectors, and (iv) governments and bureaucracies that work in transparent dialogue with these other estates.

References

Best, M. & Maclay, C. "Community Internet Access in Rural Areas: Solving the Economic Sustainability Puzzle". *Global Information Technology Report*. Oxford University Press. 2002.

Bhatnagar, S. & Schware. R. *Technology in Development: Cases from India.* Sage Publications. 2000.

Brown, J. S. & Duguid, P. *The Social Life of Information.* Harvard Busi ness School Press. 2000.

Government of Karnataka. *IT for the Common Man: The Millenium IT Policy*. Department of Information Technology. 2000.

Prahlad, C.K. "The End of Corporate Imperialism." *Harvard Business Review.* July-August 1998.

Pitroda, S. "Development, Democracy, and the Village Telephone." *Harvard Business Review.* November 1993. HBS Press.

Rajora, R. *Bridging the Digital Divide.* Tata-McGraw Hill. 2002.

Singh, J.P. *Leapfrogging Development? The Political Economy of Telecommunications Restructuring.* SUNY Press. 1999.

Sood, A. D. "How to Wire Rural India: The Problems and Possibilities of Digital Development." *Economic and Political Weekly* Vol 36: No. 43. October 27, 2001.

8

ATTITUDINAL CHANGE OF RURAL PEOPLE

With 1,000 million people and 180 million households, India is one of the biggest growing economies in the world. With the advent of the Information, Communication and Technology (ICT) revolution, India and its villages are slowly but steadily getting connected to the cities of the nation and the world beyond. India is now a powerful knowledge economy, and though India may have been slow to start, it certainly has caught up with the West and is ahead in important respects. The Government, the corporate sector, NGOs and educational institutions have supported rural development by encouraging digital libraries, e-business, e-learning and e-governance.

Most of rural India is transformed beyond imagination thanks to a host of factors which has put unprecedented wealth into the hands of farmers across the country and turned it into a huge consumer market. Latest statistics show that agricultural growth and rural income has largely been unaffected by the economic slowdown, this, despite the fact that the contribution of agriculture to total rural income has actually come down. Instead, we have a growing service industry and alternate revenue channels from horticulture, poultry, fisheries and other activities which are less rain-dependant and were virtually non-existent a decade ago. India's 6,38,000 villages, which harbour 72.2 per cent of the population, once the albatross around its neck, are now the signpost to its future. Call it a new adventurism or entrepreneurship, but most farmers have gained from a switch to new crops and technology.

8.1. Rising Rural Prosperity

India is now seeing a dramatic shift towards prosperity in rural households. To drive home the potential of rural India just consider some of these impressive facts about the rural sector. As per the National Council for Applied Economic Research (NCAER) study, there are as many 'middle income and above' households in the rural areas as there are in the urban areas. There are almost twice as many 'lower middle income' households in rural areas as in the urban areas.

Table 8.1. Distribution of people income-wise

Income groups	2001–02			2006-07		
	Total	Rural No.	per cent	Total	Rural No.	per cent
High	1.48	0.41	27.7	2.96	0.7	23.6
Middle	69.18	4.83	64.8	90.25	59.85	66.3
Low	32.29	29.52	91.42	20.41	95.8	95.7
Total	102.95	74.76	72.6	114.52	80.96	70.7

According to NCAER projections, by 2006—07, the lowest income class (i.e.Rs.2500 and below) will shrink by more than 60 per cent. The higher income classes are likely to double by 2006—07. This apparently is the result of development work, which happened under the five years plans and other special programmes such as land reforms, rural electrification rural communication, and rural credit facilities, etc. The absolute size of the rural market is thus expected to double that of urban India. But despite the high rural share in these categories, the rural penetration rates are low, thus offering tremendous potential for growth.

8.1.1. Growth in Market

The purchasing power in rural India is on steady rise and it has resulted in the growth of the rural market. The market has been growing at 3-4 per cent per annum adding more than one million new consumers every year and now accounts for close to 50 per cent of volume consumption of Fast Moving Consumer Goods (FMCG) industry. The growth rates of lot of FMCG are higher in rural markets than urban markets. In product categories like toilet soaps, talcum powder, cooking iol, vanaspati ghee, tea, cigarettes and hair oil, the share of rural market is more than 505. The table above indicates the projected market size of FMCG products in 2001–02 and 2006–07 based on the annual growth rates compounded for 1994–99 period.The estimated annual business from rural markets was Rs 1,23,000 crore, comprising Rs 65,000 crore of FMCG, Rs 5,000 crore of durables, Rs 45,000 crore of agricultural inputs including tractors and Rs 8,000 crore of two-wheelers and four-wheelers.Twenty nine per cent of the rural people own cars, 27 per cent own colour televisions, 24 per cent own refrigerators and 10 per cent own washing machines, which points to the untapped potential in the rural areas.

8.1.2. IT Penetration

Today there are over 15 million villagers in India who are aware of the Internet and over 300,000 villagers have used it! Ten years back, history was created with Public Call Office phone booths (essentially manually operated payphone facilities), opening in every corner of the country. This experiment was an instant success and contributed to hundreds of thousands of jobs. Over the next two years, WorldTel is expected to provide 1000 centres in Tamil Nadu with 2 to 20 terminals in each centre. If successful, this experiment can be replicated easily to all 27 states leading to over half a million Internet users through this experiment alone! The existing 600,000 public call offices in India will soon be transformed into public 'tele-info-centres' offering a variety of multimedia information services. The rural consumers spend time and money to access higher level information. Studies have indicated that if the content has direct relevance and will result in commercial gains, people in rural areas are willing to pay for information services. Consumerism has altered rural buying behaviour in recent years. Spending patterns of those who spend are now adapting to face the technology bug. Today's rural children and youth will grow up in an environment where they have 'information access' to education opportunities, exam results, career counseling, job opportunities, government schemes and services, health and legal advice and services, worldwide news and information, land records, mandi prices, weather forecasts, bank loans, livelihood options. If television could change the language of brand communication in rural India, affordable Web connectivity through various types of communication hubs will surely impact the currency of information exchange. As the electronic ethos and IT culture moves into rural India, the possibilities of change are becoming visible.

8.1.3. Impact of Globalisation

The impact of globalisation will be felt in rural India as much as in urban. But it will be slow. It will have its impact on target groups like farmers, youth and women. Farmers, today 'keep in touch' with the latest information and maximise both ends. Animal feed producers no longer look at Andhra Pradesh or Karnataka. They keep their cell phones constantly connected to global markets. Surely, price movements and products' availability in the international market place seem to drive their local business strategies. On youth its impact is on knowledge and information and while on women it still depends on the socio-economic aspect. The marketers who understand the rural consumer and fine tune their strategy are sure to reap benefits in the coming years. In fact, the leadership in any product or service is linked to leadership in the rural India except for few lifestyle-based products, which depend on urban India mainly.

Although globalisation has led to the economic development in the country, it has not really helped to minimise income inequalities across the country. Recent surveys say that lots of people across the country still live below the poverty line and their standard of living has gone down considerably. In fact, the poverty level in India is much more than that of China. One of the main causes of poverty in India is income inequality. While the effects of globalisation, economic liberalisation and market growth are being felt in the cities and urban sectors across the country, most of the rural areas are still not so developed and the condition has also not significantly improved. No doubt, there has been some improvement but still a lot needs to be done.

A significant portion of the rural mass does not have access to the basic amenities such as electricity, education, sanitation, drinking water, and infrastructure. The wealth distribution pattern is also uneven in the country. Recent surveys have shown that the top 10 per cent of the income groups share around 33 per cent of the total income of the country. Even after globalisation and economic progress, around a quarter of the population of the country has a earning less than the minimum level of $0.40 per day.

Globalisation has also not done much good to reduce disparities between various regions and states across the country. While some states have a high earning, there are also some states which have a very low growth rate. Some of the states which have a high income are Gujarat with 8.8 per cent, Delhi with 7.4 per cent and Haryana with 8.7 per cent. In comparison to these, Bihar with 5.1 per cent, Uttar Pradesh with 4.4 per cent and Madhya Pradesh with 3.5 per cent are some of the lowest ranking states with very little socio economic growth.

To minimise the income inequalities and regional disparities across the country, the government has taken a number of steps. Lots of rural development programmes have been initiated to make the rural mass self sufficient and financially stable. In this regard, the government has set up village cooperative banks, Regional Rural Banks and so on to help the poor and the villagers. The government also offers land for farming at cheap rates, tax relief and other incentives to minimise regional disparities and income inequality.

India saw an annual growth rate of GDP (Gross Domestic Product) of only 3.6 per cent during the 3 decades, post-independence. It's a growth of only 1.4 per cent in terms of per capita. The economy of the country only moved towards higher growth trajectory during 1980s, when it saw a growth rate of 5.4 per cent. The growth rate of GDP soared up to 7.3 per cent by 2007-08, whereas the per capita GDP saw a growth of 5.7 per cent. Due to sufficient foreign exchange reserves, moderate inflation, stable exchange rates and adequate food stocks, the country achieved a sustainable growth rate.

However, the gross state domestic product growth rates largely varied between states in India. The states like Assam, Uttar Pradesh, Madhya Pradesh and Bihar saw a growth rate of less than 5 per cent in pre and post reform period. On the other hand, states like Andhra Pradesh, Tamil Nadu, Gujarat, Karnataka, Haryana saw a growth rate of less than 5 per cent during 1980-93, which improved considerably during 1993-2006.

Finally, globalisation has had its effect on Indian economy. There also exist income inequalities and regional disparities. Yet, these shouldn't be treated as the inevitable outcomes of globalisation. There are also some other factors like politics, political institutions, political mobilisation, and policy frameworks etc. which play major role in creating income inequalities and regional disparities in the country. Political preferences often slow down the process of growing inequalities, which avert the movement from agriculture to service.

8.1.4. Rural-centred Approaches of Big Companies

It becomes amply clear that rural India has to be the hot target in future for FMCG companies as it presents a plethora of opportunities, all waiting to be harnessed. Many of the FMCG companies are already busy formulating their rural marketing strategy to tap the potential before competition catches up. With extensive competition not only from MNCs but also from the numerous regional players and the lure of an untapped market has driven the marketers to chalk out bold new strategies for targeting the rural consumer in a big way. All biggies in the industry be it HLL, Marico, Colgate-Palmolive or Britannia, are showing deep interest in rural India. However not everything is all rosy and there exist some gray areas in the rural strategies also. To increase sales, growing the consumer pie rather than sharing it, has emerged as one of the key strategies being used by FMCG majors. Offering more product variants, categories, price points, sizes and different marketing and distribution channels, all form part of a FMCG corporate's strategy.

To gauge the extent of shift in focus of the FMCG giants just sample this: recently Godrej Consumer Products Ltd (GCPL) did something that it hadn't done before; it introduced smaller pack sizes of some of its soaps and put them on the market for Rs 5. And FMCG giant HLL has just launched a green variant of Lifebuoy soap, which, it hopes will be a winner in the rural areas. Also, don't be too surprised if you village folk having their hair washed and dyed en masse as they are only taking advantage of the live demonstrations conducted by Chennai-based CavinKare Products. So it is clear that rural markets have caught the eyes of FMCG marketers and it is being targeted through experiments in a big way.

According to a study by the National Council for Applied Economic Research (NCAER), there are as many 'middle income and above' households in the rural areas as there are in the urban areas. Moreover, there are almost twice as many 'lower middle income' households in rural areas as in the urban areas. At the highest income level there are 2.3 million urban households as against 1.6 million households in rural areas. As per the NCAER projections, the number of middle and high-income households in rural India is expected to grow from 80 million to 111 million by 2007. In urban India, the middle and high-income market is expected to grow from 46 million to 59 million. Thus, the absolute size of rural India is expected to be double that of urban India. But despite the high rural share in these categories, the rural penetration levels are low, thus offering tremendous potential for growth.

With a judicious blend of click & mortar capabilities, agricultural communities in villages use internet kiosks—known as e-choupals—to access ready information in their local language on the weather & market prices. They are also able to disseminate knowledge on scientific farm practices & risk management. The aggregation of the demand for farm inputs from individual farmers gives farmers access to high quality inputs from established and reputed manufacturers at fair prices. As a direct marketing channel, virtually linked to the 'mandi' system for price discovery, 'e-Choupal' eliminates wasteful intermediation and multiple handling. Thereby it significantly reduces transaction costs. While the farmers benefit through enhanced farm productivity and higher farm gate prices, ITC benefits from the lower net cost of procurement (despite offering better prices to the farmer). Launched in June 2000, 'e-Choupal', has already become the largest initiative among all Internet-based interventions in rural India. 'e-Choupal' services today reach out to more than two million farmers growing a range of crops—soyabean, coffee, wheat, rice, pulses, shrimp—in over 21,000 villages through 4100 kiosks across six states. Whether the objective is to increase market share or to lower transaction costs, the end objective is to improve the robustness of the rural supply chain. Moreover, these are scalable and robust models, and, given the right policy environment, it should be possible to seamlessly integrate them in the months and years to come.

8.2. Globalisation and Changing Families

Globalisation is associated with rapid and significant human changes. The movements of people from rural to urban areas has accelerated, and the growth of cities in the developing world especially is linked to substandard living for many. Family disruption and social and domestic violence are increasing. Competitiveness introduced by globalisation is leading to more individualistic societies.

In a capitalistic market, multinational companies are taking the lead in establishing themselves and creating a major presence in almost every part of the world. Coca Cola, McDonalds, and Nike are examples of such growth and proliferation. The media then plays a major role in advertising the benefits of new products and services as being superiro to what the local market has. And slowly but steadily the food that we eat, the clothes we wear and the life style we lead begins to change. This process becomes consumerism within a capitalistic culture. So people as consumers are being studied for their patterns and behaviours of spending.

At one level it may appear that globalisation has no significant impact on families and that our lives are 'normal' in most circumstances. Many people are not totally aware of how they form a crucial part of this phenomenon. The reality is that every single individual is affected in one way or another. These changes affect people's identities and cultural values, which sometimes become altered significantly. Whether it is between generations, or intra-personally, new values can cause dissonance and conflict with existing deeper-rooted values. Sometimes such transitions and changes can further cause difficulty with internal growth and development.

According to Jeffrey Arnett, there are four major issues related to identity, which develop due to globalisation.

The first is the development of a bicultural identity or perhaps a hybrid identity, which means that part of one's identity is rooted in the local culture while another part stems from an awareness of one's relation to the global world. The development of global identities is no longer just a part of immigrants and ethic minorities. People today especially the young develop an identity that gives them a sense of belonging to a worldwide culture, which includes an awareness of events, practices, styles and information that are a part of the global culture. Media such as television and especially the Internet, which allows for instant communication with any place in the world, play an important part in developing a global identity. Yet, along with this new global identity people continue to retain and develop their local identity for daily interactions with their family, friends and community. A good example of bicultural identity is among the educated youth in India who despite being integrated into the global fast paced technological world, may continue to have deep rooted traditional Indian values with respect to their personal lives and choices such as preference for an arranged marriage, caring for parents in their old age. Although developing a bicultural identity means that a local identity is retained alongside a global identity, there is no doubt that local cultures are being modified by globalisation. As traditional cultural practices and beliefs change, a bicultural or a hybrid multicultural identity likely develops to include the elements of the native, local and global culture. This is especially true with immigrants.

The second issue is identity confusion, which individuals from non-western cultures experience as a response to globalisation. While people may adapt to changes and develop bicultural or hybrid, multicultural identities, some may find it difficult to adapt to rapid changes. The ways of the global culture may seem out of reach, too foreign, or even undermining their own cultural values and beliefs. Instead of becoming bicultural, they may feel isolated and excluded from both their local culture and the global culture, truly belonging to neither. The terms delocalisation and dis-placement have been used to describe these processes. For some young people, however, delocalisation may result in an acute sense of alienation and impermanence as they grow up with a lack of cultural certainty, a lack of clear guidelines for how life is to be lived and how to interpret their experience. Identity confusion among young people may be reflected in problems such as depression, suicide, and substance use. A variety of cultures have experienced a sharp increase in suicide and substance use among their young people since their rapid move toward joining the global culture.

The third change brought about by globalisation is the growth of the self-selected culture, which means people choose to form groups with like-minded persons who wish to have an identity that is untainted by the global culture and its values. The values of the global culture, which are based on individualism, free market economics, and democracy and include freedom, of choice, individual rights, openness to change, and tolerance of differences are part of "western values." For most people worldwide, what the global culture has to offer is appealing. One of the most vehement criticisms of globalisation is that it threatens to create one homogeneous worldwide culture in which all children grow up wanting to be like the latest pop music star, eat Big Macs, vacation at Disney World, and wear blue jeans, and Nikes. This outcome is unlikely since most people will develop a bicultural identity that includes a local identity along with their global identity. Besides, while most young people may jump with accept globalisation and its changes, there will e other who will remain out of it by joining a self-selected culture of fellow dissenters. Such groups can have a religious basis, which can result in fundamentalism or espouse clear non-religious anti-global views.

The fourth consequence of globalisation is the spread of emerging adulthood. The timing of transitions to adult roles such as work, marriage and parenthood are occurring at later stages in most parts of the world as the need for preparing for jobs in an economy that is highly technological and information based is slowly extending from the late teens to the mid-twenties. Additionally, as the traditional hierarchies of authority weaken and break down under the pressure of globalisation, the youth are forced to develop control over their own lives including marriage and parenthood.

The spread of emerging adulthood is related to issues of identity. Where a period of emerging adulthood is present, young people have a longer period for identity explorations in love and work before they commit themselves to long-term choices. By experiencing different love relationships, different educational possibilities, and different jobs, they learn more about themselves and they clarify their preferences and abilities. Emerging adulthood is possible only in societies where economic development is high enough that the labour of young people is not urgently needed. They are allowed to spend their late teens and early to mid-twenties exploring possibilities for self development because there is no pressing need for them to contribute to the economic well-being of their families. For young people in developing countries, emerging adulthood exists only for the wealthier segment of society, mainly in urban areas, whereas the rural poor have no emerging adulthood and may even have no adolescence because they begin adult-like work at an early age and begin marriage and parenthood relatively early. Young people who are poor and/or live in rural areas are more likely to suffer from what Amartya Sen has called the "unfreedoms" of poverty, lack of education, and restricted, economic opportunities.

To sum up, globalisation appears to be a significant force in the psychological development of the people of the 21st century. Globalisation has been going on in some form or another for centuries: Cultures have long influenced each other through trade, migration, and war. As a consequence of globalisation, the challenges of creating a viable identity are perhaps greater than they have been in the past.

8.3. Social and Cultural Changes

India is a culturally diverse country. Sixteen per cent of the world's population lives in the country. There are over 826 languages and thousands of dialects spoken. The difference in regions, topography and climate allow for different types of lifestyles and culture. Although about 70 per cent of the populations live in rural areas, India is rapidly urbanising with more than 225 cities with over 100,000 population, and at least ten cities alone with over a million people.

By United Nations standards, Indian has begun to age. Over 7.7 per cent of the population is above 60 years and this number is expected to reach 12.6 per cent by the year 2025.. Improved sanitation, increased attention to maternal health and better childcare facilities greatly reduced infant mortality rates. Globalisation is hardly a new force affecting India. To think so is to ignore a diverse and pluralistic long-standing civilisation that was shaped by a long list of "invading" (globalising) cultures that became what we now know as India. The previous globalizers of India include the Aryans, Greeks, Turks, Afghans, Muslims and most recently, the Europeans, Portuguese, French, Dutch and finally the English. The former globalizers that came with invading armies have increasingly been replaced by less violent but equally powerful globalizers. Television is arguably the most dominant gateway of globalisation affecting India today. While TV was launched inIndia in the late 1950s it only became widespread in the .980s, after the governments ended their monopoly as the only broadcaster. Satellite TV arrived in 1991, bringing with it far reaching consumerism.

In terms of people, India faces some resource and infrastructure constraints. Increased longevity has led to the emergence of many health and social issues. Fragmentation of the traditional family network is leading to an erosion of the available support within the immediate and extended family. Migration of younger generations from rural to urban areas and from one urban center to another as well as transnational migration has resulted results in the elderly being left to fend for themselves at a time when family support becomes more crucial. With more women joining the workforce system, the care of aged within families has declined. For those who live within extended families the elderly have to live in harmony with the younger generation that has to face a highly competitive world of globalisation. While the nuclear family system is increasingly becoming the norm, modern life-styles, changing professional and personal expectations are impacting relationships of marriage and commitment. In cities young people are starting to choose their own partners. Arranged marriages, however, continue. Meanwhile, as divorce rates increase especially in cities, the concept of single parenthood has not caught on in the Indian culture.

Consumerism has permeated and changed the fabric of contemporary Indian society. Western fashions are coming to India: the traditional Indian dress is increasingly being displaced by western dresses especially in urban areas. Indian MTV, soap television, and films set a stage for patterns of behaviour, dress codes and jargon.

Despite prohibition of child labour by the Indian constitution, over 60 to a 115 million children in India work. While most rural child workers are agricultural labourers, urban children work in manufacturing, processing, servicing and repairs. Globalisation most directly exploits an estimated 300,000 Indian children who work in India's hand-knotted carpet industry, which exports over $300 million worth of goods a year. Uncounted other children work in less formal sectors, such as the incense industry, used both domestically and exported. Reports indicate that urban Indian children and youth face significant competition and pressure to succeed. Yet, as the joint family system weakens and there is less parental supervision and support, the youth seem more restless and insecure. There are also reports of increases in violent behaviour and aggression especially in urban areas and cities.

As for women, the impact of globalisation has been interesting. On one hand, it has allowed women to become a larger part of the workforce, with opportunities for higher pay raising their self confidence and independence. Globalisation has provided a power to uproot the traditional views about women that have kept women economically poor and socially exploited. The growth of the computer and technology sector has provided middle class educated women with better wages, flex-timings, and the capacity to negotiate their role and status within the household and society. On the other hand, women continue to work in poorly paid, mentally and physically unhealthy, and insecure situations. For most women, their domestic responsibilities are not alleviated. Wage gaps have not showed any significant changes in most employment sectors other than information technology. Additionally, prostitution, abuse and dowry related suicides are on the increase despite globalisation and some say that the materialistic greed is one of the main causes.

Globalisation and marginalisation go hand in hand in India. With millions of poor farmers, rural labourers, urban unemployed, slum-dwellers, 3 million refugees, 100 million street children, and the millions displaced by 'the development' projects, poverty in this era of globalisation has assumed new dimensions. The question of "are the poor getting poorer?" related to inequality both nationally and internationally.

8.4. Changing Life Style of Rural Indian Women

Indian rural society is currently undergoing a revolutionary change. The interest and ambition to have a good education and better life style is helping to change and transform the political, social and economical idealism as well as cultural values of the rural women. The growing industrialisation is another factor effecting greater change in the life style of rural people here.

The social status of rural women has so far been suffering into contradictory situations. At the one hand these women are looked down upon and at the other they're worshipped and regarded as Goddess. The economical condition of rural women is not entirely satisfactory; they're exploited lot more, in comparison to male labourers. Most of the women make their entry in economical sector at very young age as a child lab our and get married at the earliest. The family responsibility and host of other social problem like –illiteracy, blind faith, conventionalism, customs and generally a male-dominated society hinder their progress at physical and mental level.

Those women who're well educated are more aware and making their niche in the family and society. The upper class women seem more advanced than the backwards and tribal women. In villages which are close to towns and cities, women are found to be more politically conscious than their counterparts in far flung remotely located villages. Earlier the rural women were generally not allowed to work outside but those living in villages which're close to town and city are being allowed to work now. Not only this, the social and family status of these working women seen with very high regard. The rural women of India have realised that the only intellectual conscience and self – reliance could get their constitutional rights and they're enjoying it all really. Using a trendy scooty and talking on mobile phone prove all this.

8.5. Changing Caste Attitudes

India's thirst to establishing the predominance of one's own caste has roots in the existence of human being. Every one thinks that their caste is superior and try dominates the rest. This creates religious violence in India. And presently, it is the major problem India is facing.

The decline in the 1970s of the "village studies model" of Indian anthropology enabled a shift of focus from caste and the caste system towards other and larger structures such as class, religion, and violence. But it is noteworthy that debates on class formation in India have long been dominated by economists, historians, Marxists, development sociologists, and some political scientists. There is, however, a small body of classic anthropological works that have dealt with caste and class and some more recent works. The anthropology of India arguably is still weak on discussing political and economic issues, especially those that integrate the traditional strengths of studying caste with attention to issues of class. The materiality of caste needs some emphasising due to the tendency to treat it as either ideological (as a mask for class or economic exploitation) or as an idealised social structure without any material basis.

In India, there are four major *varnas*: Brahmin (priestly class), Ksatriya (military and ruling class), Vaisya (merchants and traders), and Sudra (labourers). At the bottom and separate from the *varnas* one finds the Dalit, formally called untouchables. Dalit are considered unclean, and as a result, in the past interaction with those outside their group had not been permitted. There are also subgroups called jatis found within the varnas. Varnas and jatis are typically understood to make up the Indian caste system, which determines the social hierarchy in India. However, changes are taking place in India concerning how people view the caste system and how it shapes their lives.

Increasing nationalism could be one of many responses to the erosion of one's cultural identity", and that "the youth are not rejecting India, but what they consider outmoded in their culture.

Most middle-class Indians have learned to de-emphasise the importance of ethnic markers to their sense of identity that they feel as Indians". The forces of globalisation and liberalism have been at play in India for some time, the author takes a close look at how women have been effected by the diminished importance of traditional ideas pertaining to the caste system and religion.

Despite changing perspectives, dalit women are worse off than upper-caste women in terms of standard of living. The conduct and behaviour of upper-caste women is more heavily regulated than Dalit women, and as a result, Dalit women enjoy greater autonomy in their lives. The majority of Dalit women are not allowed to decide how to care for themselves, nor do their husbands consult with them in making decisions that affect the whole family. Furthermore, Dalit women are also more prone to domestic violence and abuse. An assessment of the material aspects of the gender-caste overlap suggest that more than fifty years after Indian independence, the economic condition of women continues to be defined and constrained by their caste status.

So despite changes in how the caste system is regarded, inequalities left behind by the powerful distinctions it imposed are still an important issue in India. So one sees that the importance of caste is disappearing as people are more willing to interact and associate with those from different castes, including the Dalit. Religion has taken on a less significant role in the lives of Indians, and traditional ideas pertaining to the caste system have been challenged even by the privileged youth of the upper castes as well as by college students.

To conclude, forces of liberalism and globalisation have been at play, as western influences serve to weaken the status quo. Nevertheless, despite such changes, inequality, poverty, and discrimination are still the reality among women at the bottom of the social ladder. Unfortunately, even as caste distinctions disappear, problems pertaining to class inequality still remain. Thus, in light of caste distinctions being less visible now, the consequences of such distinctions continue to manifest themselves plainly.

References

Bhalla, A., *Uneven Development in the Third World: A Study of China and India.* Basingstoke. 1995.

Bhatnagar, Subhash and Robert Schware. *Information and Communication Technology in Development: Cases from India.* New Delhi. Sage Publications. 2000.

Deshpande, Ashwini. "Assets Versus Autonomy? The Changing Face of The Gender- Caste Overlap in India." *Feminist Economics.* Vol. 8, No. 2. 19-35. 2002.

Ruggie, John Gerard. "Territoriality and Beyond: Problematising Modernity in International Relations." International Organisation 47; 139-74. 1993.

Sankaran, S. *Indian Economy: Problems, Policies and Development.* Margham Publications. 1994.

9

EMPOWERING RURAL WOMEN

Since eternity, women have played a role more important than men and that is no exaggeration. The world would not have been the same lovely adorable and liveable place without wonderful contribution so selflessly made by women. It has been said that, you teach a female and you build up a nation and truth can't be closer than that. Women have always carried the burden of being a wife, mother, sister all on their own and we need not to explain how magnificently they have carried this position. Men and women complement each other. If men were supposed to handle outside stuff then women were more responsible for internal affairs. The only difference in this notion is, today women are equally competent behind the veils and outside world. They are more confident and one can find them in every possible sphere of human's life. No male bastion is untouched by females and that's a wonderful sign of strides made by women.

Urban women in India always had more advantages and opportunities than women residing in rural places. Better education, better economic resources, and more availability of required things for urban women and yet rural women have made rapid improvements despite lacking in basic facilities. No, we have yet to attain the state of complete women empowerment but signs of gradual improvement are definitely there. India in last few decades has remained more of a male-dominated society.

Women used to command acute power and importance in our ancient culture. The proof of this fact can be found in all the scriptures and even our mythological stories. We worship Goddess Durga, Lakshmi, Saraswati and many others. That shows how Indian civilisation had revered the female form. Things have not remained the same in last few decades or even centuries. The social fabric has acquired completely new dimensions. The women are considered less powerful and important than men yet situation is not entirely bleak. Thanks to the efforts of government, NGOs, social welfare organisations and many such institutions, there has been a drastic improvement. Many private corporate bodies have also taken a keen interest in improving the economic status of women and the results are extremely encouraging.

However, the lives of women in rural India have to improve quite a lot. Majority of Indian villages do not have sustainable economies, and only through oppression of women and lower castes can the landlords, upper castes, and government officials support a better life for themselves. The social injustice that underlines this perennial problem cannot be addressed by a frontal attack on women's issues by targeting women alone, but it requires a comprehensive effort in which communities develop through sustainable and integrated programmes that impact everyone.

Issues of rural poverty and health have traditionally been the concern of governments. In the past, and even today, most programmes designed to benefit rural India are funded and managed exclusively by the government. Private initiatives are lacking as the government, to preserve its power, has placed obstacles and disincentives at every step. For example, modern healthcare for all of rural India is a free government service, but the reality is that the delivery of primary health care has failed miserably. A number of charitable institutions and non-governmental organisations (NGOs) have played a positive role, often assisted by government grants and foreign donations.

The World Bank has been the major source of external funding through loans to governments (never directly to private institutions) for specific projects. Very few projects have ever met their goals; in fact, most rural projects have been dismal failures. Unbearable bureaucracy, terrible inefficiency, and corruption at all levels of the government have wasted much of the money allocated to rural development. Furthermore, the local officials who manage projects that target women do not themselves believe in the potential of women. Yet the process continues, without an alternative. International agencies continue to pour money into these programmes, only to benefit the middlemen. Clearly, a new approach is required to have an impact on the lives of women in rural India, and to ultimately help stabilise population growth.

9.1. Empowerment of Rural Women

Empowerment of women involves many things—economic opportunity, social equality, and personal rights. Women are deprived of these human rights, often as a matter of tradition. In rural areas, women are generally not perceived to have any meaningful income generation capacity, and hence, they are relegated mainly to household duties and cheap labour. Without the power to work and earn a good income, their voices are silenced. Even in matters of sex and child bearing, women often do not have the ability to oppose the wishes of their men. In a society where men control the destiny of women, how is it possible to empower women? Simply encouraging women to resist the wishes of men would not only fail, but would create mistrust of any goodwill attempts from "the outside" to help rural communities. Women will gain power only when both men and women begin to respect and accept the contribution of women. Developing women's capacity for income generation without threatening men is key.

Past experience has taught us that attempts to control the number of children through behavioural changes in men have failed because families do not see the benefit of fewer children. Children, especially boys, are viewed as extra hands that can provide income and help with family chores. The poorer the family, the more children they seek. Hence, it is evident that the economic status of the family plays a major role in family planning. Birth control and reproductive health of women are behavioural issues affected mostly by economics, access to health care, and education. Until this reality is accepted, the desired changes may not be attainable in the foreseeable future.

Education plays an important role in bringing about awareness on women's rights. When both boys and girls grow up with mutual respect and understanding of their capabilities and roles in the society, women are more likely to find their rightful place within the family and the community. But, sadly enough, rural education perpetuates the myth that boys are inherently superior to girls. This is further reinforced by the family, where even mothers tend to give more attention and opportunities to their boys.

There is no easy or quick fix to the problems related to women's empowerment and reproductive health in rural India. The real solution lies in a holistic approach that deals with all the major interrelated issues of economic welfare, social justice, education, health, and traditions/spirituality.

The three key ingredients of success are *trust, infrastructure for delivery, and financial incentives.*

Behavioural change can be initiated and promoted only by those who have earned the trust of the people they claim to serve; government officials are amongst the least trusted, and hence, they are the most ill-suited for the task. People listen to those whom they trust, but still may not act without financial incentives that are offered through economic opportunities, and without actually seeing the infrastructure for delivery of services. Hence, projects run exclusively by private and non-governmental institutions (funded directly by government, international agencies and private donors), without unwanted governmental interference, have a better chance of success.

Private initiatives in rural areas need not always be charitable or non-profit. In fact, products and services, including education and health services, paid for through fees based on income levels can be very effective in stimulating a village's economy. Private companies need to be encouraged to deliver products and services for profit, but at affordable costs. When non-profit institutions work with profit-oriented private companies in a competitive environment, products and services are delivered at an economic cost that even most rural people can afford.

When villagers realise that they are indeed the beneficiaries of projects, they begin to trust and have confidence in those providing the services. This then opens up the opportunity to educate people on delicate topics such as sexual behaviour, use of condoms, family planning, alcoholism, abuse of women and children, and others. Institutions that are best suited for communicating these messages are the villages' health clinics, schools, community centers, and religious institutions. When project leaders become part of these institutions, they come closer to the people they serve.

In most rural areas, the primary symbol of wealth and respect is in owning cultivable land and/or cattle. When a woman earns and saves enough to buy either one on her own, she automatically gains immense respect and voice in her family and within the community. Many of the traditional barriers that have kept her silent begin to break down. Her husband and other elder members of the larger family are now prepared to listen to her and accede to her personal needs. She then has a bigger voice in how she brings up her children and in how the family is run.

It is important to note that men are more likely to support approaches to women's empowerment if they are also beneficiaries of those programmes. Without the involvement of men, women are unlikely to gain new rights. It takes a concerted effort to break age-old traditions and what men perceive to be in their self-interest.

Let us consider the case of Dharmapuri District in Tamil Nadu. This district has been identified as one of the most backward districts in the nation in terms of health and development. This District is remote and the project described below is carried out in an area about 24 kilometers from the nearest city, Hosur. Infrequent and irregular public transport hinders quick access to government emergency health services. Education facilities are limited to government primary schools of poor quality, and the nearest high school is located 10-15 kilometers from many of the villages served by The George Foundation's projects.

Large sections of the communities in this area belong to "lower castes" and backward groups, some of those often-called "untouchables." These people are largely landless labourers who have no fixed assets. There are very few non-farming occupations in this area. Communicable diseases including HIV/AIDS and Hepatitis, respiratory infections, tuberculosis and leprosy are widely prevalent. More than 75 per cent of women and children suffer from anemia or malnutrition. Chronic diseases often result in loss of precious man-hours and income. Sociological problems such as alcoholism, wife and child abuse, and discrimination of lower castes are consequences of poverty and ignorance.

A tragic and widely documented feature of this District is the prevalence of female infanticide practices. Despite some government efforts, there has been little impact in curtailing this practice. Women have very little voice in matters of human reproduction and reproductive health. The government has a primary health center located at Bagalur and there are no major voluntary agencies working in this district.

In Dharmapuri District the Foundation has attempted to facilitate the development of a model community consisting of several villages that prosper from sustainable and integrated economic activities. Health and education facilities are being renovated, and economic opportunities are being shared, especially among the socially disadvantaged castes and women.

The project started four years ago with Shanti Bhavan, a world-class residential school for children from poor backgrounds from some 25 villages in the District. Educational standards of government schools in the area are also being improved through other initiatives such as teacher incentive programmes, construction of facilities for higher grades and a library, merit scholarships, and purchase of reference books. These programmes have brought us closer to many children and their families in the community, allowing us to communicate our messages clearly.

In the health arena, the Foundation now "co-manages" a government run Primary Health Center (PHC) that serves nearly 80,000 people. Within a short period of six months starting in October 2000, the facility has been completely refurbished, better procedures have been instituted, and PC based record keeping and diagnostic software that assists in the delivery of healthcare has been implemented. Additionally, the Foundation has built a new medical and community center that focuses on outpatient and emergency care, prevention, health education, veterinary services, and other community-oriented programmes. These initiatives have earned considerable trust of the people, especially the women whose children have benefited from the many activities.

Attempts are made to preserve the rich and ancient culture of the people, while trying to meet their spiritual needs. Toward these ends, an arts and crafts museum has been built, and an arts village is being created. Two temples have been renovated, while a third one was newly built, and an ancient chariot was reconstructed. By associating the Foundation's work with the communities' social needs, it has become possible to reach them in many other areas.

All of these activities have generated considerable employment for the local population. Local labour has been used extensively, and many non-technical products and services are also being locally procured. The Foundation has persuaded the government to improve the roads by partially funding the project, and to bring electricity and telephone service to the community. All of these changes have occurred in less than four years, significantly improving their quality of life.

To reach women, especially those from poor families, the Foundation has recently launched a major project to economically empower them. To start with, we purchased nearly 150 acres of land that had been previously left uncultivated. Each woman is assigned approximately ¼ acre of land, which has already been properly prepared with ploughing by tractor, grading, soil preparation, drainage and fertilisation at commencement of the program. She is provided at no cost the basic tools for farming, and is trained in proper cultivation and farming methods—an "earn while you learn" scheme. The produce of the farm is sold centrally, and a part of the proceeds is given to each farmer periodically for daily living, while a major portion is kept in interest bearing savings. Ten to twenty percent of the sale price is retained for the purchase of seeds, fertilizers, pesticides and other resources required for the next crop. While women work in the farm for four to five hours each day, their children under the age of five years enjoy the facility of a day-care center that takes care of their educational and nutritional needs. The expectation is that within four to five years, each woman will have saved enough from the money retained to buy her own piece of cultivable land and/or cattle, and will have also learned modern farming techniques.

Despite the difficulties that are likely to be encountered, we believe it is possible to bring about major improvements to the lives of women in rural India. Well-planned and properly managed private initiatives can succeed in empowering women, provided the approach taken is sufficiently holistic. Effective and sustainable programmes can be executed with limited initial investment, while ensuring that significant benefits flow to families with low income and socially disadvantaged status.

Government run rural development projects, as practiced today, are unlikely to significantly improve the social and economic status of women in the foreseeable future. Hence, privately funded and managed initiatives on a large scale need to be tried to bring about sustaining changes. Such undertakings should seek government involvement only as a facilitator, as opposed that of a "manager" or "partner."

The time has come to go beyond small pilot projects that hardly ever lead to major undertakings. There has been much needless suffering for too long by a majority of the world's population. It would be a noble and worthwhile effort to prove the concept on a large scale, probably for several million people in an area. That would require considerable organisational skills and management talent, with a clear focus on accomplishing set goals in a time-bound fashion. The success of such a programme would be the model that international funding agencies and philanthropic institutions can build upon, and serve as a departure to the failed policies and programmes of the past.

9.2. Women and Sustainable Livelihood

Over 35-40 per cent of the rural population in India is living in poverty, deprived of basic amenities and food security. They are unemployed or underemployed and this is the primary cause of poverty. Most of them are illiterate, suffer from ill-health, suppressed by vested interests and are deprived of their due share and rights in the development due to poor governance. They are often addicted to alcohol, narcotics and other vices, which further de-motivate them from involving themselves in sustainable livelihood activities. Over 85 per cent of the rural families are dependent on agriculture for their livelihood. However, due to denudation of natural resources, sub-division of their land holdings and fluctuations in climatic conditions, the income from agriculture has been dwindling steadily. Furthermore, introduction of new technologies and farming practices have given tremendous benefits to resourceful and educated farmers on the one hand, while depriving the small land holders of such benefits on the other hand.

Women contribute to 65-70 per cent of the labour in agriculture. As most of them are illiterate and unable to attend formal training courses leaving their domestic responsibilities, rural women trail in adopting new technologies and in taking advantage of modern scientific and information technologies. Furthermore, introduction of any new programme for promoting livelihood will further add to their burden, as they are already suffering from drudgery, ill-health, suppression and deprivation of their basic rights and status in the society. Therefore, women empowerment should be an important and integral component of the sustainable livelihood programme in rural India.

Poverty has a direct influence on food security and the rural poor and women in particular suffer the most during such scarcities and calamities. Thus, ensuring food security through women empowerment should be the primary goal of sustainable rural livelihood.

In rural areas, particularly among weaker sections of the society, women are illiterate and suppressed, the women empowerment should focus on the following aspects:

i) Drudgery reduction
ii) Gender sensitisation
iii) Capacity building
iv) Promotion of micro-enterprises

While promoting women empowerment in rural areas, the participant women and the communities have recognised the success of the programme through two important indicators. Firstly, the women and their family members considered women's ability to enhance their family income as an important indicator of success apart from the improvement in hygiene, sanitation, education of children and community health. At the community level, the ability of the women to take active part in various social development activities was considered to be the most important indicator of success. In many women empowerment programmes, which did not include promotion of any livelihood activities, women started demanding support for initiating various income generation activities. It can therefore be concluded that income generation or livelihood support activities should be an integral aspect of the women empowerment programme, while dealing with poor rural communities.

India's declining sex ratio caused through foeticide, infanticide and systematic neglect requires urgent and comprehensive action. It is well evidenced that low literacy, endemic under nutrition and social inequality are closely related gender inequality is a crucial antecedent to endemic undernutrition.

9.2.1. Education

Women's education is extremely important intrinsically as it is their human right and required for the flourishing of many of their capacities. It is, however, noticed that most programmes for education of girls and women in India have reinforced Gender roles specially motherhood in curriculum as well as impact evaluation. The huge study of nearly 94 per cent of India's population done by Drez and others looks at female literacy and its negative and statistically significant impact on child mortality.

The questions of power are interlinked and we understand that what is necessary is both objective power in terms of economic resources, laws, institutional roles and norms held by others as well as subjective power in terms of self efficacy and entitlements. Empowerment of women is closely related to formal and informal sources of education. Late 19th century & 20th century reformers advocated women's education as a principal strategy to answer the 'women's question'. Many innovative efforts are accelerated after the NPE. In UP a renewal process of correcting gender stereotyping was initiated in 1998 looking at textbooks and training besides infrastructure and community mobilisation. There is marked improvement in girls enrollment and steady decline in drop out rates.

Despite statistically positive trends closer studies show that privileged spaces in classrooms are occupied by boys. Girls are rarely addressed by their names. Girls sit in last rows in classes of mathematics and rarely muster courage enough to come close to the board where the teacher sits (usually a male in most remote areas? Private school initiative for gender concerns is rare Madarsas have large number of girls but like convents and Arya Kanya Pathshala's gender transformation is not their agenda. Moral science text books still have preponderance of men. Women as agents of social reform are not mentioned. CSO efforts have very often shown greater enhancement of girls self-esteem but in many cases there is poor cognitive development generally attributed to low paid, low qualified but highly motivated instructor. Kanya Vidya Dhan, free uniforms, mid-day meal, school attached crèche, mothers meetings have all had positive results.

In various surveys conducted by ISST it has been apparent that parental apathy or opposition to girl child education is fast reading even in traditional male dominated states of north Indian. Given the right infrastructure-schools located in neighbourhoods, preferably with female teachers parents would allow girls to study "as long as they would like to". It may however be noticed as evidenced by researchers, the same families who are willing to see girls in college react violently if the girl decides to choose her partner in marriage or challenge other norms of feminine behaviour.

9.2.2. Health

2005-06 National Family Health Survey (NFHS –3) conducted through 18 research organisations between 2005 December and August 2006 provides us with several important data based insights not provided by earlier surveys. There has been a steady increase in institutional delivery percentages from NFHS—1 to 3 from 26 to 41 the increase in rural from 17 to 31 is more promising than urban from 58 to 69. Overall fertility rate has declined from 3.4 to 2.7. The states of Punjab and Maharashtra have reached the replacement level of fertility, i.e. around 2 children per woman. Women in Chatisgarh and Orrissa are expected to have an average of about 2.5 children at current fertility rates. The urban areas in five states studied by NFHS, Chattisgarh, Gujrat, Maharashtra, Orissa and Punjab have reached below replacement level fertility. There is a difference between the fertility of women with no education and those with 10 or more years of schooling. Trends in antenatal care have remained more or less constant in NFHS—1 and 2 between rural and urban women but have increased from 65 to 77 per cent total. The five state study shows regional imbalances in post natal care from only 23 per cent in Chhatisgarh to 54-59 per cent in Maharashtra, Punjab and Gujrat.

More than 40 per cent ever married women and about one third men in orissa and Gujrat are thin for their height, undernutrition is much lower in Punjab (12-14 per cent) obesity is the major problem in Punjab 38 per cent women are overweight. Overweight or obese women percfedntage hjas incrfeased in the last 7 years from 16 to 20 per cent in Gujrat from 12 to 17 per cent in Maharashtra and from 4 to 7 per cent in Orissa. The extent of overweight is greater in women than men. Overall 14.8 per cent women are obese. Except in Punjab in the other states more than 50 per cent of the children of women without any education are underwseight. The percentage of anaemia ranges from 38 per cent in Punjab to 63 per cent in Orissa. Anaemia prevalence is alarming among pregnant women 57.9 which is more than last recorded 49.7 per cent. 33 per cent of women still have BMI below normal, which has declined from 36.2. IMR has gone down but gender differences persist. This is true also of under 5 mortality. Life expectancy of women however stands a level higher than that of men. From 1961 to 2001 both in total population as well as in the population of 0-6 there has been a decline in sex ratio from 943 to 935 and 976 to 927 respectively. There is a fear that overall reduction of state resources in the welfare sector and specially less than 1 per cent investment in health is going to exacerbate the existing gender bias in society.

9.2.3. Political Participation

Women's political participation has been considered a major measure of women's empowerment. Globally, through histories of the world we have records of very few regents, sovereigns, and active agents in nobility who were women. Champions of liberalism like John Stuart Mill had advocated women's participation in governance by the struggle for women suffrage in the self avowed liberal west very well illustrates the entrenched nature of Patriarchical resistance to women's empowerment. In the last century more women heads of state could be counted in Asia as compared to Europe and the struggle for women suffrage in India was physically less violent but this is not reflective of greater acceptance of women in decision-making in public spaces.

To measure women's empowerment now GEM takes 3 indicators, women's participation in economic, political and professional activities. Within political power what is measured is mainly women in parliament, judiciary or in local bodies. Women's empowerment or disempowerment has to be seen in all areas physical, socio cultural religious, political legal and economic.

It is also now often pointed out that women's empowerment must be seen as a process where in we must consider women's awareness consciousness, choices with live alternatives, resources at their disposal, voice, agency and participation. These are all related to enhancement of women's capabilities and decisions they take individually or collectively for themselves.

Several programmes in India like Mahila Samakhya have accepted the process nature of women's empowerment. The understandings of empowerment in PACS has also been similar but planning of activity, time and budgets to ensure the empowering processes need greater scrutiny. Women's education, livelihood and personal exercise of agency have to be systematically promoted.

The 73rd and 74th Amendments of the Constitution have impacted nearly 600 million Indian people in 500,000 villages. Interestingly the percentage of women at various levels of political activity have risen from 4-5 per cent to 25-40 per cent. Both nationally as well as at the state and local levels women in elected bodies have been very few and even those who have been elected when observed from closer quarters present a complex picture. The money and muscle associated with the electoral process inhibits a large number of women from joining politics. Restriction on mobility, lack of control over resources and low literacy rates are well known obstacles but recent panchayat elections have evidenced a phenomenally large number of elected leaders much beyond reserved 33 per cent seats. Areas where PACS, Mahila Samakhya or other CSO initiatives are working women are more articulate and vigilant and have used opportunity to improve ICPS centres, primary schools sanitation and have also publicly dealt with issues of misbehavour with girls, violence and alcoholism as well as sensitive issues of widowed women dressing in coloured clothes. Women are increasingly demanding not only basis but also land literacy and fuller longer trainings instead of being short changed through orientations.

It is obvious that a more active Gram Sabha which is sensitive to women's specific issues is a much desired goal as a woman *sarpanch* or BDC member in a gender hostile *panchayat* may not be able to accomplish and sustain much for the benefit of women or the village community at large. More women in grass root organisations; better law and order will ensure better engagement of women in decision-making.

More than one million women have now entered political life in India and 43 per cent of the seats are occupied by them district, province and national level. Women's participation is understood in terms of voter turn out, number of women contestants apart from the number of those who succeeded in winning.

In an interesting study sponsored by State Planning Commission in U.P. 2006 about 45 per cent women both rural and urban reported being influenced by men of the family (father/ husband) in decision-making in the exercise of their ballot. 9 per cent reported external influence while 46 per cent exercise independent choice.

However, the battle to make the PRI's affective instruments of local rural governance is a battle, a struggle of the grass roots, population (women and men) against administrative apathy and listlessness, against ignorance and low awareness. For women these odds are accompanied and intermeshed with deep rooted patriarchal practices that determine and sanction norms of speech and behaviour both within and outside the home.

Thus while Pre election trainings of voluntary organisations and CSVOs serve to build awareness about the duties, responsibilities of PR's and about voting practices, the presence and working of women's voluntary organisations at the grass roots have served to sharpen women's understanding about the operation of patriarchy in personal lives and work places and the methods and practices to overcome and combat them individually and collectively.

Organisations such as Mahila Samakhya working to conscientise and organise women in groups and sanghas are able to address the issue of women and their participation in a two fold manner. On the one hand they organise intensive training programmes for women PRI representatives to make them effective functionaries and on the other hand tghere own programmes with their members within there collectives serve to build a culture of questioning, critical thinking, collective decision-making and mobilisation on public issues.

A mobilised community of women is thus able to raise issues of significance to the local community within the meetings, demand accountably from representatives and administrative officials regarding financial and procedural matters and intervene with creative suggestions.

It is thus that the dominance of patriarchy money power, party politics muscle power are steadily undercut and eroded and women's concerns are gradually pushed to the forefront of local politics.

Drawing from intensive discussions at the level of sanghas and mahasanghas and the experiences culled called from functionaries and from trainings, Mahila Samakhya has drawn out learnings to strengthen women's participation in the Panchayats. A memorandum incorporating these has been presented to the Panchayat Raj Department. It states —

- It is imperative to inscribe the budget for the village on the Panchayat Bhawan.
- Thefre should be rules and strategies to train and activate women members who have been elected to the post of Pradhans or members.
- There should be strict rules for ensuring the participation of 2/3 voters in the open meeting.
- The signatures of the people in the executive register of the open meeting should be ensured.
- It should be compulsory for the Pradhan/Secretary to sit in the panchayat Bhawan.
- The development plan should be widely disseminated so that it can reach the general public.
- The dates and time of the panchayat meetings in the state of U.P. should be decided in advance.
- The venue of the meeting should be either the Panchayat Bhawan ofr a public place, to enable all gram sabha members to present their problems.

Thus it is apparent that women see effective and efficient functioning of panchayats closely linked to the issue of active women's participation.

Entry into public space, utilisation of authority in practice, trainings by government and non-government agencies are all part of a process of gradual growth of knowledge, self-esteem and empowerment, which gives women the agency to function effectively in the political process.

Even proxy and dummy candidates may experience this process of empowerment women who stand and win from general seats are more likely to have a higher commitment towards, and an understanding of the political process.

Having a high participation of women at the local self government level can create an environment which is enabling for other women, receptive to the idea of gender based initiatives and can serve to monitor and implement community and gender based programmes of the government related to education, nutrition and health.

It offers a potential opportunity which can be utilised at an optimum level by appropriate trainings both capacity binding and information enhancing—by government departments and the NGO Sector.

9.2.4. Decision-Making

In terms of decision-making NFHS II had reported in the rural areas women take 71 per cent decisions regarding "what items to cook" 26 per cent decisions regarding obtaining health care fro herself 10 per cent in purchasing jewellery or other major household items. 12 per cent decisions were taken by women with reference to staying with their parents or siblings and 37 per cent about how to spend money, which they had earned. In the urban areas these figures were 71 per cent, 35 per cent, 13 per cent, 18 per cent and 57 per cent respectively. Women between ages 15 to 19 nearly 24 per cent are not involved in any kind of decision-making only. 14 per cent do not ask permission to go to the market. In rural sector 10 per cent are involved with any decision-making and 74 per cent need permission for going to the market. In urban sector however only 7 per cent are not involved with any decision-making and 53 per cent need permission for going to the market. Survey reports that of the 52 per cent illiterate women 74 per cent of urban resident and 55 per cent of rural resident have access to money. Small studies on elected Panchayat leaders show episodic increase of their decision-making in personal, social and political spaces. Studies of the NFHS scale are necessary to retrieve such data specially in PACs programme areas. This could be done with reference to internal lending of SHG's as well as leveraging through other agencies in terms of both economic status enhancement and their decision-making. Interestingly some studies reflect that women's working outside home in paid job does not always translate into appreciably greater autonomy within the household for most women. In a sample study at Sonepat and Noida 66 per cent need to consult somebody and take permission before changing jobs 27.6 per cent women in Noida and 35.3 per cent in Sonepat said they are allowed to buy nothing at all.

Working outside home women do believe that they have more experience (91.6 per cent), enlarged social networks (48.3 per cent) and stronger personality (32.2 per cent) and an increased self esteem 985.3 per cent) besides their decision-making power (62.2 per cent). The researchers however observe that objective state of affairs do not bear this out and women's decision-making is concentrated to making small purchases. In buying and selling assets they have no say.

Methodologically here there is a dilemma about privileging of perspective—that of the responmdent or that of the urban middle class educated researcher. This is particularly pertinent as the sense of being empowered is also importantly about "feeling empowered".

9.2.5. Self Help Groups

Most of the women Self Help Groups promoted under different development and micro-credit programmes are involved in savings through periodic collection from the members, recycling of this money among the members as micro-credit for consumptive and productive purposes and training of women members for initiating various micro-enterprises. Many Self Help Groups have progressed further to deal with various social issues such as education for girls, prevention of child marriages, struggle against liquor sale, promotion of community health, sanitation, establishment of community grain banks and protest against violence. Promotion of micro-enterprises and various income generation activities is an important aspect of women empowerment. Although it is extremely difficult to find remunerative self-employment, there are enormous untapped opportunities in the rural sector. These include both on-farm and off-farm opportunities.

9.2.5.1. Agro-Based Activities

While promoting various income generation activities, agro-based activities have advantages because of the following reasons:

i) Target groups are acquainted with most of the basic skills.
ii) Easy access to inputs.
iii) No problems of marketing, as most of the outputs are locally consumed as food.
iv) Market outlets for even cash crops have been well established.
v) As over 75-85 per cent of the rural families own land and livestock, income generation activities can be initiated immediately without heavy capital investment.
vi) Risk of failure due to improper technology, poor quality, low demand and poor price recovery are very low. Hence, the chances of success are high.

Infrastructure required for promotion of on-farm activities has been very well established. Hence, the entrepreneurs can progress even in backward regions, which are deprived of regular power supply and electronic information connectivity. It is therefore advantageous to tap all the opportunities to promote various on-farm activities.

The best strategy to promote income generation activities through SHGs is to analyse the on-going agro-based activities undertaken by the members and introduce suitable interventions to enhance the production. There are also excellent opportunities to improve post production management of the produce through grading, storage, processing and marketing. Establishment of direct linkage with the consumers through establishment of consumer stores and farmers' open markets in small and large towns will not only reduce the cost of marketing but also help in receiving feedback from the customers. Such direct interaction with the customers will help the farmers to improve the quality and variety of produce and enhance the profitability.

Most of the agricultural products have stable prices and steady demand. Hence, the risk of price fluctuation and market glut is limited. As these products have good local demand, marketing cost is low. Most of the surplus can be stored to ensure food security in the future. In case of non-farm activities, most of the skills and inputs will have to be brought from outside. There is very limited scope for marketing these products locally. As some of the activities are new to the local women, the cost of starting the enterprise is very high. As a result, chances of success and sustainable growth of these enterprises are also very high. The non-farm enterprises are often affected due to glut in the market, fall in prices due to competition and poor market distribution and outlet network. The enterpreneurs are not able to sustain such shocks and end up in deep financial crisis, which threaten their food security as well. It is therefore suggested that agro-based activities be promoted, followed by different non-farm activities, which will have greater chances of success and risk bearing ability. While the on-farm activities address food security, supplementary non-farm activities can contribute to rural prosperity.

9.2.5.2. Micro-enterprises through Women SHGs

With careful planning, many opportunities can be created to generate gainful employment for the rural families, particularly for women. Some of the important enterprises are listed below:

On-farm activities:

i) Crop production
ii) Forestry, Sericulture
iii) Agro Service Centres
iv) Processing of food and forest products
v) Production of Agricultural inputs
vi) Bio-fertilizers
vii) Bio-pesticides
viii) Vermicompost
ix) Mushroom spawn production

x) Seeds and Plants

xi) Cattle feed

Off-farm activities:

i) Cottage Industries
   - Pottery, Smithy, Carpentry
   - Textile
   - Production of building materials

ii) Services
   - Automobile hire and repairs
   - Electrical works
   - Civil construction
   - Consumer stores

Following support is needed to promote micro-enterprises through women SHGs.

i) Motivation of the target communities, particularly women

ii) Formation of Self Help Groups and their Federations

iii) Introduction of drudgery reduction activities

iv) Gender sensitisation

v) Training and capacity building

vi) Micro-finance—provision of credit facilities and linkage with banks

vii) Development of infrastructure, particularly through the SHG Federations to provide necessary support services and marketing

viii) Trade networking and establishment of market outlets

ix) Village level information centre/e-*Chaupal* for dissemination of useful information

A multi-disciplinary team can interact with the SHGs to explore the potentials for development of various enterprises and extend necessary support for dissemination of technologies, procurement of inputs, training of members and establishment of linkage with the market. There should be some agency to provide guidance to the entrepreneurs as and when needed.

9.2.6. Violence against Women

The questions regarding crimes against women are most entrenched, as most of them are committed within the family NCRB records that the highest percdentage of crime against women is torture (37.7 per cent) followed by Moleslation (22.4 per cent), Rape (11.8 per cent), Kidnapping (8.8 per cent) and immoral traffic (3.7 per cent). 4.6 Dowry Death and 6.5 per cent eve teasing were recorded. the further details report that in victims of rape 532 were below 10 and 1090 below 14. 3189 within ages of 30-50. No age is safe for women. In U.P. nearly 32 per cent crimes against women were committed within the family by husbands and relatives. This figure when compounded with 12 per cent dowry deaths makes 45 per cent of crimes domestically located. Incidents of honour killings and battery through not large are often threats to women's functioning and their emotional development is severely blighted. In caste ridden society women's caste membership increase her vulnerability. Small efforts to train police by UN agencies and state initiatives are encouraging but very small in scale. They require follow-ups and support monitoring.

9.2.7. Women and Work

Women's work is statistically less visible non monetised and relegated to subsistence production and domestic side this accounts for 60 per cent of unpaid family work and 98 per cent of domestic work. The non paid work includes domestic chares like cooking, cleaning, child care aand care for the elderly and the handicapped-traditonally understood as women's work. Subsistence activities like pitches gardening post harvest processing, feeding farm hands, live stock maintenance, gathering of fuel, forest produce, unpaid family labour in family farm or enterprise are done by women who are reported to be non working housewives Census estimates 51.93 per cent men & 25 per cent women workers while NSS estimates 52.7 male and 25.68 female workers. Most men are in stable employment. Micro studies report many challenges—20 out of 104 women reported in a survey as non working were actually winnowwwing, thrashing or paraboling (WB). S. Mukhopadhyaya in her study reports [illegible] times more work participation in her study. Female work participation rate in U.P. is reported as 11 per cent with a Gender gap of 52 per cent equal to. West Bengal but less than Punjab. 56 per cent women are in community service 17 per cent in Manufacturing & 8.6 rural women in agriculture. Only 4 per cent women as against 10 per cent men are in the formal sector. If women's work is rendered visible specially unpaid household work there will be many dramatic results. Studies show that working women but 664 hours & others put 872 hours on child care, womens' share of work in 55 per cent women's unpaid work is 51 per cent while men's is 33 per cent. R. Malathy's extrapolation estimates 23,773 core as the value of wowmen's household reserve rendered by women in the urban sector alone. From 17 per cent women's contribution will increase to 33 per cent of agricultural earning will include unpaid household work. Restriction on women's mobility, complete child care responsibility ideology of female seclusion, vulnerability to abuse, low access to information and mass media, low literacy, assumption that women's supplementary and confinement to largely manual untrained tasks leads to women's poor access to income.

9.3. Women and Economic Reforms

It is often argued that economic reforms have had a differential gender impact but there are further complexities. The reforms have meant more openness in trade regime and progressive decontrol of domestic production sector. There seems a steady withdrawal of state presence from the production sector arguing that this would promote greater efficiency and accountability. There has however been much protest that this will leave labour more vulnerable as profit motive alone drives the market. Market argue that since women are crowded towards the bottom end of labour market they will be more adversely impacted. The 55th round of National Sample Survey organisation (1999-2000) generally reflects that over the years specially in urban areas gender differences in the structure of industrial and occupational distributions and distribution of labour status categories seems to have lessened. There is higher demand of female labour in some sectors which can be linked to a thrust towards export orientation and deregulation in the domestic production sector. According to Swapna Mukhopadhyaya changes in structure of job opportunities have not translated into overall reduction in the degree of market segmentation along gender lines. There is marginal decrease in employment of men and marginal increase for women in urban India. Educated women in the labour market who are unemployed are for more than their male counterparts 62.7 per cent unemployed women in rural areas as compared to 56.9 per cent men. It seems IT enabled sectors in recent years may have benefitted educated women. There is not enough reliable data but persistently low wages of women to the tune of 50 per cent to 80 per cent compare to men suggest systematic wage discrimination. Wage earnings in casual female workers in 1999-2000 were 64.70 per cent of corresponding male earnings in rural India are even lower at 60.57 per cent in urban India. 2005 HDR reports that women spend 457 minutes at work as compared to 391 minutes per day for men.

9.4. Ownership of Land

A recent legislation of the Central Government, the Hindu succession Amendment Act 2005 has also moved towards women's equality in property rights. It makes Hindu women's inheritance rights in agricultural land legally equal to those of men. All daughters including married daughters age Co-parceners in joint family properly daughters now have the right to claim partition and to become 'Karta'. All daughters, married or unmarried can reside, seek partition of the parental dwelling place. This law of the centre well have the power to displace any conflicting laws of the state which are unequal to women. this is a far reaching message to assure women control over property.

According to a recent study made by Bina Agarwal in Kerala, women's risk of physical violence from husbands is dramatically less of they own hand or a house. The incidence of violence is 49 per cent among women without property, but 18 per cent among land owning women and 7 per cent of they own both land and house.

Recent initiative of the state of U.P. (ordinance of 23 Feb. 2006) regarding the reduction of stamp duty on the purchase of land from 7 per cent 6 per cent has worked in the direction of more land being bought in the name of women in the family. This transfer of asset in favour of women though initially used by male members of the family to save family money will gradually contribute to build women's agency. 2,97715 transactions have been done in the name of women in 68 districts of Uttar Pradesh between April 2006 and August 2006. The women move out of their homes to sign the papers in Tehsils and in many cases it is their first exposure to an office. This initiative developed with women's trainings on legal, land and human rights literacy will go a long way. However, this effectiveness is greatly linked with the willingness of the state administration to devolve effective administrative and financial power to the local self-governing units, and the responsiveness and sensitivity of the lower echelons of the administrative machinery to the aspiration and needs of the local population. Alcohol has not favoured women and increase in indirect taxes has also impacted them poorly. The thrust of budgets also seems to push people to private providers.

Government schemes could be seen as *Relief policies* like widow pension schemes. *Gender reinforcing assistance* like mother support schemes in health and *Empowering schemes* for women to demand and enjoy full human rights.

9.5. State Initiatives

Development writers are so often used to repeating that focus of women development in India has shifted from 'welfare' in the 50's to development in the 70's and now to empowerment. This is hardly borne out in the programmes on the ground. There are largely schemes for relief like old age and widowhood schemes and major schemes related to Gender reinforcing assistance related to reproduction National Institute of Public Finance and Policy (NIPFP) undertook the first gender budget exercise and categorised expenditure in 3 categories.

NIPFP undertook the first gender budget exercise and categorised expenditure in 3 categories.

i) Specifically targetted expenditure on women.

ii) Pro women allocation—composite expenditure in the women component (at least 30 per cent).

iii). Mainstream expenditure with gender differential impact.

It was understood that public expenditure can be clustered in terms of four categories:

i) Protective and welfare services accounting for 67 per cent
ii) Social service-education, water housing health 26 per cent
iii) Economic resources-self employment training fuel supply management 4 per cent
iv) Regulatory services—awareness generation NCW 3 per cent

Allocation for women directed scheme is pitiful. Only ten ministries/Departments have specially targetted schemes for women in India. The share of women specific programmes in departments like education, agriculture, tribal affairs and social justice is also only around one percent. No proper administrative mechanism for execution and monitoring of expenditure. Heads still under ruberic of benefits for mother and child. Shelter homes and counselling centres are still low on priority. NIPF observed that reduction in cost of foreign liquour has not positively impacted them.

It is, however, necessary that even though schemes are relief oriented the process of accessing them has often been an individual and collected struggle which has sometimes led to empowerment and at others disheartening.

There are several critical issues to ensure a just an equitable state with reference to gender. Some issues are not addressable due to procedural limitations of data collection which makes specific recommendations difficult. There is need to develop a workable gender audit system for govt. & CSO programmes which would look at targets, training recruitmentspromotion, infrastructure and decision making opportunities. The verbal change from women welfare to women rights needs to be converted into reality. This has some direct fall outs. Pitiful allotment for Vriddha and Vidva Pension and minimum wages will have to be reconsidered in terms of living wages, recent work and human right to opportunities for highest form of physical and mental health.Greatest inequity exits in family but poverty alleviation schemes address only the family. Just as one poverty calculation takes per capita consumption it should also address per capita income enhancement not family.

Gender budgets need participation of other departments besides the existing ones. Gender auditing of all organisations is necessary.

As is evidenced in many studies level of awareness of government schemes is very low so more effective publicity is necessary. A more effective MIS system for monitoring women welfare, women empowerment programmes is to be developed which is simple, transparent and involves both government and non government functionaries. Gender resource centres with autonomy need to be established in all states and in case of larger states there must be more than one such centre involving academic and activities.

Practically no schemes exist to encourage women in non stero typical occupations. Training of women in leadership market research and entrepreneurship with follow ups must be institutionalised. At the national as well as state levels we need a full fledged mechanism to ensure gender sensitive policy, implementation through a participatory apex body. Clearer definition of work, Joint Pattas for women and men will ensure better control of women over resources as well as their acknowledgement in National income. Country's inclusive agenda requires a consistent engendering at all levels.

References

Greive, Margaret and Bingham Rose. *Women as Catalysts for Social Change.* New York: The City University and McAuley and the Howard Samuels Center.2001.

Narasimhan, Sakuntala. *Empowering Women: An Alternative Strategy from Rural India.* Sage Publications. 1999.

Narayan, Deepa (ed). *Empowerment and Poverty Reduction: A Sourcebook.* Washington: World Bank. 2002.

Reserve Bank of India. *Report of the Internal Group to Examine Issues Relating to Rural Credit and Microfinance.* July 2005.

Sadik, N. "Women, the Center of Development." *Development,* 1988, Vol. 1, 30-31.

Sen, Gita and Caren Grown. *Development, Crises, and Alternative Visions: Third World Women's Perspectives.* New York: Monthly Review Press. 1987.

World Bank. *Engendering Development: Through Gender Equality in Rights, Resources, and Voice.* New York: Oxford University Press. 2001.

Woolcock, Michael. "Learning from Failures in Microfinance: What Unsuccessful Cases Tell Us About How Group Based Programmes Work." *American Journal of Economics and Sociology.* 1999. Vol. 58, No. 1.

10

POVERTY ALLEVIATION IN RURAL AREAS

In India, over 70 per cent of the population lives in rural areas. Agriculture and related activities in rural India contribute to 33 per cent of the Gross Domestic Product, and is responsible for the employment of over 60 per cent of the workforce. Hence, when one talks of socio-economic progress in India, what is mostly relevant is how the lives of the rural people have changed. Overall statistics such as the national GDP could mask the reality in the rural life.

One of the great success stories of India is the nation's achievement in food production. The Bengal famine of 1943 was responsible for the deaths of over 4 million people and catapulted the Green Revolution in 1967. New agricultural methods incorporating the use of genetically improved seeds, double cropping and expansion of farming land brought about national self-sufficiency in grain production. Constant innovations in farming techniques continue to increase unit output, but this remarkable success has not yet fully insulated the country from the impact of drought and declining water sources. Nor has the contribution of the rural sector to the nation's economic prosperity brought about the desired improvement in the lives of the 300 million poor who mostly live in the villages.

The real story of rural India must be told with over 300 million characters who live in poverty with less than a dollar a day in income for a family of four, and whose social status in their communities is relegated to below the holy cow, the potent snake and the spirited monkey. It is a land where the elites of the villages—the upper class and the landlords—prey on the helpless, often in collusion with government officials who are supposed to help and protect them. It is a life where hope for a better future is as distant as the burning sun, and nothing that happens around them, including the so-called "IT revolution," brings about solace.

Consider the national statistics on adult literacy; it is claimed to be around 65 per cent. Rural literacy is slightly lower. Most of those "literate" village folks have hardly benefited from the schools they might have attended wherein poorly trained teachers irregularly hold overcrowded classes that often combine several grades or standards for want of enough teachers. Similarly, primary health care is delivered to the rural population through a network of over 150,000 primary health centers (PHCs) and sub-centres, but the reality is that the system is badly broken, as revealed in the words of one Central Health Secretary (in a private conversation with me), it is "beyond redemption." While grain production has been growing at an average annual rate of around 1 per cent in recent years, only a handful of farmers have the means to cultivate or own cultivable land in most villages. Rural infrastructure is barely visible beyond those villages that are close to rural towns; interior villages still wait for electricity, and their muddy roads get washed away with each heavy rain. Discrimination based on caste has been prohibited from the early days of the nation's birth, but the dalits of India still huddle in broken huts within the secluded sections of villages. To deal with all these situations, considerable funds are being allocated by central and state governments, and bilateral and multilateral agencies are also making their contributions, and yet, the intended beneficiaries have realised only marginal gains in the past fifty or so years. Even to a layman it is obvious that something is awfully wrong, and something different must be done if we are to expect the situation to improve in the next fifty years.

To the rural poor, deprivation is both economic and social, which in turn is the direct result of exploitation and lack of opportunities. The condition of life for the rural poor is characterised by malnutrition, illiteracy, sufferings from diseases and long-term health problems, inadequate shelter and unhygienic conditions, high infant mortality, oppression of women, and social treatment devoid of human dignity. Much of it is concealed from view, as outsider interaction is usually limited to village heads and "authorities," unless one chooses to study the

Harijan colonies and interior villages that are not easily accessible. That is not to say that government programmes do not target these people, or non-governmental organisations (NGOs) do not work in these areas. What is missing is adequate emphasis in dealing with the root causes of these closely interrelated problems.

The hindrances faced by the poor in overcoming their deprivation is not limited to the lack of opportunity to gain a good education and to have a steady source of income. These people are the victims of what appears to be a permanent social and economic arrangement wherein the local elites—landowners, merchants, money lenders, officials—maintain a choke hold over the poor by consolidating more wealth and power through appropriation of additional land (either by purchase or through government lease allocations), and by employing the poor at low wages, while enforcing "discipline" and silence through punitive measures. Urban interests also gain from market-based exploitation wherein rural products and services are kept at such low prices that without government subsidies, there is no profit to be gained. Similarly, urbanisation of villages for cheap labour may generate employment for some of the poor, but it also perpetuates their exploitation and misery. Excess supply of labour, limited access to markets and market information, and financial weakness of the rural farmer all contribute to this inequity. This powerlessness of the poor is clearly evident in their inability to obtain even those benefits intended for them from the government, without the local elites and administrators siphoning out most of the financial resources for themselves. Many of the programmes currently in place benefit their administrators more than their intended beneficiaries.

The poor get even poorer when they face social obligations such as dowry and weddings, when they are unable to work due to illnesses, or when natural disasters strike their sources of livelihood or their dwellings. They get more indebted to landlords and moneylenders, a condition they can hardly expect to overcome in their lifetime. Without an external social support system and an income-generating asset, there is no reasonable way out of this human bondage.

Altruism, idealism and a spirit of service motivate many to do good. Needless to say, compassion is not enough; what the poor want is financial and material help, and guidance and support to create opportunity for themselves. The poor do not prefer handouts over permanent and sustainable solutions to overcome their condition. Lasting solutions can be found only when the nation is prepared to face and deal with the root causes of this social and economic injustice. Some big steps in new directions need to be taken, combined with many small steps forward; diversity in approach is fine as long as the ultimate goals are consistent.

10.1. Anti-poverty Strategy

Poverty eradication has been one of the major objectives of the development planning process. Indeed, poverty is a global issue. Its eradication is considered integral to humanity's quest for sustainable development. Reduction of poverty in India, is, therefore, vital for the attainment of international goals.

The rural poor consists of agricultural wage earners, small and marginal farmers and casual workers engaged in non-agricultural activities etc. Small land holdings and their low productivity are the cause of poverty among households dependent on land-based activities for their livelihood. Poor educational base and lack of other vocational skills also perpetuate poverty. Due to the poor physical and social capital base, a large proportion of the people are forced to seek employment in vocations with extremely low levels of productivity and wages. The creation of employment opportunities for the unskilled workforce has been a major challenge for development planners and administrators.

In India, poverty alleviation has been one of the guiding principles of the planning process. The role of economic growth in providing more employment avenues to the population has been clearly recognised. The growth-oriented approach has been reinforced by focusing on specific sectors which provide greater opportunities to the people to participate in the growth process. The various dimensions of poverty relating to health, education and other basic services have been progressively internalised in the planning process.

Central and state governments have considerably enhanced allocations for the provision of education, health, sanitation and other facilities which promote capacity-building and well-being of the poor. Investments in agriculture, area development programmes and afforestation provide avenues for employment and income. Special programmes have been taken up for the welfare of scheduled castes (SCs) and scheduled tribes (STs), the disabled and other vulnerable groups. Antipoverty programmes that seek to transfer assets and skills to people for self-employment, coupled with public works programmes that enable people to cope with transient poverty, are the third strand of the larger anti-poverty strategy. The targeted public distribution system (TPDS) protects the poor from the adverse effects of a rise in prices and ensures food and nutrition security at affordable prices.

The Government's policy and programmes have laid emphasis on poverty alleviation, generation of employment and income opportunities and provision of infrastructure and basic facilities to meet the needs of rural poor. For realising these objectives, self-employment and wage employment programmes continued to pervade in one form or other.

10.2. Jawahar Gram Samridhi Yojana

Jawahar Gram Samridhi Yojana(JGSY) is the restructured, streamlined and comprehensive version of the erstwhile Jawahar Rozgar Yojana (JRY). Launched on 1 April 1999, it has been designed to improve the quality of life of the rural poor by providing them additional gainful employment. The objectives of the Yojana are: creation of demand-driven village infrastructure including durable assets for increasing the opportunities for sustained employment, and generation of supplementary employment for the unemployed poor in the rural areas. People living in villages constitute the target group of JGSY. Preference is given to SC/ST families living below the poverty-line and physically handicapped persons.

The programme is being implemented entirely at the village panchayat level. District Rural Development Agencies (DRDAs)/ Zila Parishads (ZPs) will release the funds including State matching share directly to village panchayats. Village panchayat is the sole authority for preparation of annual action plan and its implementation with the approval of Gram Sabha. 22.5 per cent of JGSY funds have been earmarked for individual beneficiary schemes for SCs/STs. Three per cent of annual allocation would be utilised for creation of barrier free infrastructure for the disabled. Wages under JGSY will be fixed by the State government. Village panchayats will have the power to execute works/schemes up to Rs 50,000 with the approval of Gram Sabha. However, for works/schemes costing more than Rs 50,000, after taking the approval of the Gram Sabha, the Village panchayat shall seek the technical/administrative approval of appropriate authorities. Village panchayats are allowed to incur expenditure up to Rs 7,500 or 7.5 per cent of funds, whichever is less, in a year on administrative expenditure/ contingency and for taking technical consultancy. 15 per cent of funds can be spent on maintenance of assets. The funds to the village panchayats would be allocated on the basis of population without any ceiling of Rs 10,000 as at present. DRDA/ZP/Intermediate Panchayats will be responsible for overall guidance, coordination, supervision, monitoring and periodical reporting.

10.3. Swarnjayanti Gram Swarozgar Yojana

Swarnjayanti Gram Swarozgar Yojana (SGSY) is the single self-employment programme for the rural poor. Launched on 1 April 1999, the programme replaces the earlier self-employment and allied programmes—Integrated Rural Development Programme (IRDP), Training of Rural Youth for Self-Employment (TRYSEM), Development of Women and Children in Rural Areas (DWCRA), Supply of Improved Tool-Kits to Rural Artisans (SITRA), Ganga Kalyan Yojana (GKY) and Million Wells Scheme (MWS), which are no longer in operation. The Yojana takes into account all the strengths and weaknesses of the earlier self-employment programmes. It aims at establishing a large number of micro-enterprises in the rural areas. A significant aspect of SGSY is that every family assisted under this programme will be brought above the poverty-line in three years and as such the programme aims at creating substantial additional incomes for the rural poor. It is proposed to cover 30 per cent of the rural poor in each block in the next five years. The programme has been designed to provide proper support and encouragement to tap the inherent talents and capabilities of the rural poor. It will target at least 50 per cent SCs/STs, 40 per cent women and 3 per cent disabled.

It is a holistic programme of micro-enterprises covering all aspects of self-employment, viz., organisation of the rural poor into self-help groups and their capacity building, planning of activity clusters, infrastructure build up, technology, credit and marketing. It lays emphasis on activity clusters based on the resources, occupational skills of the people and availability of markets. Selection of key activities will be with the approval of the Panchayat Samitis at the block level and the District Rural Development Agency (DRDA)/Zila Parishad (ZP) at the district level. The activities will be taken up in suitable clusters to enable extension of appropriate facilities.

The major share of SGSY assistance will be in activity clusters. SGSY will adopt a project approach for each key activity. SGSY focuses on Group approach. This would involve organisation of the poor into self-help groups (SHGs) and their capacity building. Efforts would be made to involve women members in each SHG. Group activity will be given preference and progressively majority of the funding will be for self-help groups. In each Panchayat Samiti, at least half of the groups will be exclusively women groups. The Gram Sabha will authenticate the list of families below the poverty-line identified in the BPL census. Identification of individual Swarozgaris will be made through a participatory process. SGSY is a credit-cum-subsidy programme. Credit will be the critical component in SGSY, subsidy being only an enabling element.

Accordingly, SGSY envisages a greater involvement of the banks in the planning and preparation of projects, identification of activity clusters, infrastructure planning as well as capacity building and choice of activity of the SHGs, selection of individual Swarozgaris, pre-credit activities and post-credit monitoring including loan recovery. It seeks to promote multiple credit rather than a one-time credit 'injection'. The credit requirement of the Swarozgaris will be carefully assessed and they will be encouraged to increase their credit intake over the years. Subsidy under SGSY would be uniform at 30 per cent of the project cost subject to a ceiling of Rs 7,500 (for SCs/ STs it would be 50 per cent and Rs 10,000 respectively). For self-help groups, subsidy would be 50 per cent of the project cost subject to a ceiling of Rs 1.25 lakh. There will be no limit on the subsidy for irrigation projects. Special emphasis has been laid on skill development of the Swarozgaris. Closer attention to technology and marketing needs of the Swarozgaris would be the hallmark of SGSY. SGSY will provide for promotion of marketing of the goods produced by the SGSY Swarozgaris.

10.4. Employment Assurance Scheme

Employment Assurance Scheme (EAS) was launched on 2 October 1993 for implementation in 1,778 identified blocks in the drought prone areas, desert areas, tribal and hilly areas of different States. Later, the scheme was extended to the remaining blocks of the country in a phased manner. The scheme being implemented in all the rural blocks of the country has been restructured from 1 April 1999.

EAS is now the single wage employment programme being implemented at the district/block level throughout the country with focus on areas suffering from endamic labour exodus. The objective of the EAS is to provide gainful employment in manual work to all needy able bodied adults in rural areas during the lean agricultural season and the creation of community, social and economic assets for sustained employment and development. The EAS would be open to all adult rural poor. A maximum of two adults per family would be provided wage employment, subject to availability of funds.

The scheme had Central allocation of Rs 1,990 crore during 1998-99. The Central share has been released to States/UTs. Up to March 1999, 4,165.31 lakh mandays employment was generated by spending Rs 2,819.76 crore. Since inception of the scheme, the total number of registered wage seekers is 4.29 crore.

10.5. Rajiv Gandhi National Drinking Water Mission

The Accelerated Rural Water Supply Programme (ARWSP) was introduced in 1972-73 by the Government of India to assist the States and UTs to accelerate the pace of coverage of drinking water supply. The programme was given a missionary approach with the launch of the Technology Mission of Drinking Water and Related Water Management, also called the National Drinking Water Mission (NDWM) in 1986. The NDWM was renamed as the Rajiv Gandhi National Drinking Water Mission (RGNDWM) in 1991. Rural water supply being a State subject, the State governments have been implementing the rural water supply programme under the minimum needs programme (MNP). The Central government, through the RGNDWM supplements the efforts of the State governments by providing assistance under the Accelerated Rural Water Supply Programme.

The salient features of the revised policy for implementation of Accelerated Rural Water Supply Programme during the Ninth Plan period are: (a) The present allocation criteria of funds under ARWSP to the States based on normative criteria should be replaced with a need-based approach. The States having large number of Not Covered and quality affected habitations and which are in drought prone, desert regions and hard rock areas would get more allocation than the States well endowed with water resources, (b) Decentralisation of powers to the States for implementation of Sub-Mission programmes, (c) Enhancing ceiling for Operation and Maintenance from the present level of 10 per cent to 15 per cent of the annual plan allocation, (d) Providing 100 per cent funds for the nascent programmes such as HRD, R&D, IEC and Management Information System, (e) Institutionalising community based demand driven rural water supply programme with cost sharing instruments by communities, gradually replacing the current supply-driven, centrally-maintained non-people participating rural water supply programme, and (f) Institutionalising water quality monitoring and surveillance systems.

Out of 1.43 million rural habitations in the country, 1.40 million habitations have now access to safe drinking water. Special efforts are being made for ensuring sustainability of the facilities provided under the Accelerated Rural Water Supply Programme by initiating action to institutionalise community based rural water supply programme. Special emphasis is being given to areas affected with quality problems due to excess fluoride, arsenic, iron and other pollutants.

10.6. Rural Housing Schemes

10.6.1. Indira Awaas Yojana

To meet the housing needs of the rural poor, Indira Awaas Yojana (IAY) was started in May 1985 as a sub-scheme of Jawahar Rozgar Yojana. From 1 January 1996 it is being implemented as an independent scheme. The Indira Awaas Yojana aims at helping rural people below poverty-line belonging to SCs/STs, freed bonded labourers and non-SC/ST categories in construction of dwelling units and upgradation of existing unserviceable kutcha houses by providing grant-in aid. From 1995-96, the IAY benefits have been extended to widows or next-of kin of defence personnel killed in action. Benefits have also been extended to ex-servicemen and retired members of the paramilitary forces as long as they fulfill the normal eligibility conditions of Indira Awaas Yojana. Three percent of funds are reserved for the disabled persons living below the poverty-line in rural areas.

Salient features of the scheme are : Allotment of the house is done in the name of the female member of the household or in the joint names of husband and wife. A minimum of 60 per cent of funds are to be utilised for construction of houses for the SC/ST people. Sanitary latrine and smokeless chulah are integral to an IAY house. Selection of beneficiaries under IAY is done by the Gram Sabha. Selection of construction technology, materials and design is left entirely to the choice of beneficiaries; and Upgradation of unserviceable kutcha houses at the rate of Rs 10,000 per unit has also been introduced from the year 1999-2000. 20 per cent of IAY funds are allocated under this head.

10.6.2. Credit-cum-Subsidy Scheme

The Credit-cum-Subsidy Scheme for Rural Housing has been conceived for rural households having annual income up to Rs 32,000. However, preference will be given to rural households below poverty-line. Salient features of the scheme are: Subsidy up to Rs 10,000 per eligible household in plain areas and Rs 11,000 in hilly/difficult areas. Loan up to Rs 40,000 per household; and sanitary latrine and smokeless chulha are integral part of the house. The scheme has been launched with effect from 1 April 1999 and is in the process of implementation. For the scheme, funds are shared by the Centre and State in the ratio of 75:25.

10.6.3. Innovative Stream for Rural Housing and Habitat Development

With a view to encouraging the use of cost effective, environment-friendly, scientifically tested and proven indigenous and modern designs, technologies and materials, a scheme called Innovative Stream for Rural Housing and Habitat Development has been launched with effect from 1 April 1999. The objective of the scheme is to promote/propagate innovative and proven housing technologies, designs and materials in the rural areas.

10.6.4. Building Centre Movement

The Building Centre Movement popularly known as the Nirmithi Movement was started in 1985 in Kerala with the aim of technology transfer, information dissemination, skill upgradation through training and production of cost effective and environment friendly building components. The rural building centres will be involved in transfer of technology from lab to land. A rural building centre can be set up by the State government, rural development agencies, credible NGOs, private entrepreneurs, professional associations, autonomous institutions and corporate bodies including public sector agencies. For setting up of a rural building centre Rs 15 lakh will be provided as one time grant.

10.6.5. Samagra Awaas Yojana

Samagra Awaas Yojana is a comprehensive housing scheme launched recently with a view to ensuring integrated provision of shelter, sanitation and drinking water. The basic objective of the Samagra Awaas Yojana is to improve the quality of life of the people as well as overall habitat in the rural areas. The scheme specifically aims at providing convergence to various rural development activities such as construction of houses, sanitation facilities and drinking water schemes and ensure their effective implementation by suitable and sustainable induction of technology, IEC and innovative ideas. In the first phase, the scheme is to be implemented in one block each of 25 districts in 24 States and one Union Territory. Intended beneficiaries under the scheme are the rural poor, preferably those below the poverty line.

10.7. Centrally-Sponsored Rural Sanitation Programme

Rural sanitation is a State subject. The State governments implement the Rural Sanitation Programme under State sector

Minimum Needs Programme (MNP). The Central government supplements the States' efforts providing financial and technical assistance through the Centrally-Sponsored Rural Sanitation Programme (CRSP).

The CRSP was launched in 1986 with the objective of improving the quality of life of the rural people and to provide privacy and dignity to women. The concept of sanitation was expanded in 1993 to include personal hygiene, home sanitation, safe water, garbage and excreta disposal and waste water disposal. The objective of the programme is to accelerate coverage of rural population, especially among households below the poverty-line with sanitation facilities, complementing the efforts in Rural Water Supply. Generation of felt need through awareness creation and health education involving voluntary organisations and Panchayati Raj Institutions, eradication of manual scavenging by converting all existing dry latrines into low cost sanitary latrines and encouraging cost effective and appropriate technologies to support other objectives.

The revised policy for implementation of the Rural Sanitation Programme during the Ninth Plan period has been approved.. The salient features of the policy are: (a) To raise sanitation coverage to at least 50 per cent by Ninth Plan, (b) Total Sanitation Campaign (TSC) in select districts with 50 per cent allocation during first year, (c) Balance 50 per cent for existing 'allocation-based' programme, (d) Switch over from allocation based programme to a demand driven one, (e) Shift from 'high subsidy to low subsidy regime', (f) Greater beneficiary participation and private sector involvement, (g) Active participation of NGOs/cooperative institutions, etc., (h) Emphasise school sanitation, and (i) Increased technological options and adoption of "Vertical upgradation" concept.

10.8. National Social Assistance Programme

The National Social Assistance Programme (NSAP) came into force on 15 August 1995 to provide social assistance to poor households. It includes three benefits, as its components, viz., (i) National Old Age Pension Scheme (NOAPS) - Central assistance is available at the rate of Rs 75 per month to persons who are aged 65 years or more and are destitutes. The State governments may add to this amount from their own sources. Upper ceiling on the number of beneficiaries for a State/UT is prescribed by the Central government; (ii) National Family Benefit Scheme (NFBS) - Central assistance is available as a lumpsum family benefit for households below the povertyline on the death of the primary bread winner in the bereaved family. The amount of assistance is Rs 10,000. The age of the primary breadwinner should have been more than 18 years but less than 65 years. The maximum limit of the total number of beneficiaries of a State/UT is prescribed by the Central government; and (iii) National Maternity Benefit Scheme (NMBS). Central assistance is available to pregnant women belonging to households below poverty-line up to the first two live births, provided they are 19 years of age and above. A lumpsum cash assistance of Rs 500 is disbursed several weeks prior to the delivery.

10.9. Extension Training Centres

The National Institute of Rural Development (NIRD), an apex Training and Research Institute was set up in 1965 to impart training to the rural development functionaries as well as Panchayati Raj Institutions through class room interaction and field work. Thereafter, 25 State Institutes of Rural Development (SIRDs) and 87 Extension Training Centres (ETCs) have been set up in the country for intensifying training related activities. In 1983, a NIRD North-Eastern Regional Centre was established. Schemes on strengthening/establishment of SIRDs, ETCs and organisation of training courses, seminars/workshops are also being implemented by the Ministry.

10.10. Programmes to Assist Voluntary Activities

With a view of encouraging, promoting and assisting voluntary action in rural development and with focus on injecting new technologies inputs for the enhancement of rural prosperity, Government of India, in September 1986 set up the Council for Advancement of People's Action and Rural Technology (CAPART), a registered society under the aegis of the Department of Rural Development, by merging two autonomous bodies, namely, People's Action for Development India (PADI) and Council for Advancement of Rural Technology (CART).

CAPART has a set up of nine Regional Committees/Regional Centres at Jaipur, Lucknow, Ahmedabad, Bhubaneswar, Patna, Chandigarh, Hyderabad, Guwahati and Dharwad. The Regional Committees are empowered to sanction project proposals to voluntary agencies up to an outlay of Rs 10 lakh in their respective regions. Since its inception and up to 31 December 1998, the CAPART has sanctioned 18,126 projects of Rs 495.20 crore. Against this, an amount of Rs 363.84 crore has been released. NGOs are provided financial assistance through CAPART.

10.11. District Rural Development Agency

District Rural Development Agency (DRDA) has traditionally been the principal organ at the district level to oversee the implementation of the anti-poverty programmes of the Ministry. This agency was created originally for implementation of the Integrated Rural Development Programme (IRDP) but was subsequently entrusted with a number of programmes, both of the Central and State governments. Since inception, the administrative costs of the DRDAs were met by setting apart a portion of the allocations for each programme.

However, of late, the number of the programmes had increased and while some of the programmes provided for administrative costs of the DRDAs, others did not. Besides, there was also no uniformity among the different programmes with reference to the administrative costs.

While an indicative staffing structure was provided to the DRDAs, experience showed that there was no uniformity in the staffing structure. It is in this context that a new Centrally-sponsored scheme DRDA Administration has been introduced from 1 April 1999 based on the recommendations of an inter-ministerial committee known as the Shankar Committee. The new scheme replaces the earlier practice of allocating a percentage of programme funds to the administrative costs.

10.12. Vigilance and Monitoring Committees

The Ministry of Rural Development lays great emphasis on monitoring and evaluation of rural infrastructure development programmes in general and poverty alleviation and employment generation schemes in particular being implemented in various states. The comprehensive system of monitoring and evaluation includes various mechanisms such as Progress Reports, Financial Returns, Audit Reports, Intensive inspections by officers of both Central government and the State governements, Area Officers Scheme, Review by various Committees, namely Parliament Committees as well as Standing Parliamentary Committee and Concurrent Evaluation Reports and impact research studies of the programmes of the Ministry. The Monitoring Division has introduced a high tech review system through the Video-conference as an instrument to monitor the implementation of the programmes. A Home Page regarding the details of programmes of the Ministry has been put on INTERNET so that transparency is ensured to the programmes.

The State governments have been directed to constitute Vigilance and Monitoring Committees at the district, block and village levels to monitor the implementation of the programmes. A schedule of inspection prescribing minimum field visits for each functionary at the supervisory level from the State government to the block is drawn up and strictly adhered to. Review Committee at Central/State/District/Block and Village level undertake detailed review of the overall performance of the rural development programmes.

10.13. Drought-Prone Areas Programme

The Drought-Prone Areas Programme (DPAP) was started in 1973. The objectives of the programme are: (i) to minimise the adverse effects of drought on production of crops and livestock and productivity of land, water and human resources through integrated development of the natural resources base of the area by adoption of appropriate technologies; (ii) to conserve, develop and harness land, water and other natural resources including rainfall for restoration of ecological balance in the long run; and (iii) to improve the economic and social condition of the resource poor and disadvantaged sections of society.

Since 1995-96, a new approach based on watershed development has been adopted and so far 6,454 watershed development projects have been sanctioned for implementation in 13 States through local communities. The programme also aims at restoration of ecological balance by harnessing, conserving and developing natural resources, i.e., land, water, vegetative cover and raising land productivity.

Since inception till 1994-95, as a part of core sector activities 30 lakh hectares under land resources development, 9,46,000 hectares under water resources development and 17,84,000 hectares under afforestation and pasture development have been successfully treated. The programme is being implemented on watershed projects basis since 1 April 1995. At present, 5,956 watershed projects out of 6,465 are under implementation at various stages.

10.14. Desert Development Programme

The Desert Development Programme (DDP) was started in the year 1977-78. The programme was started both in the hot desert areas of Rajasthan, Gujarat and Haryana, and the cold desert areas of Jammu & Kashmir and Himachal Pradesh.

The thrust of the programme is on capacity building and empowerment of village community, ensuring participation of Panchayati Raj Institutions and NGOs in the programme implementation at grassroot level and transfer of funds as well as decision-making power to local people. Since 1995-96, a new approach based on watershed development has been adopted and so far 2,202 watershed development projects have been sanctioned for implementation in seven States through local communities. A watershed project is required to be implemented in a four-year period. Since inception till 1994-95, as a part of core sector activities, 1,85,000 hectares under land resource development, 83,000 hectares under water resource development and 2,85,000 hectares under afforestation and pasture development had been successfully treated. The programme is being implemented on watershed project basis since 1 April 1995 and 2,202 watershed projects sanctioned so far are at various stages of implementation.

10.15. Integrated Wastelands Development Project

The Integrated Wastelands Development Project (IWDP) has been under implementation since 1989-90. From 1 April 1995, the scheme is being implemented on watershed basis under the new guidelines for Watershed Development.The Scheme also helps in generation of employment in rural areas besides enhancing people's participation in the wastelands development programmes. Up to May 1999, 248 IWDP projects were sanctioned in 25 States with a total outlay of Rs 778.12 crore to treat total project area of 15.98 lakh hectares.

The Scheme is being implemented through ICAR, State Agricultural Universities, Government and private institutions having adequate institutional framework and organisational back-up.

During the Eighth Five Year Plan, 66 projects with investment of Rs 828 lakh have been sanctioned under the scheme. During 1998-99 an amount of Rs 804 lakh has been spent for the project implementation. An amount of Rs 800 lakh has been allocated under the scheme to cover 3,000 hectares of area during 1999-2000.

Under the Support to NGOs/VAs (Grant-in-Aid) Scheme 100 per cent grant is provided to registered voluntary agencies, cooperatives, mahila mandals, yuva mandals and other similar organisations for undertaking work directly or indirectly, encouraging afforestation and wastelands development. During the Eighth Five Year Plan, 234 projects were sanctioned and a sum of Rs 13.75 crore was released to voluntary agencies for development of about 20,000 hectares of wastelands. All projects under the scheme are now being sanctioned by CAPART. During 1999-2000, a provision of Rs 2 crore has been made for implementation of the scheme. In order to stimulate involvement of the corporate sector/financial institutions, etc., to pool in resources for development of non-forest wastelands an Investment Promotional Scheme was launched in 1994-95. The projects promoted by Nationalised Banks, Regional Rural Banks, Land Development Banks and Cooperative Banks are eligible for promotional grants/subsidy under the scheme. During 1998-99, three projects were sanctioned and an amount of Rs 4.20 lakh released as subsidy under the scheme. During 1999-2000, a budget provision of Rs 200 lakh has been made.

10.16. Land Reforms Policy

The Land Reforms Policy adopted since Independence aims at restructuring agrarian relations to achieve an egalitarian social structure; elimination of exploitation in land relations; realising the age-old goal of land to the tiller; increasing agricultural productivity and production and infusing equality in local institutions. The aim of Land Reforms (LR) in the successive Five Year Plans is the fulfillment of all the principles of the National Land Reforms Policy consisting of the following objectives : Abolition of intermediary tenures; tenancy reforms; ceiling on agricultural holdings and re-distribution of surplus land; and updating and maintenance of land records.

10.17. Improving Food Security

Most of the poorest of India's rural population lives in the country's semi-arid tropical region. Although the Green Revolution has transformed agriculture elsewhere, shortages of water and recurrent droughts are a constant barrier in rural India. A major impediment to improving agricultural productivity and farm income is the lack of access for both individuals and communities to the proper resources and markets needed to obtain agricultural stability.

The lack of technological resources and poor water management by the government creates a continuous struggle for farmers to produce enough food for a marketable surplus. Farmers usually have a hard time producing enough crops to feed their families and do not have markets within close proximity. Another factor creating this struggle is the lack of knowledge as to what crops can be grown for the emerging biofuels industry and how crop residues that would ordinarily be wasted can be converted into income-generating produce used in the manufacture of ethanol and electricity. Education is one of the key factors to improve food security and income of the Indian farmer.

Majority of the people in India live in rural areas, and most of them are poor. Many rural people are starting to migrate into urban areas, but three out of four of India's poor live in the rural parts of the country. For more than 21 percent of them, poverty is a chronic condition. One of the most important sources for economic growth and food production in India is the family farm. A typical family farm is about one hectare. Whole families usually run the family farms, but because of their rural location they are not always aware of the products needed in the open markets.

Most of the farmers in India do not get the proper education about how to create sustainability on their farms. Many of them do not receive any formal education beyond elementary school. Women in general are the most disadvantaged people in Indian society, though their status varies significantly according to their social and ethnic backgrounds.

Through Sarva Shiksha Abhayan (SSA), The Indian government is committed to improving the educational attainment of women so that they can be employed in higher skilled and supervisory jobs on farms and in other sectors of the economy.

10.17.1. Educating Family Farmers

Education is one of the most powerful tools in reforming a system. Educating farmers about the benefits created by growing the right crops for the biofuels market is a promising way to increase their income stream and improve food security.

A distinctive feature of rural India is a rather high population density compared to other parts of the world. A significant proportion of villages do not have a single reliable telephone connection. Rural areas in India are also characterised by very low incomes. Providing telephone and Internet service to such populations has always been a challenge. Since telephone and especially Internet connectivity are known to be powerful tools of empowerment by giving people in low-income areas access to a wide range of resources, the Internet overcomes several socio-economic and geographical barriers. It provides people with better education and access to information, thereby expanding their horizons unimaginably. Therefore, a support system using the Internet can be used to deliver expert knowledge to rural farmers.

Lack of water is another significant problem preventing increases in yields. Agriculture in India is mainly rain fed and the majority of farmers have little access to alternate sources of irrigation. Farmers are still dependent on the monsoon to sustain their livelihoods. Dependable irrigation devices are a major factor behind a large number of farmers being drawn into a poverty spell. Unfortunately, India doesn't know how to manage the country's available water resources efficiently and equitably so that its economic development continues, along with poverty alleviation and environmental conservation. Farmers can be taught techniques for rainwater harvesting—that is, collecting and storing water so that it can be used for the rest of the year. But the many political issues that surround ownership of water and public access to it must be addressed through government policies.

10.17.2. Internet Kiosk

Internet Kiosk was an innovative business model to deliver Internet services to rural areas, including the family farmer. An Internet Kiosk consists of a multimedia PC, an Uninterrupted Power Supply with battery, a digital camera, printer, and a wireless subscriber unit with related accessories. Once the kiosk is in operation, the Kiosk Operator (KO) can access a host of services. These include computer education, adult literacy programmes, agriculture-related services, health services, and e-Government services.

So, in many communities the Internet Kiosk has become a "business centre" for the village, providing access to multiple technologies. Through these kiosks and their KOs who are computer savvy, farmers are given advice on farming methods and animal diseases. They can also get access to various agricultural portals to find weather information, crop prices, and improved farming techniques. These kiosks can help with water problems and provide long-term predictions on crop prices, demand, and rainfall. By providing these resources for farmers, they can become educated about different ways to farm, and thus can increase their yield and prevent harvests from dying.

Farmers will know when to expect rainfall and can collect the water to irrigate their crops. So the problem of water can be solved temporarily. By educating the farmers about the results from agricultural yield and irrigation systems that they themselves can put in place, and by providing a means for the farmers to convert wasted crop residues into useful biofuels produce, it can greatly increase the income of the family and hence improve food security. Women could be given higher skilled jobs such as interacting with the KOs, and supervisory roles in transporting the goods to the markets.

A family could improve its quality of life and livelihood for generations to come through the implementation of such technological solutions and through proper advice as to what crops to cultivate and market for the biofuels industry. By educating a generation of family farmers about irrigation systems and the benefits from increasing their yield, the information passed down to their children will be extremely valuable. Many more people will become educated about this system, giving rise to an improvement in the livelihoods of the subsistence family farmers.

10.17.3. Implementation of Water Management Policies

International organisations such as the International Development Enterprises, India (IDEI) are trying to help the rural populations to come up with an irrigation system. The technology offered by IDEI frees the farmers from the limitations of rain-fed farming, enabling them to grow a wider variety of crops, cultivate all year round with higher cropping intensity, and to engage in priority farming. Good irrigation technologies and agricultural practices coupled with enhanced participation of the poor in the open markets are the keys to income generation. There are, however, flaws to this system. Organisations such as the IDEI are business oriented and profit driven, and do not have programmes that are affordable for subsistence farmers. This does not create the necessary food security for farmers.

Knowledge of the climatic, physical, social, cultural, economic, environmental, and institutional conditions of rural India is necessary for implementing a system. First and foremost, political support is needed before any ideas can be implemented. The probability of any policy being accepted, let alone implemented, without the support of high-level policymakers is almost close to zero. Thus, political support is a pre-requisite for acceptance and implementation of any water policy.

Water problems of India are because of poor management practices. In order to solve and manage seemingly technical problems, we need a new breed of water professionals who not only have expertise in technical areas, but also are knowledgeable on the social, economic, legal, environmental, and institutional issues within which technical solutions are to be applied.

10.18. Social Funds

India is make use of Social Funds (SFs) to uplift the conditions of the poor. So, SFs, have expanded rapidly in recent years. Social funds (SFs) have expanded rapidly in recent years. Although SFs differ in design and content, they have some common features. Characterised as 'demand driven and decentralised initiatives, their salient features are: (i) they make grant funds available to communities or municipalities to choose from a menu of projects; (ii) project design and construction are decentralised to local actors comprising private firms, NGOs, local governments and community groups; (iii) community groups contract the design or construction firms or equipment suppliers, monitor project execution and/or take responsibility for operations and maintenance; and (iv) a local contribution of 10-15 percent of project costs is often required.

SFs were meant to provide employment through public works and emergency social services in rural areas, and to compensate for lay-offs as a result of downsizing of the public sector in urban areas. By the mid-1990s, several SFs were elevated to more permanent status, in view of their potential as an alternative mode of delivery of public services.

10.19. District Poverty Initiative Projects (DPIPs)

The DPIPs are aimed to create income earning opportunities for the rural poor; to empower disadvantaged groups; and to promote more effective, accountable and inclusive Panchayats (village councils) and other local support and service organisations. The performance of existing anti-poverty programmes was unsatisfactory. So the need for DPIPS arose. The factors lead to the failure of need for DPIPs arose from the unsatisfactory performance of existing anti-poverty programmes such as Swaranjayanti Gram Swarozgar Yojana (SGSY) and Employment Assurance Scheme (EAS) are (i) high administrative costs, (ii) their supply driven nature, and (iii) limited focus on organisations and the skills of the poor.

The benefits accrue mostly to the poor, two mechanisms are proposed: one is geographic targeting and the other is group targeting. The first will involve selection of the poorest blocks and villages/habitations in 14 districts; and the second will require actively promoting collective action, organisation, information and the skills of the poorest first, so that they can negotiate better with formal organisations and demand project and other forms of assistance. The poorest are aware of funding possibilities under the project and the procedures to be followed, there is considerable emphasis on dissemination of information and communication. A communication specialist at the State level would support the district units, and PFTs would carry out communication activities at the village level.

To be eligible for sub-project financing, villagers would organise themselves into Common Interests Groups (CIGs), with the majority being poor. PFTs would help ensure inclusion of the disadvantaged by building their capacity and assisting them in accessing DPIP funds. The CIGs at the village level, would identify and submit proposals to the Village Development Committee-composed of all elected Panchayat members, and representatives of all CIGs for appraisal. The VDC would appraise them in consultation with the PFTs, and prioritise them for the given budget. The VDC would submit them to the District Sub-Committee for approval and disbursement. CIGs would be responsible for implementation and operation, and would get assistance from government, NGOs or private sources.

At the state level, the overall budgetary allocation would be the responsibility of the Board of the Society for Poverty Alleviation Initiatives (MPSPAI), chaired by the Chief Minister. Budgetary allocations in the first year would be on the basis of the target population, and in the second on the basis of performance. Project stakeholders should understand better the reasons for a project's success or failure, as well as learn from the experience in other DPIP states.

There were several innovative features for DPIP. Creation of a Board with the Chief Minister as the Chairman is designed to ensure that the project has the full backing of the state government, and considerable autonomy. The emphasis on quick and flexible disbursals through streamlining of procedures at the district and village levels seeks to remedy bunching of expenditure in the last two or three months of a financial year and large unspent balances. The shift of emphasis from supply driven to demand driven allocations with considerable attention to ensuring that the poorest have access to them and are enabled to improve their well-being is appealing. In this context, the priority assigned to dissemination of information and communication at different stages of decision-making—in particular, to making the poorest aware of opportunities for enhancing their incomes and for capacity building is noteworthy.

Moreover, the focus on not just economic betterment but also on empowerment of the disadvantaged through their more effective participation in decisions that are crucial to their well-being is a significant departure. Ownership of assets created through mandatory community contributions would contribute to their sustainability. Finally, without periodic and systematic monitoring and evaluation, the flexibility in the design and implementation of the project would be of limited value. So to avoid distortions considerable emphasis is placed on monitoring and cross-learning from DPIPs in different states.

References

Datt, G. and M. Ravallion. "Is India's Economic Growth Leaving the Poor Behind?" *Journal of Economic Perspectives* 16: 89-108. 2002.

Hayami, Yujiro and V. Ruttan. *Agricultural Development: An International Perspective.* Baltimore, MD: Johns Hopkins University Press. 1985.

Hazell, P. and S. Haggblade. "Rural-Urban Growth Linkages in India." *Indian Journal of Agricultural Economics* 46 (4): 515-29. 1991.

Mellor, J.W. *The New Economics of Growth.* Ithaca, NY: Cornell University Press. 1976.

Perry, G., D. de Ferranti, D. Lederman, W. Foster, and A. Valdes.*Beyond the City: The Rural Contribution to Development.* Washington, D.C: World Bank. 2005.

BIBLIOGRAPHY

Agarwal, S.P., and N. Kanta. *Child Education in India: Index to Scholarly Writings*. Concept Publishing Co. New Delhi. 1990.

Andy Hall. *Challenges to Strengthening Agricultural Innovation Systems: Where Do We Go from Here?* United Nations University. UNU-MERIT Working Paper Series. 2007-38. 2007.

Best, M. & Maclay, C. "Community Internet Access in Rural Areas: Solving the Economic Sustainability Puzzle". *Global Information Technology Report*. Oxford University Press. 2002.

Bhalla, A., *Uneven Development in the Third World: A Study of China and India*. Basingstoke. 1995.

Bhatnagar, S. & Schware. R. *Technology in Development: Cases from India*. Sage Publications. 2000.

Bhatnagar, Subhash and Robert Schware. *Information and Communication Technology in Development: Cases from India*. New Delhi. Sage Publications. 2000.

Braun, Joachim von, et al. "Agricultural and Economic Development Strategies and the Transformation of China and India". In Essays: Lessons Learned from the Dragon (China) and the Elephant (India) Annual Report 2004–2005. Washington DC: International Food Policy Research Institute (IFPRI). 2005.

Brown, J. S. & Duguid, P. *The Social Life of Information*. Harvard Busi ness School Press. 2000.

Burgess, Robin, and Rohini Pande. "Do Rural Banks Matter? Evidence from the Indian Social Banking Experiment". *The American Economic Review* 95(3): 780–795. 2005.

Caldwell, J.C., P.H. Reddy, and P. Caldwell. Educational Transition in Rural South India. *Population and Development Review*, Vol.11. No.1. 1985.

Chaudhuri, S., and M. Ravallion. "Partially Awakened Giants: Uneven Growth in China and India". In *Dancing with Giants: China, India and the Global Economy,* edited by L.A. Winters and S. Yusuf. Washington DC: World Bank. 2007.

Datt, G. and M. Ravallion. "Is India's Economic Growth Leaving the Poor Behind?" *Journal of Economic Perspectives* 16: 89-108. 2002.

Deshpande, Ashwini. "Assets Versus Autonomy? The Changing Face of The Gender- Caste Overlap in India." *Feminist Economics.* Vol. 8, No. 2. 19-35. 2002.

Dreze, Jean and Geeta Kingdon. School Participation in Rural India. *Review of Development Economics,* Vol. 5. (1). 2001.

Duraisamy, Malathy. Children's Schooling in Rural Tamil Nadu: Gender Disparity and the Role of Access, Parental and Household actors. *Journal of Educational Planning and Administration,* 12 (2). 1998.

Fan, Shenggen, et al. "Government Spending, Growth and Poverty in Rural India". *American Journal of Agricultural Economics* 82(4): 1038–1051. 2000.

FAO. *The potentials of microcomputers in support of agricultural extension, education and training.* Rome: FAO. 1993.

GOI. *Employment and Unemployment Situation in India: January-June, 2004,* Government of India. National Sample Survey Organisation. Report No. 506. 2005.

Goldar, B.N. *Trade Liberalisation and Manufacturing Employment: The Case of India,* Employment Paper 2002/3,4, Geneva. International Labour Office. 2003.

Government of India. *Report of the Expert Group on Agricultural Indebtedness,* Ministry of Finance. 2007.

Government of Karnataka. *IT for the Common Man: The Millenium IT Policy.* Department of Information Technology. 2000.

Govinda, R. (ed). *India Education Report—A Profile of Basic Education.* Oxford University Press. New Delhi. 2002.

Greive, Margaret and Bingham Rose. *Women as Catalysts for Social Change.* New York: The City University and McAuley and the Howard Samuels Center.2001.

Hayami, Yujiro and V. Ruttan. *Agricultural Development: An International Perspective.* Baltimore, MD: Johns Hopkins University Press. 1985.

Hazell, P. and S. Haggblade. "Rural-Urban Growth Linkages in India." *Indian Journal of Agricultural Economics* 46 (4): 515-29. 1991.

India Panchayati Raj Report-2001 Volume I & II. National Institute of Rural Development. Hyderabad. January 2002.

India: Human Development Report. National Council for Applied Economic Research. Oxford University Press. New Delhi, 1999.

Jagannathan, Shanti. *Role of NGOs in Primary Education. A study of NGOís in India.* World Bank Policy Working Paper. August. 2000.

Jaychandaran, Usha. Understanding School Attendance and Children's Work Participation in India. *Journal of Educational Planning and Administration.* Vol. 15.No.1-4. 2001.

Jodha, N. "Effectiveness of Farmers' Adjustment to Risk", *Economic and Political Weekly,* Vol. 13, No. 25, pp. A38-A48. 1978.

Kripalani, Manjeet. "The Digital Village: Fighting Poverty with Technology in India". *Business Week.* 28 June. 2004.

Mellor, J.W. *The New Economics of Growth.* Ithaca, NY: Cornell University Press. 1976.

Mishra, S. *Agrarian Scenario in Post-reform India: A Story of Distress, Despair and Death,* WP-2007-001, Indira Gandhi Institute of Development Research, Mumbai. 2007.

Narasimhan, Sakuntala. *Empowering Women: An Alternative Strategy from Rural India.* Sage Publications. 1999.

Narayan, Deepa (ed). *Empowerment and Poverty Reduction: A Sourcebook.* Washington: World Bank. 2002.

Papola, T.S.'The Question of Unemployment', in Bimal Jalan (ed.) *The Indian Economy: Problems and Prospects.* New Delhi. Viking, Penguin Books India (P) Ltd. 1992.

Paroda, R. "Sustaining the Green Revolution: New Paradigms", Lecture delivered at the 2nd International Crop Science Congress, New Delhi. 1996.

Pitroda, S. "Development, Democracy, and the Village Telephone." *Harvard Business Review.* November 1993. HBS Press.

Planning Commission. *Report of the Special Group on Targeting Ten Million Employment Opportunities.* New Delhi. Government of India. 2002.

Planning Commission. *Second Five Year Plan,* New Delhi. Government of India. 1956.

Prahlad, C.K. "The End of Corporate Imperialism." *Harvard Business Review.* July-August 1998.

Rajora, R. *Bridging the Digital Divide.* Tata-McGraw Hill. 2002.

Reserve Bank of India. *Report of the Internal Group to Examine Issues Relating to Rural Credit and Microfinance.* July 2005.

Riddell, Rogar and Mark, C and Robinson. "*Non Government Organisations and Rural Poverty Alleviation.* Clarendon Press. Oxford. 1995.

Robert Tripp. *Self-Sufficient Farming: Labour and Knowledge in Small-Scale Farming.* London. Earthscan, 2006.

Roul Chhabilendra. *Bitter to Better Harvest*. Northern Book Centre. New Delhi. 2001.

Ruedi Baumgartnet and Ruedi Hogger. (eds). *In Search of Sustainable Livelihoods: Managing Resources and Change*. Sage Publications. New Delhi. 2004.

Ruggie, John Gerard. "Territoriality and Beyond: Problematising Modernity in International Relations." International Organisation 47; 139-74. 1993.

Sadik, N. "Women, the Center of Development." *Development*, 1988, Vol. 1, 30-31.

Sampath, R.K. and C. Gopinath. "Land Distribution in India: Its Nature and Economic Implications". *Margin*, Vol.2 (3): 43-70. 1979

Sankaran, S. *Indian Economy: Problems, Policies and Development*. Margham Publications. 1994.

Sarkar, K. Gautam. *Agriculture and Rural Transformation in India*. Oxford University Press. Delhi. 1995.

Sen, Gita and Caren Grown. *Development, Crises, and Alternative Visions: Third World Women's Perspectives*. New York: Monthly Review Press. 1987.

Singh Katar. *Rural Development: Principles Policies and Management*. Sage Publications. New Delhi. 1999.

Singh, J.P. *Leapfrogging Development? The Political Economy of Telecommunications Restructuring*. SUNY Press. 1999.

Sinha, Amarjeet. *Primary Schooling in India*. Vikas Publication House, New Delhi. 1998.

Sinha, Basawan and Ramesh Bhatia.*Economic Appraisal of irrigation projects in India*. Agricole Publishing Academy, New Delhi. 1982.

Sood, A. D. "How to Wire Rural India: The Problems and Possibilities of Digital Development." *Economic and Political Weekly* Vol 36: No. 43. October 27, 2001.

Woolcock, Michael. "Learning from Failures in Microfinance: What Unsuccessful Cases Tell Us About How Group Based Programmes Work." *American Journal of Economics and Sociology*. 1999. Vol. 58, No. 1.

World Bank. *Engendering Development: Through Gender Equality in Rights, Resources, and Voice*. New York: Oxford University Press. 2001.

World Bank. *World Development Report 2008: Agriculture for Development*. Washington, D.C.: World Bank. 2007.

Index